Benedictine
Tapestry

Benedictine Tapestry

FELICITAS CORRIGAN

DARTON, LONGMAN AND TODD
LONDON

First published in 1991 by
Darton, Longman and Todd Ltd
89 Lillie Road, London sw6 1ud

© 1991 Stanbrook Abbey

isbn 0–232–51818–1

A catalogue record for this book is available
from the British Library

Typography by Humphrey Stone
Phototypeset in Sabon by Intype London
Printed and bound in Great Britain by
Courier International Ltd,
East Kilbride, Scotland

Contents

Acknowledgements

As at almost any time these past forty years, I am indebted above all to the assistance of my own religious community, and in particular to Dames Frideswide Sandeman and Michaela Whitmore. Dame Frideswide's monograph on the missionary Benedictines in Korea, translated by her from German and first published in *The Way*, has brought the historical survey of this book up to date; Dame Michaela not only shared her knowledge of classical Greece and Rome, but with unstinted generosity rifled for my benefit her own research over years on the life and times of St Hildegard.

I tender sincere thanks also to the friends who have allowed me to quote letters, especially to Michael and Hilary Rubinstein for permission graciously given to include so many from their father. It only remains to thank the following for leave, readily granted, to reprint from their publications: Mother Mary Clare OSB, 'What Christ means to me', *Word and Spirit* (1983); the Editor of *The Clergy Review*, 'Seeing is Believing' (May 1978); the Editor of *The Tablet* for excerpts from articles on St Gregory and St Wulfstan (1974); the Editor of *The Way Supplement*, 'Forced Labour in Korea' (spring 1981).

Preparation of the typescript owes much to the generosity of Mrs Anna Rains, ever ready to drop whatever she was about and go, hot-foot, to the typewriter in an emergency. To misquote Shakespeare's Olivia, 'Help sought is good, but given unsought is better.'

The verse scattered throughout the book is the product of the soul, mind and pen of Dame Scholastica Hebgin, with the sole exception of the *Song for an Easter Profession* (p. 116). This I found sticking out of my Gradual on the Friday of Easter week, 1938, the day of my Solemn Profession. There has only ever been this single copy, hurriedly written out on a scrap of flimsy paper by its author, Dame Cuthberta Welman my fellow-novice, shy lover of poverty, who was to depart all too soon to partake of the breakfast prepared by her Lord and Master on the further shore. Finally, I am indebted to the Revd Dr Sidney Griffith, Professor of Oriental Studies at the Catholic University of America, who initiated me into the Syriac world of the 'Singles in God's Service' that forestalled the monastic movement of the fourth and fifth centuries.

F.C.

Introduction

Whether or not it happened as it should, this book simply happened. The opening study, 'What is a monk?' requested as the Introduction to a series that came to nothing, was laid aside until the day a young housewife called, urged by a friend to find out for herself precisely what nuns were, and why and how their way of life differed from her own deeply Christian path. 'What do you *do* all day?' she asked the two figures seated in front of her. The older nun waved an arm that embraced the enormous sprawl of nineteenth-century Puginesque buildings, designed for solemn splendour rather than for human comfort. 'Do you imagine', she asked teasingly, 'that Puck puts a girdle round about the monastery and calls in the aid of Peaseblossom and Cobweb with an army of fairies to keep the entire place spick and span each day?' Laughter and commonsense saved the situation. All the same, here was a good question that called for a considered reply.

What impels girls in their twenties to turn away from noble human love, from so much that is lawful, beautiful and the gift of God, to embrace a life so demanding and austere? Shakespeare has powerfully argued the case for the prosecution in *A Midsummer Night's Dream*. Hermia, the would-be nun, is asked to consider carefully whether she has the spiritual endowments necessary to

> — endure the livery of a nun;
> For aye to be in shady cloister mew'd,
> To live a barren sister all your life,
> Chanting faint hymns to the cold fruitless moon . . .
> But earthlier happy is the rose distill'd,
> Than that which, withering on the virgin thorn,
> Grows, lives, and dies in single blessedness.

This is eloquent pleading and fine poetry — but is it true? It is readily admitted that even among fervent Christians, many can readily appreciate a Mother Teresa of Calcutta, a missionary dispensing medicines under a blazing tropical sun, a Sister of Charity surrounded by motherless orphans: all these are the hands and feet of Christ going about his healing and apostolic ministry. But the so-called contemplatives – aren't they setting themselves up as some kind of esoteric élite, a mystical aristocracy that relegates the rank and file to the status of the second class?

In many documents issued by the Second Vatican Council, it is made abundantly clear that there is no second class in the Christian Church. It was not to a chosen few that Christ our Lord addressed the words, 'Be perfect, as your heavenly Father is perfect.' Perfection is not graded. Each of us has a divine vocation, whether as husband or wife, parent, teacher, doctor, business tycoon, farmer, dock-labourer, monk or nun: what we do matters nothing; what we are matters everything. God has made hearts one by one, as the psalmist tells us (Psalm 32:15), and we mirror God according to our own temperament and personal call, some the life of Martha, others that of Mary. As Dom Augustine Baker would teach Dame Gertrude More, on whose patrimony our house was founded in Cambrai in 1623:

> Regard thy call;
> That's all in all.

Underlying 'What do you *do* all day?' is the unspoken but more deeply probing question: 'What are you doing with God's gift of life? Throwing it away? To what purpose is this waste?' To this, the only answer is: 'I'm giving my life back to God in praise and thanksgiving because he himself for his own secret purpose asks it of me. With St Augustine, all I can say is, "This is my life: to praise you, my God." Were I to refuse, I should never taste true happiness, and God will give the grace for whatever the future holds.'

Thus in the mystical Body of Christ the roles of parent and nun are complementary and need each other. A girl called to make a radical renunciation of all subordinate goals, however lawful, does so in the name and for the sake of the entire Church: at the same time, commonsense makes obvious that

without father, mother and family life there would be no potential priests, monks or nuns. So the score is fifty-fifty. Mary
witnesses to the Absolute, to God's unchanging transcendence,
to the fact that we have not here a lasting city; Martha affirms
God's immanence in the world of his creation, and applies all
her energies to the growth of the Body of Christ and the building
on earth of the City of God.

Since in common parlance and thought any man who, with
a religious aim, dons an ankle-length tunic girded by a cincture
is at once dubbed 'a monk' (Luther, 'the solitary monk who
shook the world', was not a monk; he was an Augustinian
friar), and his veiled counterpart 'a nun', the idea presented itself
of showing against a background of time, how one monastic life
has been woven on a Benedictine loom to the Stanbrook pattern.
The texture, the colour-scheme, the varying thickness of thread
and strands are symbols of the curtains and veils prescribed in
Exodus 26, cunningly woven in blue, purple and scarlet fine-
twisted linen, to adorn the holy temple of God which we all
are (1 Corinthians 3:17). The fabric is not woven easily, as will
be evident to any reader who ponders the human implications of
Dame Laurentia McLachlan's conferences on obedience which
conclude the book. She once quoted to a young rebel the fourth
degree of humility from Chapter 7 of the Rule of St Benedict:

If, in this obedience, the monk should meet with difficulties, contradictions, and even injustice, with silent mind he must hold fast to patience
and endure . . . for Scripture says, 'Thou hast brought us into the
snare' and it goes on to say, 'Thou hast set man over our heads'.

With a mischievous glint in her grey-green eyes, the abbess
added: 'And how much worse when he sets a woman over those
heads.' To be housed, shod, clothed and fed is taken pretty well
for granted, but almost certainly there will come a time in the
life of every monk and nun when the vow of obedience is put
to the test: was it made with what J. H. Newman calls 'notional'
or 'real' assent? For many Christians the Church itself presents
the same challenge, the same turning-point of crisis. That is
why, after a lifetime of experience, Dame Laurentia has used a
sharp needle to draw a crimson line of decoration right across
the pattern. The disciple is not above the Master, and acceptance

caused the God-man to sweat blood in the garden of Gethsemane:

> Cloth newly-woven is unfit to wear
> Until trodden underfoot, cleansed in fuller's frame,
> Soaked well in water, combed with teazles,
> Fluffed out and stretched tight in the tailor's hand.
>
> PIERS PLOWMAN XV 450–3

As in any woven material, the tapestry consists of warp and
weft: the warp, the lengthwise element in the construction,
strong and durable, the immutable forces of history, personalities and events that provide a firm foundation for the weft,
the crosswise element of different-coloured threads wound on
shuttles, thrown lightly backwards and forwards through sheds
in the warp, fit symbols of the transient affairs that occupy
our day's labour until Death fastens off and cuts the thread.
Following this pattern, Part One sets out the historical background of the monastic life: led by St Benedict, 'Father and
Leader of monks', preferably young, beardless and holding a
simple crook as in the English eleventh-century Arundel manuscript, followed by eminent men and women who have lived
and interpreted his flexible and enduring Rule, the procession
moves from the year 480 to the mid-twentieth century. In Part
Two the historical events and interest of Part One are projected
into the present day, mirrored for the most part in personal
letters written by the author, and reproduced as they were
written without any thought of publication.

There is no cast-iron uniformity about the interpretation of
the Rule of St Benedict, and each monastery is an extended
family. It will be clear from Part Two that ours includes animals
and birds, together with the monastery's workforce of both
men and women, and all who knock at the door in search of
refreshment whether of body or soul. Over the door of a medieval foundation was inscribed: *Porta patet, et cor magis* – The
door stands wide open, and our hearts wider still. The motto
is exemplified many times over in these days of the Welfare
State, the handicapped, and homeless. Upon the completion of
a Persian carpet, its figures and patterns were always spread
out under the eye of the beholder. This book has been called a

tapestry, and before it can be wound off the loom altogether, it too demands human eyes to discern the correspondences and correlatives of the varying patterns, and shades of colour. Only if it wins approval from that section of the monastic family will it dare to claim as its own the motto of the Canterbury weavers:

> Fair weft and fitting woof
> Weave the web that bideth proof.

On the monastic vocation

Not that they beggared be in mind, or brutes,
That they have chosen their dwelling place afar
In lonely places: but their eyes are turned
To the high stars, the very deep of Truth.
Freedom they seek, an emptiness apart
From worthless hopes, din of the marketplace,
And all the noisy crowding up of things,
And whatsoever wars on the divine,
At Christ's command and for his love, they hate;
By faith and hope they follow after God,
And know their quest shall not be desperate,
If but the Present conquer not their souls
With hollow things; that which they see they spurn
That they may come at what they do not see,
Their senses kindled like a torch, that may
Blaze through the secrets of eternity.
The transient's open, everlastingness
Denied our sight; yet still by hope we follow
That vision that our minds have seen, despising
The shows and forms of things, the loveliness
Soliciting for ill our mortal eyes.
The present's nothing; but eternity
Abides for those on whom all truth, all good,
Hath shone, in one entire and perfect light.

ST PAULINUS OF NOLA 353—431

From Dom Augustine Baker's Introduction to his
Commentary on St Benedict's Rule. Dedicated to Dame
Catherine Gascoigne, first abbess of Cambray, and
presented to her and the Community on 28 June 1631

As St Basil is termed Father of the Monks of the Eastern parts of the world, so the most holy St Bennet in these Western parts is termed the Father of Monks. The Rule that he wrote being (by the testimony of St Gregory) excellent for the discretion of it, doth instruct the professors of it more particularly in all the things which they are to doe, than doth any other Rule. The Rule of St Basil is intricate; the Rule of St Augustine is very generall and doth not descend to particulars, whereby it leaves many uncertainties and doubts; The Rule of St Francis is but short & by reason thereof it has many precepts full of scruples. But the Rule of the most holy Father St Bennet setts down everything most clearly . . .

Of the order of St Bennet there are held for known Saints to the number of 55 thousand & 7 hundred, besides the secret saints of the order unknown to men, but well known to God. There be divers orders that profess the Rule of St Bennet, who yet do differ in colour of habits and constitutions, as the Cistercians, Celestions, Camaldulenses. But yet it is only the black-Monks & Nunns that are known and called usually by the name of Benedictines.

PART ONE · THE WARP

I

What is a Monk?

In the knapsack of our minds, most of us carry about a not inconsiderable outfit of die-hard prejudices. The literary evidence — Milton, Gibbon, Kingsley, Borrow — would seem to suggest that honest and true Englishmen suffer impatience with the variety of life-styles within the Latin Church: Milton consigns the lot to hell.

> Embryos and idiots, eremites and friars,
> White, black, and grey with all their trumpery
> *Paradise Lost* III

Friars, canons, clerks regular, all who in Kingsley's phrase are men no longer but have become things, mere tools, are frequently lumped together under the generic term, 'monks', to be summarily dismissed as 'a set of idle, dissolute drones, useless burdens, if not actually injurious to the community at large'. So much for the Poor Man of Assisi, Thomas Aquinas, Walter Hilton, Ignatius of Loyola, John of the Cross, Vincent de Paul, John Bosco — the list could be prolonged indefinitely. The sweeping indictment just quoted, from the pen of Robert Curzon (1810–73), product of Charterhouse and Christ Church, Oxford, admits of one exception. 'I am inclined to think favourably', he magnanimously concedes, 'of the learned order of the Benedictines, who built most of those beautiful abbeys whose ruins in our fairest valleys attest the former wealth and magnificence of their inhabitants.' Sightseers, true enough, may explore picturesque ruins for an hour or two, a Tintern Abbey may even be immortalized in poetry, but as long as Westminster Abbey remains to witness the coronation of English sovereigns, the nation will never be able to forget the thousand years of its Benedictine past.

English Benedictines are a native growth from the day on

which Pope St Gregory the Great sent Augustine and his forty monks armed, if one may conjecture from their subsequent acts, with the double sword of Benedict's *Regula Monachorum* and his own counterpart *Regula Pastoralis*, over the salt sea to teach the islanders of Aella to sing Alleluia in thanksgiving for God's mercies. That Benedict's Rule was probably only one of several matters little in the context: it very soon superseded all the rest. The so-called 'Benedictine centuries' moulded the civilization first of England and then, through English men and women, of Northern Europe. Boniface, the English monk of Devon, with his colony of English nuns were among the chief makers of European unity. But Germany, the heartland of their apostolate, was to present the problem of the Berlin Wall as early as the sixteenth century, by a defection that gave definite shape to a long-threatened cleavage of the Western commonwealth of nations incorporated in Christ that had been Boniface's dream. In his own native land, the rupture of Christendom transformed many monasteries into country houses sold to the highest bidder, or merely left them as quarries for building materials.

Today Downside, Ampleforth, Douai, Stanbrook and all the newer foundations have replaced Glastonbury, York, Worcester, Barking and the rest, but it would be foolish in these last decades of the twentieth century to harbour medieval conceptions of an architectural demi-paradise, a fortress of religion and culture closed in on itself, against an engulfing tide of materialism. Have monks then become a quaint anachronism? By no means. Hewn down, the Benedictine tree sends out ever stronger shoots and branches. If in the past Benedictines kept the gates of knowledge for Europe, they may now be opening those gates to the whole world. Monks and nuns are busily adapting the monastic life to new forms according to individuals and circumstances in North and South America, Australia, Africa, India, Sri Lanka, Korea and Madagascar. Benedict's monastery of the sixth century, a paschal brotherhood whose primary care, the worship of a transcendent God, exercised so magnetic an attraction that it became a life-giving centre of compassion and healing for all, a place where honour, love, humility and friendship were extended to guests and strangers, those of the household of the faith and those outside it, rich and poor alike, has a curiously timeless yet contemporary ring.

The Maundy shall be administered with the greatest care to the poor, for in receiving them Christ is adored. Nor must the vicar of the eternal Christ be slow and cold in the guesthouse, delaying or neglecting the poor, while showing himself swift and fervent in service to the rich. For the rest, wayfarers shall be provided on departure with a supply of food according to the means of the house.

The admonition comes from the *Regularis Concordia*, the Monastic Agreement, drawn up by English monks, Sts Ethelwold and Dunstan, about the year 970. What was, is, and will be again. Monks will never become an anachronism.

Unlike Dominican or Franciscan friars, monks are not a product of Western thought or spirituality. A non-Christian monastic tradition flourished thousands of years before the Christian era. India would seem to have been the cradle of monastic life in the world of men. The discovery of a figurine of the god Shiva, seated in the yoga posture, under a seal of the Indus Valley civilization of 2500–1500 BC is evidence of the possible existence at the dawn of history of groups of ascetics, a claim substantiated by the Vedas, their oldest Scriptures. Whatever their title, be it Hindu rishi, Jain sadhvis, Buddhist bhikkhsu, or Christian monk, such men are in search of the Absolute, the Infinite, the Ocean of Peace. The mid-twentieth-century discoveries of the texts of Qumran have revealed Jewish communities, possibly belonging to the sect of Essenes, who withdrew into the desert, broke with the blood-offerings of the Temple worship in order to make their sacrifice the offering of a life of liturgical praise and fidelity to God's law, manifested by true conversion of heart and fraternal charity. St John Baptist may well have belonged to these Essenes. Philo of Alexandria (*c.* 20 BC — *c.* AD 50) in his *De Vita Contemplativa* describes another group, that of the Therapeutes, Jewish monks living near Alexandria, but clearly belonging to the same spiritual movement as Qumran. Both call for special mention as being contemporaries of Christ our Lord and his apostles; a knowledge of their writings brings new life and colour, for instance, to the account in Acts 2:42–5 of the first Christian community in Jerusalem.

Egypt was the first home of Christian monastic groups. As early as the second century Clement, the erudite Greek presbyter of the church of Alexandria, specifically refers to the Hindu, Jain, and Buddhist ascetics encountered daily in that city of brilliant intellectual culture. Here, influences from the East, from India, Greece and Rome confronted the faith of the Judaeo-Christian, forcing him to abandon Jewish legalism and rigidity, and come to grips with Hellenistic humanism. To teach the convert from paganism how to live as he should, Clement sketched a pattern of the thoroughly Christian man, drawing as he did so upon all the true values of a classical education and integrating them into the faith. His three works, *An Exhortation, The Tutor*, and *Miscellanies* were to exercise a strong influence on Christian monasticism. The many non-Christian ascetics thronging Alexandria may well have led Clement to formulate his theory that, in the beginning, angelic intermediaries communicated to each race a singular divine wisdom, so that each had their distinctive prophets. 'Among them,' he says, 'the chief were the prophets of Egypt, the Chaldeans of Assyria, the Druids of Gaul and the Celtic philosophers, the Magi of Persia, and the Gymnosophists of India.'

Such philosophers and ascetics are no dead phenomena: they are flourishing and gaining ground increasingly in the West — the Christian monk may come face to face with his own likeness at any street corner. Regardless of their various labels, are they all then much of a muchness? By no means: that must be said at the outset. The disciples of the Indian Gautama Buddha, 'the Enlightened One', or of Confucius, the Chinese philosopher, or of the Persian sage Zoroaster are following the teaching of masters long dead. Not so the Christian, for Christianity is not one religion among many others, but the revelation of the living God. If, as for all monks, the search for God the Absolute is his primary aim, the Christian can only meet him in the person of Jesus Christ, true man and true God. He is the only teacher, and through him the monk learns that the Ocean of Peace is not a selfless infinitude, but an immense 'Sea Pacific', to use Catherine of Siena's phrase, which bears him in the Son to the

Father through the Holy Spirit. As St Benedict, 'Father and Leader of monks' will constantly point out in his Rule, the search becomes one for a union with Christ which will gradually transform the disciple into the image of his divine model, and so enable him to fulfil a profoundly apostolic role within the Church.

The name 'monk' is not a translation but a mere transliteration of the Greek *monachos* defined in the dictionary as 'a solitary'. Christianity was largely an Aramaic phenomenon that found its final and loudest expression in Greek, becoming cabined, cribbed, and confined in the process, as we are increasingly discovering today. This non-scriptural word, first found in a papyrus fragment dated 6 June 324 to designate a Christian ascetic, may have come into use as a translation of the much richer Syriac term, *Yiḥîdāyâ*. The exploration of modern scholars points increasingly to the conclusion that the basic word underlying the Greek is this Syriac *Yiḥîdāyâ*, a biblical term that is above all else a special title of Christ, 'God the *Yiḥîdāyâ* in the bosom of the Father' (John 1:18). Its many connotations, nuances and dimensions must all be taken into account in order to listen to its echoes and overtones in the *Demonstrations* of Aphrahat, the Persian sage (d. *c*. 345), and the hymns and homilies of Ephraem the Syrian (d. 373), when the word had already become a technical term in ecclesiastical usage well before the period of monastic expansion. Fr Robert Murray SJ has summarized under three heads the meanings of *Yiḥîdāyâ*, as applied to the virginal consecrated holy ones of either sex 'who have taken on the likeness of the angels': the word implies (a) single in body; (b) single in mind and heart; (c) single in soul as being totally consecrated and united to the Single One, the Single Son of God the Father, with all that is thereby symbolized of death and resurrection.

Approaches differ, but sages of other religions almost unanimously affirm that, though their concepts be given another name, the profound reality underlying the monastic quest is the same — namely, the eternal God. In striving to reach the same goal, all have adopted similar techniques: spiritual training under an experienced guide, and a programme of self-mastery following precise rules. The fact that problems, seemingly modern and solely Christian — obedience, singleness of life, withdrawal or openness to the world, silence and speech — have faced monks of every religion and culture, enlarges perspective by bringing into strong relief the basic unity that makes past experience and judgements valid for all time. A new age is upon us, and the acute problem of adjustment to a changing civilization calls for a clear understanding of the monastic ethos, of the unity that binds monks of every tradition into a true brotherhood of an *Ordo monasticus*, a religious state of life. By entering into dialogue with ascetics and monks of other schools of thought, the Christian monk may well find a deepening of his own faith, a new way of penetrating into the mystery of the God who is Infinite Bliss and Prince of Peace, and a hitherto unknown way of making him known to those unwittingly in search of him.

It is here that St Benedict, separated from us by fourteen centuries, may prove an indispensable link. His life of seventy years or so, from about 480 to the 550s, saw the disintegration of Roman civilization, marked by profound changes in every sphere of life, political, social, economic, racial and intellectual. He was caught up in the full tide of the 'Wandering of the Peoples'. In 451, Attila, the Scourge of God, had been prevented by Pope Leo the Great from sacking Rome; four years later, the Vandals pouring in from Africa knew no such restraint. Benedict was sixteen or thereabouts when Theodoric, a foreigner and a heretic, King of the Ostrogoths, invaded and conquered Italy after the three years of war that initiated his reign from 493–526. A year later Justinian, the new Emperor of Constantinople, embarked on the re-conquest of Italy against Totila, the Gothic king. For twenty years, a war of ruin and devastation was to reduce Rome, golden Rome, immortal Rome, into a desolate waste; it remained so for the next forty years.

This is the backcloth to Benedict's life. It began and ended in war. Our sole source for the events of his career and development is the Second Book of the Dialogues of St Gregory the Great, written about 593. In his letter to Maximian of Syracuse, dated July 593, Gregory expressly asks for stories of 'miracles of Italian Fathers' to satisfy his own community of monks.

Although not devoid of historical value, Gregory's account of Benedict is not a biography in our sense of the word at all. Seven years old when Benedict died, Gregory was certainly acquainted with his close disciples, whose names and positions he is careful to cite as his sources. Whereas a newcomer to the monastic life may greet the miracle stories with a tolerant smile — pious legends and unscientific mystical experiences do not accord with a nuclear age — the seasoned monk will listen avidly year by year to the public reading, so deep and authentic is Gregory's penetration into the human psyche and the world of the supernatural. Many phrases form a kind of signature-tune of the Apostle of England; as such they are sheer delight. Gregory's authorship of the *Dialogues* was challenged and dismissed by Robert Cooke (1550–1615) as 'superstitious Romanist piety' in 1614; in 1987 Francis Clark repeated and expanded Cooke's arguments, only to have them completely demolished by Paul Meyvaert, a scholar deeply versed in Gregorian studies. In a letter to the present writer of 3 September 1974, the monastic historian David Knowles made these pertinent observations:

Do you know the judgement of the great Lutheran historian Erich Caspar? 'Were you to ask which of all the popes was the greatest Christian figure, then the palm must be awarded to Gregory.' Who are the greatest popes? Very few spring to mind. There are many very good Upper Seconds, but relatively few Firsts. Possibly because few popes had a long run, and almost all had either come up the ladder as subordinates in the Curia, or had shown pastoral qualities in a single see. Leo I, Gregory I, Gregory VII, Innocent III — they all make the First Class, but who else? Leo XIII. All the popes (save the short-lived Benedict XV) of this century make a bid for greatness — and two at least for *id quod maius est* sanctity — but it is almost always easier to suggest a non-pope as greater than a pope of the same date. But Gregory I with England, Job, *Regula Pastoralis*, Chant (?), liturgy, charitable works, capacity to rule and to foresee, warmth of personality etc *Omne tulit punctum*. Did he write the *Dialogues*? I think he did — but they are curiously unlike any other work of his, but cf. Hilaire Belloc's political novels and his *Cautionary Tales*; Housman's Poems and introduction to Manilius . . .

There is then no need to regard St Gregory's *Dialogues* as an embarrassment: they are simply the work of a great storyteller and his life of St Benedict is authentic.

Born of distinguished parents in Nursia, about 70 miles north-east of Rome, Benedict was naturally sent for schooling to the capital of the Western Empire. Education meant the Roman training for the Forum: Boethius, who preserved for Europe the subtle and precise terminology of Plato and Aristotle, was Benedict's exact contemporary. The city was still resplendent with the marble and bronze of the ancient monuments, the Colosseum, temples and palaces, as well as early Christian shrines. Rome was the seat of the papacy with a tradition of learning and scholarship, and the boy must have attended schools of rhetoric and law. But like the cosmopolitan cities of every age, evil and corruption were rife, and the student body was by no means the last to catch the infection. While some 'slept in the gutter, snoring fast', as Petronius put it, Boethius watched the inner light extinguished in the minds of Roman youth:

> He lies there, heavy chains about his neck,
> Their weight has bowed his head, so that his face
> Is downward, and his eyes
> Gaze but on sullen earth.
>
> *De Consolatione Philosophiae* I, 2

One student at least was free, his eyes fixed on the stars: Benedict surveyed the revelry and riot, turned his back on Rome and a brilliant future, and fled. *Recessit igitur scienter nescius —* the oxymoron is a typical Gregorian touch — *et sapienter indoctus —* he departed knowingly unknowing, wisely untaught. As St Peter Damian would later say: 'He forsook the world with all its attractions, to run with strong strides after the running Christ, and did not rest until he had caught up with him.'

Thirty-five miles east of Rome, in the valley of the river Arno, there stood the little town of Affile which sheltered small colonies of monks and hermits. There the fugitive found a welcome, and there possibly he became acquainted with the *Rule of the Master*, which he was to make the basis of his own Rule. But this Thebaid of his had one big drawback. His nurse 'who loved him tenderly' had accompanied him from Rome, and a Nana preparing the nursery, loudly proclaiming hers to be the most wonderful boy in the world, could embarrass a would-be anchorite. He took the only way out, gave her the slip, made his way north, and for the next three years hid in a cave in a lonely wilderness called Subiaco. Inevitably his secret dwelling was discovered, his holiness made manifest, and soon disciples flocked to him for guidance.

To this day Subiaco is impregnated with his spirit as well it may be, for it was there he spent the years of his young manhood. He established no fewer than twelve monasteries, each containing twelve monks ruled by a superior, while he became the revered father of a specially selected group of young monks of whom two, Maurus and Placid, are known to us by name. All was well until jealousy, that bitter corrosive of community relationships, reared its ugly head. Florentius, a local priest, tried to get rid of him by poison. Calmly facing facts, Benedict reorganized all his monasteries and then 'let envy have its way and set out with a few monks to find a new home'. He found it in the citadel of Campania, known now as Monte Cassino, on the road from Rome to Naples. Here he built a monastery on the site of a pagan temple, and here, supported by his monks he stood with hands upraised in prayer as he died, if tradition is to be believed, on 21 March 543, or perhaps as late as the 550s. Benedict was to urge his monks to run while they had the light of life: Gregory shows the patriarch of monks himself moving with swift step from Nursia to Rome to Affile to Subiaco to Cassino, and finally along a road streaming with pure and endless light leading to heaven beyond the stars.

No contemporary portrait of St Benedict exists except in the masterpiece of his own word-painting. 'He wrote a Rule for Monks', St Gregory tells us, 'that is remarkable for its discretion and clarity. Any one who wishes to know exactly what he was like can discover him in his Rule, for his life and teaching were one and the same thing.' A short document of some 12,000 words, half of them biblical quotation, the Rule of St Benedict consists of a Prologue and 73 chapters of prescriptions which might be summarized: 'Praise God night and day in common, pray to him apart and alone, savour and absorb holy Scripture, live by it, share all things with the brotherhood, keep silence, and obey.' The Rule proposes no special work, no economic, no social, no intellectual or even apostolic purpose. It is simply a compendium of gospel teaching of apparent simplicity and unfathomable depth, to guide his own sons to Christian perfection. But in the sixth century there were hosts of homilies, letters, treatises and even Rules to guide would-be ascetics. Why then did Benedict's 'little Rule' as he calls it, surpass and supersede all others?

Historically, St Benedict was faced with precisely the same challenge that society poses today — a highly complex civilization dissolving into chaos. And the remedy? A return to gospel values. Not for nothing did Benedict make the parable of the Prodigal Son the groundwork of the Prologue to the Rule, and the actual subject of the vow of *conversatio*, the turning-back to God our Father, the *metanoia* of every Christian on his pilgrimage to the Source. From boyhood, Benedict had been familiar with monks both of East and West, some of them giants, some pygmies. With mordant pen, Jerome had sketched the pygmies, the dumdawdlers* of the fourth century — truly there is nothing new under the sun: 'With their loose sleeves, flapping boots, squalid appearance, they sigh a great deal, call on consecrated virgins, and on feastdays eat themselves sick.' Unorganized, often irregular and extravagant, following no agreed observances or universal system, the whole monastic movement was threatened with destruction under the barbarian invasions and the separation of the Western and Eastern Empires. With Roman thoroughness and unspectacular sanity and sanctity, Benedict sat down and compiled his eminently practical, concrete, workable code to control and inspire his disciples. In so doing, he saved monasticism and gave Western Europe a reserve of spiritual nuclear energy, so to speak: it would provide for centuries the monk-bishops and statesmen who were to mould culture and religion, and it would become one of the basic documents of the Middle Ages.

In no country of Europe did the Benedictine Rule exert a

---

* A dumdawdler or slowdonothinger, from Robert Southey's Lingo-Grande letter to Stumparumper, 24 December 1822.

more powerful influence than in England. From the moment that Ethelbert of Kent gave Augustine of Canterbury and his forty companions the Church of St Martin, the monks 'began to meet, to sing, to pray, to say Mass, to preach and to baptize'; in a very short time England was a deeply Christian nation — the first stronghold of Benedictine monasticism. The life, the laws, the institution of parliament and university, the very character of the English people have been so strongly marked by the thousand years of Benedictine culture, that no change of religion or indeed lack of it has ever been able to eradicate it. At this point it is perhaps wise to remember that, according to St Gregory, Benedict had a sister, Scholastica, real enough in the flesh, but together forming symbols of the law and of love: neither is whole without the other, neither self-sufficient but each a reflection of the other. The monk-apostles of Europe all had nun-helpers at their side from English monasteries, often enough their own sisters or relatives, for English Benedictine nuns were a recognized institution from very early times: at the time of Henry VIII's Dissolution there were roughly eighty Benedictine nunneries. Under the Tudors and Stuarts, a thin trickle of young men and women escaped the persecution at home and made their way to Spain and the Low Countries where, like the Church itself after the cataclysm of the sixteenth century, they survived, revived, and in due course returned, lessened in number but rejuvenated in spirit. Unlike the nuns, the English Black Monks managed to preserve a corporate continuity with the pre-Dissolution monastic body through the agency of Dom Sigeberg Buckley, last monk of Westminster: they can therefore lay claim to an unbroken link with Augustine of Canterbury. Could anything be more English?

Like all human institutions, monasteries have had their ups and downs but, throughout history, at points of breakdown in society — when Europe had to be christianized and civilized anew, and a social fabric restored — their impact has been immediate and effective: they have bridged over the transition and set men's feet on a new path. It is now generally acknowledged that Enlightenment, Reason and Science, that trinity of false gods, have brought mankind to the verge of ruin, and in the process destroyed purity, honour, love, fidelity, everything that makes a man a man. The Rule of St Benedict is exercising an ever-increasing attraction on those filled with a need to replace 'facts' by realities. To steady the soul on eternity and reach out to the love and joy of the simplicity of God, to stand before him in worship and prayer, to look upon all beauty as a means of union with the Infinite, to recover a lost sense of mystery, to recognize Christ in one another and show forth his gentleness to all in anxiety and distress: these urgent contemporary longings can all be epitomized in the Benedictine vow of *conversatio*, that radical return of the prodigal to God our Father. In this Christian way of life, the values of a profit-oriented, competitive, consumer society have no place whatsoever.

It must be remembered that although St Benedict was an abbot, he was not a priest. Clericalization was a gradual development not completed until the twelfth century. The Rule was written simply for those dedicated to a search for God, and its spirituality has been unaffected by the lapse of time. It is not surprising therefore to find monks and nuns responding to contemporary pastoral and missionary needs. In recent years, at least 250 new foundations have been made in various countries. The English Benedictine Congregation has sent monks out to Peru and nuns to Uganda and the USA; at home, there is a lay community sharing in the monastic life, and a pastoral centre. This increasing extension of the monastic family may explain the growing interest in monastic oblates, laypeople affiliated to a specific house. From Anglo-Saxon times in England, the greater monasteries granted letters of confraternity to benefactors, thus creating a close spiritual bond. In 1530, Thomas More and his wife Dame Alice were received into the fraternity of Christ Church, Canterbury; in 1606, John Roberts, monk of St Gregory's, bestowed gifts of confraternity on the secular clergy and layfolk who would witness his martyrdom and live to keep the faith alive; in the twentieth century Edmund Bishop the liturgist, William Pantin the medievalist, and Archbishop Derek Warlock have all been affiliated as Benedictine confraters, but more recently oblates have in general ousted confraters as being socially more diversified, thus providing a more accessible and possibly more fruitful participation in monastic life.

We live in an age of pluralism on all fronts, and are witnesses to an inter-religious monastic dialogue unheard of since the days of Clement of Alexandria. On 10 September 1987 Pope John Paul II spoke of the need to strengthen the bonds which unite all who honestly seek the truth when he received a group of Zen monks together with their Christian counterparts. To the Benedictine monks present, he said:

Your specific contribution is not only that of keeping alive an open dialogue, but also of promoting a deep exchange on a spiritual level, since your life is dedicated in a special way to silence, to prayer, and to the witness of community life. There is much that you can do by means of hospitality. In opening your homes and your hearts, you follow the tradition of your spiritual father, St Benedict. To your brother monks who come from other spiritual traditions, you put into practice that beautiful chapter in the Rule about the reception of guests.

In keeping with this admonition, Dom Bede Griffiths, a monk of Prinknash Abbey, resident for many years in India, has appealed to every religious tradition to overcome its exclusiveness, to penetrate to the depths of its own wisdom and lore, and then from that deeper understanding to relate to the other religions of the world.

This study has attempted an answer to three questions: What is a monk? Who was St Benedict? What is meant by a Benedictine monk? Let it conclude by answering the questions not in the abstract, but in the concrete. Dom Henri Le Saux (1910–73), a monk of the Solesmes Congregation, after spending some twenty years in the abbey of Kergonan in Brittany, the house of his profession, was given permission in 1948 to follow his monastic call to India. Known henceforth by his Indian name of Swami Abhishiktananda, he explored as few others have done the heart and experience of Hindu rishis and saints. This integration and combination of spiritual insights, far from weakening the doctrinal foundation so firmly established by his early monastic training, gave a tremendous impetus to his awareness of God's ineffability in the mystery of the Blessed Trinity and of the divine peace radiating from Christ, his supreme Sadguru. He passed his days as a hermit at Gyansu in the Himalayas, near the source of the Ganges: writing to his sister, a Benedictine of Kergonan, he referred to his intense joy at the prospect of spending Christmas in solitary retreat in a cave, immersed in the hidden truths to be learned only at the feet of Christ his master. He was to die on 7 December 1973. True son of St Benedict that he was, in his journal of 28 December 1971 he had formulated this credo: 'If I say that I believe in Christ, that means that Christ is God for me. God-for-me, because there is no abstract God. Jesus is God's face turned towards man, and man's face turned towards God.' Let St Benedict himself have the last word:

Let monks prefer nothing whatever to Christ,
And may he bring us all together to life everlasting.

2
Gregorian Patrimony

T. S. Eliot was once asked why he drew so heavily on the past, since 'we know so much more than they did'. 'Precisely', he replied. 'They are what we know.' In *Burnt Norton*, a poem associated with the beauty of childhood in the Gloucestershire garden of his forebears, he propounds this principle:

> Time past and time future . . .
> What might have been and what has been
> Point to one end, which is always present.

In this light, it is but natural to turn to the springtide of Christianity in Britain, and more especially to that *vir incomparabilis*, Gregory the Great. This is not to minimize the work of the famous Celtic missionaries of the North: they have left an indelible mark upon English tradition and culture. Yet one can sense Bede's immense relief as a historian when after twenty-two chapters, he leaves 'the horrible doings of the Britons, which their own historiographer Gildas doth lamentably set forth in writing' — and then, like a man who has toiled up a mountain and reached the summit with its sunlit vistas, he records: 'In the tenth year of the Emperor Mauricius, Gregory, Bishop of the Roman and Apostolic See which he governed thirteen years, six months and ten days, being moved by the inspiration of God, sent the servant of God, Augustine, to preach unto the nation of the English men.' Thus began our history. Bede's trumpet call has rallied Englishmen from that day to this.

Eminent historians, English, German and French, have long debated the exact chronology of the mission to England from the evidence supplied by Bede's narrative and Gregory's own letters. Whatever their different conclusions, all agree that the conversion of the heathen English was one of Gregory's most momentous initiatives. Erich Caspar regards it as the crowning achievement and most personal act of the Pope's missionary strategy, and his principal claim to the title accorded him of 'the Great'. From Rome, Gregory sent his monks instructions never to coerce the English: they must be treated gently and with sensitivity. Keep their pagan sanctuaries intact: simply sprinkle them with holy water and so consecrate them to the worship of the true God. Let them learn by taking small steps upward: don't ask them to make a giant leap. So speaks the author of the *Cura Pastoralis*. It is to this man of moderation and charm that we owe, not only the conversion of the realm and the organization of the *Ecclesia Anglorum* as he called it, but also our integration into Europe and even our national existence. The Roman temper of his mind was strangely akin to the English — or did he help to mould it? Clear-sighted, shrewd and practical, an energetic and administrative genius, an enterprising missionary, a preacher who disliked abstractions and delighted in playful anecdote, a keen psychologist, and a lofty contemplative — such was the man of whom Bede proudly wrote: 'Although to others he is not an apostle, yet he is so to us, for we are the seal of his apostleship in the Lord.' The English Church as the direct and special creation of the Holy See — indeed of one Pope — would seem to be unique in history, and when at the last day the apostles lead into the high Jerusalem the glorious procession of the peoples they have converted, Englishmen will fall in behind Gregory the Great.

'Great' he certainly was. In an age of universal ruin and destruction as cruel, bureaucratic, corrupt and violent as our own, Gregory laid the foundations of a new Europe. He formulated no five-year plans for constructing a fresh social order; he simply laboured for the salvation of men in a dying world because the time was short. It was precisely this indifference to temporal results that made him the rallying-point for the forces of life, and the creator of that very civilization we are now doing our best to save. He created it mainly through two small books which papal Rome, in his person, promulgated to the world. Upon his election in 590, he at once set to work to complete a short spiritual treatise, long meditated, for the guidance of the pastoral clergy. In his orderly Roman fashion, he

drew up the four propositions of his thesis: the grave burden
of the pastoral office, the *ars artium*; the qualities demanded of
a pastor of souls; the psychological aspect of the office (to judge
from his forty categories of men and women, he must have
proved a wonderful confessor); and the necessity of a life of
prayer — the priest must 'return unto himself', *redeat ad semet-
ipsum*, a typical Gregorian phrase. With deliberation he called
his book *Liber regulae pastoralis* as a counterpart perhaps to
Benedict's *Liber regulae monachorum*, the technical term *regula*
denoting the ordering of a religious community. Then from his
own monastery on the Coelian Hill, he selected forty monks
under the leadership of Augustine to go forth armed simply
with treatises on spiritual perfection to reconstruct their totter-
ing world. They were to conquer first England and, through
England, the whole of Western Europe for Christ and Roman
civilization.

Until the sixteenth century, England regarded Gregory as the
fons et origo of its whole doctrine and practice. When the
Normans revised the liturgical calendar and ejected the Anglo-
Saxon saints, even Lanfranc's reforming zeal dared not delete
the red-letter feast of 12 March from the *festivitates quae magni-
fice celebrantur* ('feasts celebrated with the greatest solemnity').
At pre-Conquest Glastonbury and Worcester it ranked with the
Epiphany, major feasts of our Lady, and the twelve Apostles.
To the English monk of Whitby who wrote his first biography
about 713 he is 'our master, our doctor, our Gregory'; St Bede's
(673–735) last recorded words bequeathed *The Pastoral Care*
to Egbert of York as his greatest treasure; his contemporary,
the Devonshire St Boniface (680–754) exchanged copies of Gregory's letters with both Canterbury and York; Alcuin
(735–804), the schoolmaster of Europe, urged Eabald of York
to 'read and re-read Gregory's *Pastoral Care*'; King Alfred the
Great (849–901), who gave us the King's English, gave it in his
own translations of Gregory's *Herd-Book*, his *Dialogues*, and
Bede's *History*, in that order; Aelfric of Eynsham (955–1020)
wrote a life of Gregory in prose worthy of Dryden; Gregory is
predominant in the fourteenth-century mystics — he is the only
author Julian of Norwich quotes directly. Veneration for
England's Apostle found final and fitting public expression

when, interrupting Audeley, one of his judges, Thomas More
appealed in Westminster Hall from the narrow issues of Tudor
England to the event that made it a portion of world-civiliz-
ation:

For as St Paul said of the Corinthians, 'I have regenerated you, my
children, in Christ', so might St Gregory, Pope of Rome, of whom by
St Augustine his messenger, we first received the Christian faith, of us
Englishmen truly say: 'You are my children, because I have given to
you everlasting salvation.'

For the first time since that mission of Augustine in 597, the
primacy of Gregory was being assailed. If his name could not be
slashed out, at least the hated epithet '*papae*' could be defaced or
erased wherever it occurred. For half a century from 1549,
Anglican Church calendars make no mention whatever of him;
he reappears in 1604 simply as 'Gregorie 12 March'; in 1662
under the Restoration, he is back in full glory as 'Gregory
Magnus, Bishop of Rome, Confessor'; in 1928 the calendar
strips him of his 'magnus', a sometime trophied warrior now
in disgrace. The sixteenth-century Reformers made no appeal
to Canterbury; Luther had been an Augustinian friar and it was
to Augustine of Hippo, the Doctor of Grace, that they looked
for guidance. To meet the demands of polemic, they turned
especially to the Bible and the early Fathers. Their researches,
as Professor Owen Chadwick has pointed out, led them to
unforeseen conclusions. The closer their studies, the nearer they
drew to the traditionalists and the further they retreated from
Calvinism and non-episcopacy. They found that the ancient
Church, Ignatius of Antioch, Cyprian, Anthanasius, had all
valued virginity, considered private confession and spiritual
direction to be useful, revered the Blessed Virgin and the saints,
used formal and even elaborate liturgies. While remaining indis-
putable disciples of the Reformation, the outstanding Anglican
divines — Richard Hooker (1554–1601), steeped in Aristotle
and Aquinas; Lancelot Andrewes (1555–1626), a translator of
the Authorized Version and master of fifteen languages; John
Donne (1573–1631), poet and Dean of St Paul's, great-grandson
of St Thomas More's sister, and nephew of Jasper Heywood,
SJ; Nicholas Ferrar (1592–1637), founder of Little Gidding;

William Laud (1573–1645), Archbishop of Canterbury — these, one and all, move in an atmosphere redolent of Catholic sacramental thought and devotion. The *Preces Privatae* of Lancelot Andrewes, for instance, written originally in Greek, draw upon ancient church services, the Jewish synagogue, the Roman breviary, Irenaeus, Tertullian, Cyprian, Arnobius, Lactantius, Jerome, Ambrose, Gregory Nazianzen, Gregory of Nyssa, John Chrysostom, Cassian, Augustine, Cyril of Alexandria, Fulgentius of Ruspe, Bede, Anselm, a host of medievalists — Theophylact, Bernard, Peter Lombard, Aquinas, to say nothing of secular authors such as Euripides, Cicero, Seneca and Erasmus — but from this glittering galaxy, two names are notably absent, both of them popes and Doctors of the Church, viz. Leo the Great and Gregory the Great.

In the following century, the Age of Reason, under its high-priests, Locke and Hume, patristic study was at a discount, the Bible a mere object of higher criticism. But with the nineteenth-century patristic revival of the Oxford Movement, there came a man sent from God, whose name was John Henry Newman, to unite the two traditions. Emboldened by Catholic Emancipation, Catholics had emerged from their hiding-holes, and before long monks were busy reinstating Gregory as master and teacher. Ullathorne's *Christian Patience* was little more than a synopsis of Gregory's *Morals on Job*; in his *Lex Levitarum* Hedley was doing precisely what Bede and Boniface, Alcuin and Alfred had urged all bishops to do — instructing priests and church students in Gregory's *Pastoral Care*. In our own century, Cuthbert Butler's *Western Mysticism* has placed Gregory along with Augustine of Hippo and Bernard of Clairvaux in the trinity of the foremost contemplatives of the Western Church. But Catholic efforts pale beside Anglican erudition and the patristic studies sponsored by the leaders of the Oxford Movement. From that day to this, a steady stream of translation and expert historical research have added immeasurably to our common heritage, and leave us for ever in their debt.

Times have changed. On the one hand, St Gregory the Great is no longer ignored by our Anglican brethren — we owe them the monumental study of his life and work by F. H. Dudden;

on the other, Pope Paul VI specifically declared that the Anglican communion occupies a unique position in the Church at large.

'Truce!' cried Truth. 'You speak truly, by Jesus!
Let's clasp hands in covenant and each kiss the other!'
'And let no persons,' said Peace, 'perceive that we quarrelled!
There is nothing impossible to the Almighty.'

These words of Langland, written six hundred years ago as he stood on the Malvern Hills dreaming that marvellous dream in which he foresaw the consequences of the disintegration of Christendom, the new power-politics, and the sovereignty of money and economics, are strangely apt today. Men have walked on the moon and seen the good earth floating small and blue and beautiful amid the cold silence of the planets, an earth peopled by men whom God created to be brothers, but who have had to learn brotherhood afresh in underground cells and concentration camps where all, whatever their labels, have suffered alike for their Christian witness. A new vision is opening on the horizon. We are moving once more towards a 'United Europe'. But a Europe that is no more than a supra-national republic of scientists, sociologists, writers and teachers will be doomed to failure unless it includes theologians and saints. It is here that St Gregory the Great, Apostle of the English and maker of Europe, has a vital role to play.

In the eighth-century biography, the monk of Whitby repeats the legend that, long before election to the papacy, Gregory had extorted permission from Pope Benedict I to slip away from Rome and fulfil his heart's desire to evangelize England. The Romans, distraught at hearing of his flight, stormed the papal palace with strident cries of, *'Petrum offendisti; Romam destruxisti; Gregorium dimisisti!'* ('You have insulted Peter, ruined Rome, sent Gregory away!') There is a moral for us in the tale. We are Gregory's handiwork; we must never let him go. Kathleen Raine has defined tradition as 'vital memory'. While we look at a universe, terrible in its destructive potentialities, we must remember the rock from which we were hewn, that steadfast shepherd hemmed in by swords, with pestilence, famine and death at his very doors. For fourteen years, his heart steadied on eternity, his vision clear, his will one with God's, his frail body faced the labour, the pressure, the sufferings of his awful charge with a solicitude, a sweetness and tenderness that knew no bounds. Having proclaimed Christ's gospel to the distant race of the Angles, he received Augustine's report with a cry of joy: 'Glory to God in the highest!' Once an apostle, always an apostle: he is 'our master, our doctor, our Gregory'.

> What we call the beginning is often the end
> And to make an end is to make a beginning.
> The end is where we start from.

3
An English Monk

Liturgical reform is a disease recurring with rhythmic regularity every fifty years or so. But when saints are cast out of the calendar, they have a habit of creeping back stealthily perhaps, but none the less surely. St Wulfstan of Worcester, last and one of the greatest of the Anglo-Saxon bishops, had to stand by in silence and watch the Norman Lanfranc, who never got beyond the mere rudiments of Englishry, suppress the traditional English feast of our Lady's Conception, substitute the translation of St Benedict's relics to Fleury for the ancient *transitus* on 21 March, and cast clear out of the calendar all the saints, including even Dunstan and Alphege, to whom the English had paid the profoundest veneration from time immemorial. It must have seemed the end of all things English — but was it? Wulfstan himself was to prove the enduring link between old and new. He would withstand all the bewildering tides of the times, a sturdy massive figure, jutting out of the maelstrom of contemporary history, a rock of stability amid the eddying waters of dissolution which engulfed the world to which he belonged.

One's first reaction to a life of an Anglo-Saxon bishop is possibly boredom. It is almost certain that the man will be treated, in R. A. Knox's phrase, as an umbrella stand on which to hang heroic virtues. We prefer our hagiography served up palatably by Graham Greene or Evelyn Waugh. Quite. But our chief authority for Wulfstan's life is a remarkably sober and reliable document written by Coleman, the saint's chaplain, a monk of Worcester, in one of the last great prose works to be written before the English language was temporarily submerged beneath the Latin-French culture of the Normans. This account was sent to Rome for Wulfstan's canonization on 21 April 1203, where it may still repose in the Vatican archives. Now the figure that emerges from Coleman's pages is no stained-glass window saint, but rather a man intensely alive and intensely human. The newly-ordained priest who with youthful appetite stood watching the goose for his dinner being spitted and roasted over an open fire until 'his soul melted with delight and his mouth ran with water' and then, to punish himself, bade farewell to fat goose and flesh meat for ever; the prior who gave an impudent woman a resounding smack on the face; the bishop who whipped out of his pocket the knife he kept for paring his nails, snipped off an offending lock from the flowing tresses of a kneeling young man and held it out to him with the smiling invitation to shorten the rest to match; the old man who kissed and fondled children, reflecting how lovely must be the God who made such lovely little creatures, and who stooped to smooth out the creases in the cassocks of his untidy altar-servers; the blunt Englishman that administered a sound snub to the patronizing and polished Norman, Geoffrey of Coutances, who upbraided him for wearing cheap lambskin when sable or fox would better become his dignity ('Wulfstan answered that Geoffrey and men versed in worldly prudence should use the fur of cunning beasts; he for his simplicity was content with lambskin. Geoffrey had at him again and bade him at least put on catskin. Believe me, quoth Wulfstan, we sing the Lamb of God oftener than the Cat of God') — a man such as this is no pious puppet on a medieval stage. Coleman tells none of the tall stories that raise sophisticated smiles in our machine-age of hard facts — he even concedes that Wulfstan's nose was large and red, too large and red, and notes with satisfaction that in death 'even his nose which in his life stood forth overmuch minished and grew white.' For the rest, he relates the incidents for the saint's life among the plasterers and builders and farmers of Worcestershire — the Outy Grimkelsons and Turstan Dubbes and Gouse Gamelsons and Spurt Lunsers — with such a wealth of careful topographical detail, that anyone who has fallen under the spell of the quiet villages of the Severn valley where to this day the tenor bells of the thirteenth-century parish church of Kempsey, site of Wulfstan's manor-house, answer across the river the deep-toned bass carillon of Worcester Cathedral, whose magnificent crypt built by Wulfstan in 1084 still stands, will feel inclined to agree with Coleman when he says of his hero: 'I think Wulfstan will never lack for readers so long as the stars turn about the pole, and there is any writing in the world.'

Wulfstan's life falls naturally into two divisions: as a monk of Worcester Priory until he was fifty-three years of age; and as Bishop of Worcester for a further thirty-four years. The two phases may be considered to coincide roughly with the pre-Conquest and post-Conquest period; had there been no Conquest, Wulfstan would not have played the important part he does in English history. When he was born in 1008 a few miles from Stratford-on-Avon in the county which Henry James has called 'the core and centre of the English world, midmost England', Lanfranc was already two years old, so that they were exact contemporaries when, sixty years later, they met and measured each other's strength. Coleman does not record at what age Wulfstan became a monk — he was already a priest — but what he has said of the observance at Worcester Priory sufficiently answers those who see in Anglo-Saxon monasticism before the Conquest little but decadence. Wulfstan, successively schoolmaster, precentor, sacristan and prior, became famed as preacher and confessor. Later as bishop, he continued as far as possible to reside in the monastery and to live the life of a simple monk. He followed the monastic timetable, insisted on taking his weeks in singing the daily High Mass, noticed absences of defaulters at the Night Office and gave the absolution and blessing at Compline. Under his rule the priory prospered, and from twelve monks the community grew to fifty. He refounded the priory of Westbury and — an important fact in view of the post-Conquest flowering of eremitical life — gave his support to one of his monks at Worcester who wished to found a community of hermits at Malvern.

St Wulfstan has often been depicted as a simple, unlettered, bluff Anglo-Saxon bishop, *rudus* or *idiota*. This is to fly in the face of facts. True, he had not the acute subtlety, the eager, brilliant, progressive spirit of Lanfranc, for he was cast in the mould of Wilfrid, Dunstan and Oswald; but a glance at the literary achievement of Worcester and the extant books of Worcester Library under Wulfstan as prior and bishop should be sufficient to dispel any notion of illiteracy, and to prove that under his leadership Worcester became a most active centre of intellectual life and culture. He showed an astonishing adaptability. He not only accepted the Normans but he appreciated their learning and sent his favourite disciple Nicholas to Canterbury, to profit by Lanfranc's world-famed teaching. It was from this Nicholas that the school of Worcester — Coleman, Florence and John the chroniclers — was derived. Worcester gave unique opportunities for the survival of the English tradition, for Wulfstan in his long rule bridged over the period of transition, and the monastery was ruled by a succession of English priors, Wulfstan's disciples, until the mid-twelfth century. The early manuscripts of Worcester Cathedral Library provide far more than a pedantic excursion into the realm of palaeography, for whereas the Carolingian revival of learning in Europe directed attention to Augustine's theological works and Jerome's exegesis, thus paving the way for the Schoolmen, England itself stood largely apart from the movement which Englishmen such as Alcuin had inspired, retaining her unique and abiding love of her own apostle, Gregory the Great.

Of the four most ancient eighth-century Worcester fragments, so ancient that only Durham possibly possesses their equal, two contain works of the apostle of the English, the third is a gospel-book of the eighth century derived from a standard text brought to Canterbury presumably from Rome in the early days of St Gregory's mission, the fourth is a fragment of St Jerome's Commentary on Matthew. The two Gregorian fragments are a Latin manuscript of the *Cura Pastoralis*, probably copied at Worcester, and an anthology of St Gregory's writings compiled by his contemporary, Paterius. (Manuscripts of Paterius have never been common: those of Paris, the Vatican and Durham are assigned to the twelfth century.) Two more copies of the *Cura Pastoralis* — this time in English — are the glory of Worcester. One is the very presentation copy which Alfred the Great sent to the church of Worcester. It still contains the name Wereferth, bishop of the see, and bears Alfred's inscription: 'This book shall go to Worcester.' It is preserved today in the Bodleian (MS Hatton 20), while Corpus Christi College, Cambridge possesses a second copy, undoubtedly of Worcester origin, made under Wulfstan, probably to save King Alfred's copy from wear and tear. A considerable number of manuscripts, written wholly or partly in English, for the most part in the eleventh century when Wulfstan was either prior or bishop, are scattered among various libraries — St Gregory's *Dialogues*, in both Latin and Anglo-Saxon, a composite volume containing extracts from Bede, and works such as St Jerome on the Psalms, Augustine's *City of God, Letters* of St Leo, extracts from Isidore, Fulgentius, Maximus, Eusebius, Severinus, Peter Chrysologus, Origen, Ambrose and Chrysostom, all bear witness to the sound scholarship of Worcester Priory under Wulfstan's rule.

Such a library would redound to the credit of any bishop in any century. For Wulfstan belongs essentially to that splendid body of English diocesan bishops whose task lay, not in reforming abuses or guiding others by writings of spiritual counsel, but in giving the gospel to all classes of men, in being the *forma facti gregis ex animo* of which St Peter speaks, the living practical embodiment of the qualities which St Gregory demands of the pastor of souls in the *Shepherd's Care* so familiar to Wulfstan. In the pages of his biography, you meet him among kings and princes, among his fellow-bishops and priests, among nuns and simple labourers, among rough soldiers, and children in their mother's arms. We hear much in these days of the necessity for priests to get to know their people. Seven hundred years before Wesley fulminated against the black slave-traffic at Bristol, Wulfstan had wiped out the white slave-traffic there by going and living among the citizens and quietly studying the problem at first-hand for three months together. Then, not by any Wesleyan spectacular mass conversion but 'little by little', by Sunday sermons and by endless private contact with those concerned, he blotted out the disgrace.

In considering St Wulfstan as the pattern of an English bishop, one is tempted to wonder whether the Benedictine Rule and the social setting of his time would not have produced a similar type anywhere else in Europe. England itself provides the answer. Lanfranc of Canterbury, Wulfstan of Worcester, Anselm of Bec all held responsible office at exactly the same time, were trained by the same Rule, shared the same ideals — yet how different they were. They represent two entirely different epochs, two entirely different cultures. Wulfstan differed in nothing from Chad and Wilfrid, Dunstan and Oswald. Anselm looked backward to Augustine, forward to Aquinas. The intellects of Wulfstan and Anselm are not to be compared, yet England never recognized either Lanfranc or Anselm as her own; Anselm left little or no impress on English thought whereas he has left an indelible mark on European letters. Wulfstan on the other hand was England's darling, and even in our sophisticated age, children in Worcestershire are proud to hear his name. His type has persisted throughout the history of the English church: Wulfstan and John Fisher, Wulfstan and Challoner, and above all, Wulfstan and Bernard Ullathorne who held jurisdiction over the same see. Ullathorne, the last of the vicars apostolic; Manning, high-souled, energetic, determined, deeply versed in the art of statecraft; Newman, combination of sanctity and luminous, penetrating intellect — all three reproduce in the strange way history has of repeating itself the *dramatis personae* of Wulfstan, Lanfranc and Anselm almost a thousand years earlier.

Prayer used by St Wulfstan of Worcester

O Lord, for thy great mercy's sake, through the love and merits of all thine holy ones, have mercy upon me a sinner, according to thy glorious will. Strengthen and stablish my heart in thy will.

O my Lord, let me never depart from this wretched life by sudden death; but whensoever my appointed time shall come and it be thy will that I leave this worthless life, let me end my days in quietness. Also, I pray my dear Lord for thine own name's sake, through thy goodness, that thou let me not depart from this world ere through thy great mercy I have forgiveness for all I have ever wrought against thy glorious will, by day or night, wittingly or unwittingly, in word or in deed or in my secret thought. High King of heaven and redeemer of all the earth, have mercy upon my wretched self, according as may be thy glorious will, and grant me merciful forgiveness from mine offences both in this life and in that to come. Grant me, my Lord, true repentance, confession, and atonement for my sins, and turn me away from mine unrighteousness to thy will and mine own need.

Grant me, my Lord, right faith and true charity, humility and piety, purity and contrition, strength against the temptations of the devil, patience in adversity, and moderation in prosperity. Soften thou, my Lord, the hardness of this stony heart of mine, and grant me abundant tears that I may bewail and repent those misdeeds that in my misery I daily commit against thy will. Enlighten, my Lord, the thought of my heart with lively understanding, enlighten my words and deeds, my body, my soul, and my life with the outpouring of spiritual gifts, and grant me thy mercy both in this life and in the life to come.

To thee, my Lord, Almighty God, and to all thy holy ones, be praise and glory and thanks for ever and ever, for all the gifts, and benefits thou hast ever granted me, and for all the mercies bestowed upon me a sinner. I humbly pray thee, Lord, to help me and all my friends and kinsmen, and all those who desire and confide in my prayers, both living and departed, granting to the living prosperity in this life, and in the life to come joy everlasting; and to the departed merciful forgiveness of all their sins, and the bliss of the kingdom of heaven for ever and ever. Likewise I beseech thee, my Lord, to show mercy to all those who have done good to me and shown me the knowledge of good, and to grant everlasting forgiveness to all who have spoken or thought evil against me, or may yet intend to do so.

O Lord, high King of heaven, strengthen them according to thy will, and be merciful to all Christian folk, living or departed, to all that have received the cleansing of baptism, for thy name's sake. Amen.

Translated by Dame Scholastica Hebgin from the Anglo-Saxon

This prayer and the short extracts from Latin which follow are drawn from St Wulfstan's own book of prayers, known as the *Portiforium*, preserved in the library of Corpus Christi College, Cambridge. In the life of his hero, the monk Coleman often refers to this stout little volume of 724 pages, a kind of mini-breviary, which Wulfstan always carried with him, whether behind the locked doors of a secret oratory 'known only to his servants, that he might not seem to make a show of religion', or on horseback when he 'began a psalm as he mounted, and he and his attendants recited psalms without pause until he reached his journey's end'. There is nothing original about the prayers, except that they are those of a typical Englishman: they are clear, practical, deeply-felt but not at all emotional. One, numbered 16 in the manuscript, is of particular interest in the present context. A petition for pardon passes to praise of the Blessed Trinity, and concludes with a protracted litany centred round the Book of Revelation. The Virgin Mother of God, the four and twenty ancients, the angels, the apostles, all are there in force. Matheus, Marcus, Lucas, Joannes appear in small script and then suddenly there starts out of the page in bold capitals (our Lady and St Peter alone share the honour), the petition: *SANCTUS GREGORIUS* et omnes sancti famuli Dei intercedant pro me. The Apostle of England is the sole non-scriptural saint in the long litany: Wulfstan is firmly rooted in the tradition that stems from Bede.

From the Portiforium of Saint Wulfstan

Have mercy, Lord: have mercy, Christ:
    free me from uncleanness of heart and body
      and quench the fires of lust.
    free me from the devil's wiles.
    free me from all evil.
    free me from impure thoughts.
    may my soul live in thee.
    may my flesh rejoice in thee.
    may my life reach its goal in thee.
    Father, my glory, my life.
    Saviour, my salvation, my strength.
Mercy, O Holy Paraclete, my comfort, my enlightenment.
Mercy, Lord God, Trinity and Unity.

Prayer: Lord God, magnet of virgins, attract us also to yourself, and so prepare us to join the maiden throng that will be led into the Courts of the King. Through Christ our Lord.

No. 2109

In this concluding prayer, the terms employed in translation derive from the direct spiritual tradition of Dunstan, Ethelwold, Aelfric and Chaucer: applied to both men and women, they were the common coinage of English speech as far at least as 1600. At what point and why did the concepts maide, maidenhede, and virginitee yield in modern usage to celibacy and celibate, words devoid of any Christian resonance?

Etymologically the Latin *coelebs* from which the English derives is described as 'a word of dubious origin'. The Oxford Dictionary states that *coelebs* and *coelibatus*, the only cognate Latin words, are employed by classical authors such as Pliny,

Horace and Ovid, chiefly in reference to plants and animals, although Horace speaks of a *coelebs senex* — an aged bachelor or widower — and Cicero makes the adjective almost a noun: *Coelibes esse prohibento* — they should not be unmarried. The word was treated as a third declension adjective of one termination, and belongs to the same group of words as *plebs* and *urbs*: cf. *particeps, inops, anceps*. Two laws, the *Lex Julia* and the *Lex Papia Poppaea* of Emperor Augustus (+ AD 14) severely punished any who chose to live unmarried. Since linguistic science is comparatively modern, the word found its way at least once into the liturgy, where it is sung to this day at the monastic office of Sunday Vigils in a hymn of unknown authorship, sometimes ascribed to Pope Gregory the Great:

Quo carnis actu exules	Freed from human desire
Effecti ipsi coelibes,	Minds fixed on heaven,
Ut praestolamur cernui	Bowed low in worship
Melos canamus gloriam.	Let us hymn your glory.

The meaning has undergone a subtle change. Presumably, to the Christian hymnographer *coelebs* was connected with the Latin *coelum*, the abode of the blessed, inhabited by *coelibes* — heaven-dwellers or angels — a term increasingly applied to monks. As Hildegard of Bingen would assert in her *Scivias*: 'Monks are like angels, protecting God's people from the devil by their constant prayer and service.' To Émile Littré (1801–81), the eminent French scholar and lexicographer, the word *coelebs* was anything but angelic in meaning. Admitting that its origin was obscure, he derived it from a Sanscrit root *coe* = sansoeil, one-eyed, combined with *libere* or *lubere* = a liking for solitude. This powerfully evokes an image of the Cyclopes of Odyssey 9, the savage race of one-eyed giants, island-dwellers free of all social ties and ignorant of cultivation. When finally the word *coelebs*, doffing its Hindu ochre *kāvi* and its Graeco-Roman pallium, donned an English silk cravat and perfumed peruke, did the one-eyed anti-social solitary commend itself to the ironical eighteenth-century mind as a fitting symbol of permanent bachelorhood? Indeed, 'that great Cham of literature', Dr Johnson, who considered that monks and nuns who indulged a 'youthful passion for abstracted devotion' practised a solitude that was 'dangerous to reason without being favourable to virtue, certainly luxurious, probably superstitious, and possibly mad', was himself responsible, as was no other, for the absorption of the word 'celibate' into the language. Johnson's contemporary, the Swedish naturalist Linnaeus (1707–78) had followed the classical model of associating *coelebs* with plants and animals. Observing that flocks of chaffinches tend to congregate during winter in flocks of males or females, he labelled the charming little fellow whose song in April on an English orchard bough filled an English poet with homesickness, *fringilla coelebs*.

It is perhaps pertinent to the discussion to note that whereas the *lex continentiae* was obligatory from the fifth century, the expression *lex coelibatus* does not appear in any conciliar text of the Roman Church until the sixteenth century, at the synod of Sens in 1528; its appearance in any text of a General Council was withheld until *Lumen Gentium* of the Second Vatican Council. One of the prime targets of the Protestant Reformers had been the abolition of the law forbidding the clergy to marry. When it was repealed in England in 1549, the Latin *coelebs* was at hand to designate an arid, loveless and negative state of life. Latin had for so long held the field as the universal medium of expression, it was but natural that the classical past should be ransacked to provide words that could be stripped of all trappings and clothed in English 'russet yeas and honest kersey noes'. The printing press and the Renaissance accelerated, facilitated and transformed the English language. So it was that *coelebs* became the English word 'celibate'. It was not easily accepted. First recorded in the New World (possibly imported from East Anglia), it appeared in English print only in 1614 in the *Vitis Palatina* 21 of John King, Bishop of London (1559–1621): 'Solitude and celebate, a single monasticke life agreeath not to it.' The word reappeared at rare intervals — 1659 (Evelyn), 1663 (1 Corinthians) and 1754 (Hume) — but it was not until Samuel Johnson sat down in a rickety chair at an 'old crazy deal table' in the dictionary workshop of 17 Gough Square, and included the word 'celibate' as one of more than 40,000 words in his *Dictionary* published in 1755, that it became part of a living language. Moreover Johnson himself put it to use. Boswell assures us that his hero 'preferred ill-assorted marriage to cheerless celibacy', and his much-travelled Rasselas, Prince of Abyssinia, making a choice of life, reached the philosophical conclusion: 'Marriage has many pains, but celibacy has no pleasures.'

This is a far cry from the Syriac *Yiḥîdāyâ*, single from wife or family, single in heart, united to the Single One, the Only-Begotten; far removed also from Hildegard of Bingen's beautiful play on the words *vir, virgo, viriditas* — man, maid, flowering branch, power to grow green. The Englishman's virgin and maid, divided now into 'single gentlemen' and 'old maids' are seen in the pure light of the nineteenth century in J. H. Newman's *Historical Sketches:*

Bachelors are just the most selfish, unaccommodating, particular, and arbitrary persons in the community; while ancient spinsters are the most disagreeable, cross, gossiping, and miserable of their sex. Dreariness unmitigated, a shivering and hungry spirit, a soul preying on itself, a heart without an object, affections unemployed, life wasted, self-indulgence in prosperous circumstances, envy and malice in straitened; deadness of feeling in the male specimen, impotence of feeling in the female, concentrated selfishness in both; such are the only attributes with which the imagination of modern times can invest St Ambrose, bishop and confessor, or St Macrina, sister of the great Basil.

Newman's reference to St Ambrose, the Christian Julius Caesar, the man who united the Roman fatherland and the Christian faith in a single loyalty and hope, lawyer, orator, administrator, greatest of bishops, is apt at this point, for he is the exponent *par excellence* of the ideal of Christian virginity. Born in 339 from noble and Christian parents, his forebears reckoned a virgin-martyr Soteris among their number. As long as Christians had been a proscribed people living under constant threat of death, the Church in general had maintained standards of holiness and discipline derived from the Apostles themselves. When, however, in 312 after the Battle of the Milvian Bridge (only seventeen years before Ambrose's birth), Constantine the Great granted liberty of worship to all his subjects, the cessation of persecution opened the door to dissipation and worldliness. This ever-recurring rhythm, whether in history or in human life, was to be neatly summed up by Shakespeare's Jesuit contemporary, Robert Southwell, poet-ancestor of Shelley:

> Times go by turns, and chances change by course,
> From foul to fair, from better hap to worse.

Following the pattern, laxity in its turn provoked strong reaction. In a spirit of penitence and from a desire for Christian perfection, zealous laymen in their hundreds fled to the seclusion of desert wildernesses to escape contamination. The Egyptians Antony and Pachomius had already blazed the trail for Christian monks but not, be it noted, for Christian women. The women had long anticipated the action of the men: a nun is not a female monk.

4
What is a Nun?

Love, light for me
Thy ruddiest blazing torch,
That I, albeit a beggar by the porch
Of the glad Palace of Virginity,
May gaze within, and sing the pomp I see . . .
There of pure virgins none
Is fairer seen,
Save One
Than Mary Magdalene.

COVENTRY PATMORE

In the length and breadth of the Old Testament, nothing what-ever foreshadows the relationship portrayed in the gospels between God-made-Man and woman. In the three great *Fiat*s of holy Scripture, the first — *Fiat lux*, Let there be light — is spoken in the opening page of Genesis by the triune God; the third — *Fiat voluntas tua*, Let thy will be done — is the cry wrung from the lips of God the Son made Man in Gethsemane; and between the two, the *Fiat mihi*, Let it be done to me, of Mary of Nazareth, a wholly human creature, gives consent to God's plan of incarnation and redemption. Again, whereas none but men occupy the central position as recipients and guardians of the Old Covenant — Abraham 'our father in the faith', Moses the law-giver, Elijah the prophet — in the New, peerless and alone, stands the same young girl, Ark of that Covenant who is God's Only-Begotten Son.

When in due time Christ entered upon his public ministry, women called forth his full humanity. On a natural level, they prepared his meals, provided what comforts they could, watched him play with their children, caress them and send them off with a blessing; on a supernatural level, with subtle, quick, feminine instinct, they gave him what he had come on earth to seek — faith. The prostitutes were among the first to believe, to say nothing of the woman who had disposed of no fewer than five husbands and heard from his lips, over a pail of water drawn from a well in Samaria, the sublimest teaching that the Word of God ever uttered. Our Lord flouted the false standards of his day: he scandalized the 'unco guid' and rigidly righteous Pharisees and surprised even his own apostles; the Almighty was not constricted by laws of culture. He spoke and consorted openly with women of every rank and class of society, ate with them, accepted costly gifts, defended them under attack, and after the resurrection made a woman of ill repute the first apostle to proclaim the Good News.

Three days previously, knowing that his hour had come as the gospel puts it, Jesus Christ our High Priest had sat surrounded by the Twelve, to celebrate the love-feast of the New Covenant in his Blood. Only after he had placed himself unreservedly in the hands of each — 'Take and eat. This is my Body' — was Judas, in possession now of his prey, able to go out with his Master's permission from that supper-room of divine light and self-giving into the black self-chosen chaos of betrayal and despair. As for the Eleven, all seemed well as they accompanied Jesus to the Garden of Olives singing psalms of joy and thanksgiving, until they came face to face with a mob armed with clubs, whereupon they fled in fear. Not so the women.

'Standing by the cross of Jesus were his mother, and his mother's sister, Mary the wife of Clopas, and Mary Magdalen' — the three archetypes of womanhood, the virgin, the wife and mother, and the harlot. For ever and aye they stand as embodiments of that love, special to womankind, which no waters of affliction can quench. From the sixth to the twentieth century, the liturgy of the Roman Church made no obvious distinction between Mary of Bethany, Mary Magdalen, and the sinful woman of Luke 7. Today biblical critics discard the identification of Magdalen with the unnamed sinner, a view accepted in the liturgical reform of Vatican II. Mary Magdalen is accounted a woman of means out of whom our Lord had cast seven devils (not a bad innings); with deep love she followed him, providing for him out of her substance. But is the damage, if any, likely to be rectified? The word 'magdalen' has become a common noun in Christian usage whether in literature or life, to denote 'a reformed prostitute' (*OED*). The Maries beneath the Cross are likely to remain a mystery of love and of divine irony. The poets succeed where the theologians fail:

> The only hope, or else despair
> Lies in the choice of pyre or pyre—
> To be redeemed from fire by fire.

T. S. Eliot has summed up the Holy Spirit's perfect restoration of innocence in wounded souls who have gazed upon the face of God:

> To become renewed, transfigured, in another pattern.
> Sin is Behovely, but
> All shall be well, and
> All manner of thing shall be well.

It goes without saying that men as well as women were influenced by contact with Jesus Messiah, and were led to dedicate their lives to God in prayer, poverty and perpetual chastity, as the Acts of the Apostles prove. But the first to seize upon the exact implications of the gospel with its new and revolutionary evaluation of woman was precisely woman herself. At a single stroke, the prohibition of divorce translated the moral equality of the sexes into deeds; but that did not go far enough. It was left to the virgins, 'God's chosen ones, brides of Christ', to proclaim their right to the full prerogatives of human personality: a fulfilment of their womanhood, no longer dependent on physical qualities but attained through spiritual and intellectual values. To be childless would cease to be a synonym for withered barrenness, to be unmarried neither misfortune nor curse.

Whereas Christian monasticism dates roughly from AD 300, consecrated virgins are of apostolic origin. Acts (21:9) refers to Philip of Gaza's four virgin daughters who prophesied; Tertullian (160–225) the African church Father, speaks of the *virgines sacrae* devoted to psalmody and prayer; Origen of Alexandria (185–254) observes that their number was unbelievably great; in 280, before going into solitude, the Egyptian Antony, Father of Monks as he is called, placed his young sister in a well-established parthenon of 'known and trusted virgins'. When later on the monastic ideal spread, men and women tended to join forces and work in close collaboration. Elder sisters of a family played an important part in moulding the character and outlook of brothers who were to assume leadership. Thus in Cappadocia, Macrina (d. 379), eldest of ten, took in hand her brilliant brother Basil when he returned home, laurel-crowned and insufferably conceited after completing his studies in Constantinople and Athens, and transformed him under her tutelage into the humble monk whom Benedict, Patriarch of the West, was to salute in his Rule, as 'our holy Father Basil'. Two more brothers, Gregory of Nyssa and Peter of Sebaste find a place in the calendar of saints; Peter, her youngest brother, revered her as 'father, teacher, guide and mother'. Her task of education complete, Macrina continued to live in the family estate, presiding over a large community of nuns. When she came to die, a few months after her brother Basil, she did so stretched on two wooden boards, her face turned towards the East. Whispering prayers for forgiveness of her sins, she finally sealed eyes, mouth and heart with a large sign of the cross, drew a deep breath, and closed life and prayer together, just as the lamps were being lit for Vespers. Gregory (whose theological influence since the Second Vatican Council equals, if it does not surpass, that of Thomas Aquinas) insisted on laying out her virginal body with his own hands, but such was her poverty that he himself had to supply the linen, since her personal possessions amounted to little more than the coarse veil of her consecration, and a hood. All these early Fathers together with John Chrysostom, Patriarch of Constantinople, who drew upon Olympias and her two hundred and fifty nuns for support of every kind in the heavy trials that beset him, belong to the Church of the East. The East had never been very interested in the West; to the cultured Greek, the West was barbarian, its Roman balance and common sense mere mediocrity; but this fourth century of the Christian era was to see a constellation of men of genius and sanctity in both East and West who would renew the face of the known world, and transform the *urbs aurea aeterna* of Horace and Virgil into the *Roma nobilis* of Sts Peter and Paul, the goal of Christian pilgrims yesterday and today until tomorrow.

It staggers the mind to realize that St Athanasius to whom St

Antony left his sheepskin cloak was but thirty-three and recently ordained as Bishop of Alexandria when Basil of Caesarea was born in 329, his bosom-friend Gregory Nazianzen one year, and his brother Gregory of Nyssa two years later. These three were boys when John Chrysostom was born about 347. In 360, St Benedict's hero, Martin of Tours, was forty-four, Ambrose twenty-one, Jerome nineteen, Paulinus of Nola seven, Augustine six. Almost all came into direct contact with one another, sometimes as friends, occasionally as foes. Many of the Eastern Fathers were monks; in the West, Jerome alone had embraced the monastic life, and it was he, the Latin educated in Rome, Antioch and Constantinople, who resolved the tension, built the bridge linking East and West, and set the pattern of monastic life that was to permeate the Middle Ages. The pages of the Rule prove that St Benedict had studied Jerome assiduously; he quotes directly from him six times and, like Jerome, has little time for monks who lived alone or in twos or threes as self-will dictated. 'Live in a monastery under the control of one father and with many companions', Jerome wrote to Rusticus (Epistle 125). 'Things at first compulsory will become habitual' (cp. Prologue to Benedict's Rule).

No art is ever learned without a master and these will teach you, one humility, another patience, another silence, a fourth meekness. You will eat what you are told to eat, wear what clothes are given you, obey one you do not like, go to bed tired out, be forced to rise before you have had sufficient rest.

No room here for gyrovagues or sarabaites.

This digression is not alien to the purpose of the present study for no century so much resembles our own as the fourth: we are its heirs. To it belong the Vulgate translation of the Bible, the *Confessions* and the *City of God*; the codifying of Roman law; the great Latin hymns of Prudentius; and the grouping of men and women ascetics in the West that was to lead almost inevitably to Subiaco and Monte Cassino, to St Benedict, and to Boethius, who gave the Middle Ages the deepest concept of its philosophy, the *simplicitas Dei* — the simplicity of God, so striking a quality of the Benedictine Rule. With determined vigour this small group was pursuing a new ideal of knowledge.

Steeped as they all were in the pagan literature of the ancient world, they were aiming at nothing less than a restructuring of human thought, in much the same way as theologians today.

The problem, acutely relevant then as now, was the attitude the Church should adopt towards the world: in the fourth century it was the old paganism, in the twentieth, the new. Even in the Church there was a double morality — one for men, who often had concubines, another for women, whom the law would punish for adultery. History repeats itself in a cyclic pattern, and as in the Apostolic Church it was the women who spread the gospel, so in the crisis of the fourth century it was women, especially those consecrated to God, who provided inspiration and antidote. When, in 382, Jerome the *doctor doctorum* of John of Salisbury, 'the only champion, expositor and light of our religion' of Erasmus, exchanged Constantinople and his beloved master Gregory Nazianzen for Rome, Pope Damasus, and the work of revision of the Latin Psalter and Gospels, he made a discovery important for the direction of his own life. Among the throngs of fashionable women who plastered their faces with rouge and antimony, loaded their heads with other people's hair, and showed a front of maidenly timidity amid a troop of grandchildren (the description is from Jerome's own pen), he found on the Aventine a community of women bearing the noblest names of antiquity, living a life of extraordinary asceticism. Many are numbered among the saints: Sts Marcella, Asella, Albina, Lea, Melania, Fabiola and, more important than all the rest, Paula and her daughter Eustochium. Eustochium, a child of twelve or so when she decided to give her life completely to God, put herself under Jerome's spiritual direction, and drew from this fiery caustic critic hidden reserves of deep tenderness. The opening apostrophe of a letter he addressed to her would be copied by Abelard in a letter to Heloise: 'My Eustochium, daughter, lady, fellow-worker, sister — the first to your age, the second to your rank, the third to your religious vocation, the last to the place you hold in my heart.' When, as was inevitable in a society so corrupt, slanderous gossip assailed Jerome's good name, both he and Paula, with their retinue of monks and nuns, made their way to Bethlehem and there established two famous monasteries. It was in strong contrast to the wealthy Roman palace on the Aventine. Paula divided her nuns into three communities housed in low, poor buildings, each under a superior; they all dressed alike, all ate the same frugal fare, all assembled in a common oratory for the Divine Office on weekdays, and the neighbouring Church of the Nativity on Sundays, where they sang the psalms in the original Hebrew, and devoted whatever time was left to a study of the ancient codices under Jerome's direction, helping him by their expert knowledge of Greek in the translation of the Vulgate. Jerome summed up their daily round: 'They trim lamps, light fires, sweep floors, wash vegetables, cook cabbage, lay tables, run to and fro to wait on others.' It sounds very familiar. Paula paints a slightly more idyllic picture in a letter urging Marcella to join them:

In this little villa of Christ, everything is rustic, and apart from the singing of psalms there is silence. The ploughman driving the share sings an alleluia; the vine-dresser clipping the shoots with his curved pruning-knife (cp. Virgil's *Eclogues*) hums some snatch from David. This is what the shepherds whistle; these are the popular love-lays.

(Marcella as events proved, was to meet a more painful and glorious end. In 410 Goths plundered Rome, trampled on her and tortured her while she begged them to spare Principia, the young nun who attended her — a favour the ruffians granted — before she breathed her last at St Paul's-outside-the-Walls.)

In a century so like our own, when women were finding a place in law and medicine, when they cut their hair short and dressed like men, it is good to find so abrasive a tongue as Jerome's filled with praise for the scholarly group of women at Bethlehem who gave him such invaluable help, and at whose request he wrote his commentaries on St Paul's epistles, for 'these women were more capable of forming a judgement on them than most men'. When Paula died in 404, grief forced Jerome to lay aside for a time his biblical labours, but when Eustochium was laid in the same tomb as her mother in 419, it was not long before Jerome followed her, to be buried near both his friends in the grotto of the Nativity, traditionally the birthplace of the Christ-Child. Not a vestige remains of the buildings raised to provide a roof 'so that if Joseph and Mary chance to come to Bethlehem, they will not fail to find shelter and welcome', but as the Benedictine of the eighth century, Hrabanus Maurus, would observe, 'the written word alone flouts destiny':

> God's finger made its furrows in the rock
> In letters, when he gave his folk the law.
> And things that are, and have been, and may be,
> Their secret with the written word abides.

Jerome's biblical translations, his treatises and letters remain his enduring monument.

As might be expected, his moral and ascetical writings have exercised a considerable influence to our own day. When Jovinian crossed swords with our Lady's knight-errant by denying her perpetual virginity, Jerome was quick to point out that in the Old Testament men were virgins — Elijah, Elisha, Jeremiah, Daniel, John the Baptist. His letter to Eustochium (Epistle 22) written on the occasion of her public consecration as a virgin, but obviously aimed at a wide audience, to judge from its scathing criticism of unworthy religious, and studied today in many a monastic noviciate, is a guaranteed kill-or-cure recipe for prudery (not to be confused with purity). Yet it was not Jerome, it was Ambrose, our Lady's troubadour, principal commentator on St Luke's Gospel, who was to exercise on Christian thought ideas that have possibly been overstressed or even distorted with the passage of time. The two men were exact contemporaries, both of them highly civilized scholars, but with a difference.

Ambrose, son of the prefect of Gaul, had returned to Rome with his family on his father's early death. He was fourteen years of age when his sister Marcellina, 'dearer to him than life and eyes', received the veil of a consecrated virgin in St Peter's on Christmas Day from the hands of Pope Liberius, before a vast concourse of people. The two brothers, Ambrose and Satyrus, were products of her training. The family residence in Rome was daily thronged by eminent ecclesiastics, splendid targets for a mischievous little boy to follow, aping their walk and mannerisms, extending an imaginary jewelled hand to be kissed. The elder sister's pedagogy clearly never cramped her brothers' style, but it may well have contributed to the making of one of the most attractive saints of all time. Following in his father's legal footsteps and in high favour with the Emperor, Ambrose rose to the position of Governor of Liguria, resident in Milan, the administrative capital of the West. In 374 the Arian bishop died; Ambrose as Roman consul went to the cathedral to quell rioting between opposing factions. Suddenly the rafters rang with the cry: 'Ambrose bishop!' Although openly Christian, Ambrose was still only a catechumen and, appalled, attempted flight in vain. Bowing his head to the will of the populace, he surrendered all civic honour, was baptized, ordained priest and bishop within a single week, and took just one year to create a model diocese in the midst of a tumultuous world of imperial intrigue, heretical wrangles and widespread moral decline. From the outset, he felt deeply the teaching responsibility of a bishop; it was not long before he was catechizing his flock rather in the style of Pope John Paul II. Never lacking in quiet courage he sifted evidence, with legal mind separating doctrine from custom. So it was that in his running commentary on the first psalm, he admitted that he liked to hear girls singing the psalms, and even thought that the apostolic precept bidding them keep silence in church might be set aside, because they sang so sweetly and so well. In a single bound, he had transferred the sung liturgy from the choir to the nave. Needless to say, the girlery was quick to spot a protector, and soon Ambrose was facing a youthful spellbound audience avid to hear him extolling virginity as *the* Christian virtue, when practised from supernatural motives hand in hand with moral purity. In his campaign to restore gospel values, he could not have chosen a more cunning weapon. To appropriate Charles Kingsley's diatribe versus John Henry Newman fourteen hundred years later: 'Cunning is the weapon which heaven has given to the saints wherewith to withstand the brute male force of the wicked world which marries and is given in marriage.' (In the ancient world inherited by Ambrose, Juvenal mentions a woman married eight times; Seneca talks of women who reckoned dates according to the names of their various husbands.)

Ambrose tranquilly countered fierce opposition. 'Am I decrying marriage? On the contrary, I encourage it. Those who denounce marriage and procreation prove that they should never have been born. "The world is dying", you say. Tell me, has any eligible young man on the look-out for a bride ever failed to find one?' No wonder that while girls from all over northern Italy and as far afield as Morocco flocked to Milan, there were none from Milan among the congregation — they had been locked indoors by parents determined to shield their daughters from that siren eloquence. 'Parents cry, NO; if you overcome your family, you overcome the world!' In the face of freedom and fashion, Ambrose had soon enrolled a 'monstrous regiment of women', all consecrated virgins, grouped most often in communities under a superior, that quickly spread throughout Western Europe counteracting moral corruption and spiritual sloth by lives devoted to the praise of God, to prayer, biblical study and works of charity.

No fewer than five treatises of Ambrose on virginity are extant. All have exercised a strong and unbroken influence on the Church's thought and practice. It was in his fourth treatise *De Institutione Virginis* that he reached the heart of his doctrine. As Hildegard of Bingen was to do later, he argues that man cannot come to perfection without woman. The two sexes, characterized by essential differences, are complementary. While others inveigh against Eve as temptress and cause of the Fall in Eden, Ambrose maintains that her guilt was less than Adam's: weak and exposed to greater temptation, she atoned by frank confession, and in working out her punishment, set man an example of repentance and amendment. 'Finally, Eve's fault was cancelled by Mary, the Virgin-Mother, who restored and exalted her sex.' Here he has reached the very core of his theological thought. Virginity, he observes, is of divine origin and institution — a fact that refutes all criticism. 'Who is the author, if not the spotless Son of God whose flesh saw no corruption, whose divinity suffered no loss? Christ is the bridegroom of the virgin, for virginity is of Christ, not Christ of virginity. He is the Virgin who was espoused, the Virgin who bore us, who fed us with her milk.' Quoting from Jeremiah, he refers to Christ the Rock who receives the gift from the Father in the Holy Spirit: 'This is the Trinity which waters the Church, the Father, Christ, the Spirit.' From the Trinity, he passes to the Church, a virgin in her sacraments and a fruitful mother to her children. From her, it is a small step to our Lady, pattern of virginal life, image of purity, mould of all virtue. In his *Commentary on St Luke* (ii, 87–8), Ambrose anticipates the Second Vatican Council, which firmly established our Lady as the chief glory of the Church:

Let God then come, let him build woman, Adam's helpmate, but this one, Christ's. Come, Lord God, build such a woman, build the city of God. See her now, this woman who is mother of all: see her, the abode of the Spirit: see her, Christ's beloved, a glorious bride, holy and spotless. This woman is the hope of the Church.

Such praises and insight provide a delicate prelude on strings to the beautiful orchestration of medieval devotion to Mary, the virgin-Mother of God.

Yet even during his own lifetime, while Ambrose's theology in essence was unassailable, in practice undesirable elements manifested themselves in varying forms, until the Church in Vatican II set about redressing the imbalance. In the great basilicas of the fourth century, for instance, Christian virgins were given a place of special honour, screened from public view by balustrades of pure white marble — talisman of holiness — safely placed between the altar and the congregation, which included the solid block of public penitents cut off from the sacraments. A society that admires nothing less than a saint may easily put the sinner to flight: the Roman matrons would pause on leaving the basilica to exchange the kiss of peace with the chaste virgins. Which is the more essential Christian virtue — virginity or love proceeding from faith? Perhaps the most terrifying parable in the gospel is that of the Ten Virgins, and the warning issues straight from the mouth of God. Ambrose's own contemporary, John Chrysostom, saw the danger; he said of the Manichaean elect what the seventeenth century would say of Port Royal: 'The worst licentiousness is not so wicked as their chastity.' A whole millennium later, William Langland exposed the fallacy in *Piers Plowman*:

Therefore chastity without charity will be chained in hell:
It is lifeless as a lamp whose light is out.

To revert to the three women standing beneath the cross on Calvary: Magdalen's past sins were so far from hindering love that they acted, as Gregory the Great points out, as manure to fructify the seed of Divine Love, and form a bride of Christ more innocent than any maid. The Church in her liturgy never uses words idly: there is a striking collect which opens: '*Deus, innocentiae restitutor et amator*' — 'God, lover and restorer of innocence'. Can innocence once lost be restored? The answer is to be found at the foot of the cross: both the virgin and the prostitute have poured out from love the alabaster jar of their entire lives: they have nothing left to give. In the virgin, love issues in motherhood; in the prostitute, virginity restored; Our Lady, Mother of a Church containing good and bad alike, subsumes in herself every aspect of womankind. It was no mere poetic flight of fancy that moved Crashaw to hymn Teresa of Avila's 'lives and deaths of love' as being responsible for the thousands of souls awaiting her in glory:

> sons of the vowes
> The virgin-births with which thy sovereign spouse
> Made fruitfull thy fair soul.

Mention has just been made of St Gregory the Great, that commanding figure who stands at the cultural crossroads of East and West, a Roman of the Romans, well acquainted with Constantinople and Syria, imbued with the learning of the ancient world, and traditionally hailed as the Father of medieval Europe. By nature he excelled in storytelling, and in his *Fioretti*, as his *Dialogues* may well be called, he devoted Book II chapters 33–4 to an account of the last meeting between St Benedict and his sister Scholastica. The clever men up in London, or should it be Oxbridge, who follow the contemporary fashion of 'deconstruction', would argue that nothing can be known for certain, historical fact is agonizingly difficult of demonstration, and Scholastica has been 'misidentified'. She is

> a phantom of delight . . .
> A lovely apparition, sent
> To be a moment's ornament

— no more than a projection, a feminine symbol, of Benedict's contemplation. Really? An actual prayer to St Scholastica might reveal upon nearer view, 'A spirit, yet a woman too'. She belongs without question to the time-honoured syndrome of the brother–sister relationship of an Antony, Pachomius, Augustine, Caesarius, and the spiritual partnership of a Jerome and Paula, John Chrysostom and Olympias, Francis and Clare, Jordan of Saxony and Diana d'Andalo, John of the Cross and Teresa of Avila, Francis de Sales and Jane Frances de Chantal, Vincent de Paul and Louise de Marillac — a pattern that has persisted down the ages.

Like the gospel parables, Gregory's narrative is simple only on the surface. Scholastica, 'who had been consecrated to God in early childhood, used to visit Benedict once a year, in a house belonging to the monastery a short distance from the entrance'. So far, two statements call for comment. Speaking to the cultured circle of his own monks whom he is preparing to hold high office in the Church, the Pope need say no more than that Scholastica was a consecrated virgin. Her parents' dedication of their child to God in infancy was a devout act, not unknown even today, following the precedent found both in the Old and New Testament. It had no binding force. Canonical legislation from at least the fourth century expressly forbade any formal consecration, before a candidate had reached maturity and was capable of making a deliberate choice: Marcellina, Ambrose's sister, was twenty-three; Blaesilla, Paula's daughter and Jerome's spiritual protegée, was twenty. Like Macrina, Basil's sister, Scholastica seems to have spent her infancy and girlhood in her parents' home in Nursia. We do not know whether she ratified their dedication and received the veil of virginal consecration at the hands of the bishop in full church assembly in the province of Nursia, or in the city of Rome. If in Rome, then her young brother Benedict, in his teens, was just about to don the toga of full citizenship in order to enter the schools of grammar and rhetoric. What is certain is that it was she who blazed the trail. Far from being a disciple, the roles were reversed. Benedict's nurse may not have known his whereabouts when he responded to God's repeated calls, but Scholastica undoubtedly did; when she went to see him every year, she was treading a well-known path of the elder sister sharing and guiding, a perfectly natural God-given sequence in any Christian family. To quote the wise saw of Helen Waddell, who had eight brothers: 'There is motherhood in that relationship always: the woman who has cared for a brother is not childless.'

The visit Gregory has chosen to describe in some detail was to be the last meeting of brother and sister on earth, and she may well have known it. After spending the day together, a meal was set before them in the lodge at the foot of Monte Cassino, obviously provided by the monastery for the reception of women guests, since men were free to enter the monastic enclosure. Evening was drawing in, and Benedict grew restive: he must return home. Gregory the Great's factual reportage strikes a note of authenticity:

Scholastica. Please don't leave me tonight. Can't we go on talking just for once until daybreak?
Benedict. What? Are you suggesting that I shouldn't return to the monastery for a whole night? Utterly impossible!
Scholastica buries her head in her hands where they rest on the table. There is silence. After a while, as she raises her head, there is a roar of thunder, blinding flashes of lightning, and floods of rain.
Benedict. God almighty forgive you, what *have* you done?
Scholastica. What have I done? I asked you, my brother; you said NO! I then asked our lord, and He said YES! Very well; let us go. You see me safely on to the road, and then get back to your cell — *if you can!*

The voice is by no means gentle as any sucking dove: there is here no hint of the meek admirer drinking in every word, as set forth for instance in Paul Claudel's Ode: 'Scholastica le regarde et tremble et loue Dieu qui l'a rendu si grand!' ('Scholastica observes him with quickening pulse, praising God who has raised him to such a height!')

On the contrary, it is the voice of a teasing elder sister affectionately exposing the all too legalistic oddities, not yet eradicated, of a brother she knows inside out. Before bidding him a final farewell, she teaches the patriarch of the monks of the West an essential lesson: monks have not been made for his sacred night silence any more than man was made for the sabbath: there may be times however rare when the law of charity becomes absolute and supersedes all others.

So whether he liked it or not, the monastic lawgiver was

made to break his own rule and resume converse with his sister. One naturally wonders what they discussed for a whole day and night, and St Gregory's phrase offers perhaps a clue: *Per sacra spiritualis vitae colloquia sese vicaria relatione satiarent* ('they wanted an uninterrupted talk together on the things of God'). The operative words are *vicaria relatione* — a mutual exchange. Brother and sister enjoyed a spiritual feast that night as they capped one another's heavenly longings. Abelard was to take it for granted that a community of monks should be at hand for Heloise's consolation and instruction — as if nuns were baby sparrows waiting with wide-open beaks for kind brethren to drop grubs of advice and encouragement as food for famished souls. Have nuns nothing to give? Gregory's words suggest that Scholastica gave at least as much as she received. Is it just conceivable that in her yearly pilgrimage to visit Benedict over a lifetime consecrated to God, she should live out and compare notes with him over his 'little book of holy gifts', as Smaragdus, the ninth-century abbot was to call the holy Rule? For a century or two there had been as many monastic rules as there were communities. Does the fact that the Benedictine Rule speedily surpassed and replaced all others, that it spread throughout the world, and proved an inspiration to both men and women for its loftiness, sobriety and humanity, suggest that two minds, two souls, two personalities, feminine as well as masculine, were involved in the making? Was it Benedict who thought of providing two cooked dishes and *young* vegetables at dinner for queasy stomachs, or was it his practical sister? Who wanted the abbot loved rather than feared? Who, looking on the sick as Christ, ensured that they receive meat, baths and every possible comfort? It was surely the woman.

In opening his narrative of this last meeting of brother and sister by a quotation from 2 Corinthians 12:7, Gregory after his usual fashion had prepared the alert reader to search out hidden nuances. Like St Paul, Benedict was deliberately humbled, the strong lawgiver unmanned by weak woman. Even more significant is Gregory's considered judgement in his summing-up. With insight and economy of phrase, he analyses the victory: *Plus potuit quae plus amavit* — she prevailed who had the greater love. The phrase echoes Luke 7:42 and 7:47, Christ's verdict on the notorious sinner, who pushed her way into the house of Simon the Pharisee, poured out her precious nard over the Master's feet with copious tears of repentance, and rose with innocence restored, *quoniam dilexit multum*, because of her great love. (The Syriac tradition of set purpose systematically superimposed the Maries of the Gospel.) Gregory avoids any overstress. Both brother and sister were possessed of *virginitas carnis*, physical virginity, the bodily integrity — *corpus intactum* — of the evangelical counsels; but *virginitas cordis*, virginity of the heart, the *fides incorrupta*, inviolate faith, takes precedence. Even in outward seeming, Gregory does not repeat Ambrose's overstatement. He portrays Benedict reflecting a Divine Wisdom constricted and confined by human caution put to flight by the unbounded trust of a Scholastica, reflecting the Holy Spirit of Love.

Little remains to be said of this parable of intercession. The siege of Monte Cassino during World War II shows the force of Scholastica's prayer of petition. Rain, whether of bullets or of heaven's waterspouts, discharged from the crest of that fearsome hill, could paralyse any movement below. Benedict had no option but to light the candles, wait for the fury of the storm to abate, and possibly forgive his sister's smile. Her parting words to him next day might well have anticipated those of Ethelburga, abbess of Barking in Essex, quoted by Bede (*Ecclesiastical History* IV, 8): 'Burn now your candle as long as ye will: it has naught to do with me, for my light cometh when the day breaketh.' It broke for Scholastica three days later, when the abbot of Monte Cassino, standing at the window of his cell, saw his sister's soul ascending to the glory of heaven, and had her body brought to his monastery for burial in the tomb destined to receive his own.

Pope Gregory the Great's small relief carved in words has set the scene for the relationship between Benedictine monks and nuns in general — one of family affection, of frank yet harmonious interchange on spiritual and intellectual levels. It is perhaps not too much to claim that wherever monks have realized and witnessed by their lives to a high ideal of monastic life, the nuns have attained to it by a simpler route, and arrived more speedily at the summit. It was in England, in the early years of the

seventh century, that the Rule saw its first expansion: the grop-
ing and searching ceased, and St Benedict took command. St
Hildegard would chart the progress of monastic history under
the symbol of light: 'The first light of day represents the apostolic teaching; dawn represents the beginning of that way of life
which first flourished in the desert; sunrise however symbolizes
the clear well-ordered way of my servant Benedict.' Soon English kings and nobles vied with one another in founding and
endowing houses for both monks and nuns, and so brought
into being such famous nunneries as Barking, Ely, Coldingham,
Wimborne, Wilton, Shaftesbury, Winchester, Ramsey and Min-
ster, built, as a rule, in close proximity to the monks. Their
declared purpose was to erect churches worthy of God for
solemn liturgical worship. Within a century, split oak covered
with reeds was replaced by walls of polished masonry, leaden
roofs, lofty towers, and glass windows. In the church built
before 700 by Eadburga, daughter of the King of Wessex, the
principal altar was covered with cloth of gold surmounted by
a cross encrusted with gems; the chalice and paten 'which bore
the sacred body and blood of Christ' consisted of a cup of pure
gold chased with precious stones and a dish of silver of great
magnificence. These monasteries and nunneries with their wide
human and cultural implications, have been described as alternative societies in miniature. Abbesses, who were often of royal
blood, attended synods — no fewer than five signed the Acts of
the Synod of Becanheld in 694 — and were frequently decisive in
disputes of Church and State.

A distinguishing mark of English monastic life was the double
monastery with its centralized government under the abbess.
The Saxons retained the ancient distinction between church
virgins who, after consecration by a bishop, resided in their own
homes, and those who lived in community under a superior. The
first, known as 'nonna' were classed with priests; the second
were known as 'mynekins', a word derived from the Saxon
'munic', because they observed the rule of the monks. While
monks and nuns might profess their obedience to a particular
monastic rule in the hands of abbot or abbess, the virginal
consecration, considered of greater importance, was still exclus-
ively reserved to the bishop, the ceremony being attached to the

principal festivals of the year, notably Epiphany and Easter. With the organization of religious Orders within the Church, individual consecration became rarer yet never died out. Sts Catherine of Siena, Rose of Lima, Gemma Galgani among the better-known, passed their lives in the houses of parents or friends; less familiar are the 'Christian Virgins' of China who have played such a prominent part since the sixteenth century, in fostering and preserving the faith during times of stress and persecution. The legislation of the Second Vatican Council has given a fresh impetus to the ideal of the consecrated virgin living in her own home and devoting her life to the service of the ecclesial community. The wheel is come full circle. Whereas the pagan Danes levelled the Saxon double monasteries to the ground, so that by the ninth century, after its period of great glory, the monastic institute had ceased to exist in England, double monasteries have begun once more to flourish in the Church. As yet, in spite of the feminist movement, they have not produced a second Hilda of Whitby (d. 680) who was not only present at the Synod that united Romans and Celts in 664, but trained her monks to become bishops, abbots, and scholars of renown, and left an indelible mark on history.

Nevertheless, it was the man from Crediton in Devon, born in the year that Hilda died who, according to Christopher Dawson, had a deeper influence on the history of Europe than any Englishman who has ever lived. Educated from the age of seven in English monastic schools (he composed the first Latin grammar for English children), Boniface had become a monk at Nursling in the diocese of Winchester, and from there had gone out in 718 to evangelize the heathens of Saxony, Thuringia and Hesse. In the process, before the final crown of martyrdom, he was ordained bishop, appointed primate of Germany, founded bishoprics throughout the Empire, set English monks to rule them, and by means of English Benedictine nuns educated and civilized his undisciplined flock. Nuns in mission fields are no nineteenth-century innovation, as is commonly supposed. These Anglo-Saxon nuns who spoke and wrote Latin fluently, produced exquisite embroidery and illuminated manuscripts, were just as much at home in bakehouse and brewhouse. They also managed to keep up a lively correspondence with Boniface and his companions. From her abbey of Wimborne, a young nun Lioba related to him by blood sent him a little gift to remind him of her, with a Latin verse for his correction, 'to draw tighter the bond of true love for ever'. It is hardly surprising that in 748 Boniface appealed to the abbess of Wimborne to send him help from her community of 250 nuns. Her response was generous and, with amazing courage and adaptability, thirty volunteers set out, speedily transplanted their tradition, and soon peopled Germany with daughter-houses, under Lioba's leadership. Like Hilda of Whitby before and Hildegard of Bingen after her, Lioba was consulted by men of affairs in Church and State. The Emperor Charlemagne whose queen was her close friend, listened to her counsel with reverence but, for all his powers of persuasion, failed to retain her in his court at Aachen to adorn his already large company of English saints and scholars. Noted for her smiling loveliness, Lioba insisted on returning to the solitude of her monastic cell. Boniface had always loved her tenderly and directed that after death, they should share the same tomb to await together the resurrection. Having modelled Fulda on Monte Cassino, and himself on the Patriarch of monks of the West, he was not to lack a Scholastica.

Some eleven centuries later in 1865, General Chapter of the English Black Monks appointed Dom Laurence Shepherd, a monk of Ampleforth, to be *vicarius* to the newly-settled community of nuns at Stanbrook in Worcestershire. After the shattering trials they had endured — violent expulsion from their home in Cambrai, nearly two years of hunger, illness and death in the prison of Compiègne during the Revolution, followed by return to their native land penniless and homeless — the nuns were longing to regain their ordered traditional way of life. In the spirit of Boniface, Father Laurence at once identified himself heart and soul with his charges, and spent himself in their service. His first care was to collect funds by every means in his power to build a beautiful church for the full liturgical and choral celebration of Mass and the Divine Office. To this end, he translated eleven volumes of Dom Guéranger's *L'Année Liturgique*, accepted no salary, undertook financial appeals, and for himself asked only roof, food, and an occasional coin to cover his fare to Worcester. In order to raise the standard of

observance, he gave commentaries on holy Scripture, taught
Latin to the community, and built up a splendid patristic library.
Truly Laurence Shepherd deserves the veneration paid him as
the second founder of the Benedictines of Stanbrook. Worn out
by labours and suffering, he lay dying at the age of fifty-nine
in the Stanbrook presbytery. Among his farewells on 30 January
1885, he sent a parting message to the novices, among whom
was his special favourite, his 'dearest Maggie' as he always
called her. A few months previously, she had been given the
Benedictine habit and his name: she would be known henceforth
as Laurentia McLachlan. 'Tell them they must be saints', he
said. 'They must be grand Benedictines of the seventh century.'
He lies entombed in the Holy Thorn chapel of the Stanbrook
Abbey church. Some yards away against the outer side of the
wall, Abbess Laurentia's body awaits with his the glory of the
resurrection. Thus it is that St Benedict's sons and daughters
call to one another across all boundaries of time and space;
they speak the same language, and are united in the same loyalt-
ies and love.

5
Contrasts: Sic et Non

HELOISE AND HILDEGARD

Every four centuries or so, holy Mother Church would seem
to go into labour, and bring forth a generation of intellectual
and spiritual giants. It would be difficult to surpass those born
into the twelfth century, that watershed between the declining
monolithic civilization of a post-Roman world, and the dynamic
new society of spiritual unity in national diversity called Western Christendom. All roads now converged, not on Rome, but
on the river Rhine, no longer a moat guarded by a handful of
Roman legionaries, but bearing on its waters the commerce of
the whole of the known world, both East and West. This age
of conflict and reform, of creative thought and culture, broke
down feudal barriers of class and territory, and made monk,
bishop and knight equally conscious of their participation in a
common cause. In addition to the Crusades and three General
Councils, the century saw the emergence of two new monastic
Orders, the white-clad Carthusians and Cistercians, the latter
interpreting the Rule of St Benedict afresh under a strong centralized government — was the undyed white wool of their
monastic apparel a sign that they had turned away from scholarship to become agriculturalists, to reclaim and replace swamps
by corn and pastureland, breed horses, rear sheep, and trade
their produce to earn their subsistence rather than look for
patronage? During these years also were born the Norbertines
or White Canons, the Reformed Carmelites or Whitefriars, the
Victorines of Paris, and the Military Knights Templar, whose
memory is perpetuated to this day in the church that stands in
the City of London's courtyard of the Inner and Middle Temple,
built in 1185 on the model of the Holy Sepulchre.

After a lengthy period of 'iron, lead and darkness', as Baronius the sixteenth-century annalist was to call it, instead of dire dissolution there rose from seeming chaos a republic of teachers, thinkers and saints: Bernard, Anselm, Bruno, Stephen Harding, Norbert, William of York, Thomas Becket, John of Salisbury.... But were there no women? Political upheaval and social unrest clearly called for women's obstetric hand to mould and control the onrush, and women were not slow to answer the need. It is only in recent years that scholarly research has concerned itself with the role of women in monastic reform and revival: historical records are far from abundant, but the more the so-called Dark Ages are subjected to scrutiny, the more they become flooded with light and colour, and the more impressive does the feminine influence appear. Two contemporaries of the twelfth century arrest attention, both Benedictines, both abbesses: Heloise (c.1100–63), abbess of the Paraclete, one of the most distinguished nunneries in France, and foundress of no fewer than six daughter-houses; and Hildegard of Bingen (1098–1179), called in her lifetime 'the Sibyl of the Rhine', foundress of two monasteries, St Rupertsberg and Eibingen. The two women stand at opposite poles to one another: the first, typically French, beautiful, romantic, looking over her shoulder to the past, haunted by a twofold vision of pagan and Christian Rome, uncertain as to whether she herself is the second Pompey's Cornelia or Jerome's Eustochium; the second, a Teutonic epic figure, a singularly practical contemplative and visionary, standing like a twelfth-century Queen Boudicca, challenging men to cower and look for cover in the battle for Christ while she, a woman, meets the onslaught, prepared either to win or to perish. With equal efficacy, her strong hand could wield the abbatial crosier, the apothecary's pestle, the dramatist's pen, or the whip of the prophet.

The historical record of Heloise's early life yields few incontrovertible facts. Her father is unknown, her mother only by name — the necrology of the Paraclete calls her Hersinde. A windflower growing in the shade of Notre Dame, Paris, Heloise was a niece of Fulbert, cleric and canon of the cathedral; it was probably he who sent her to the Benedictine nuns of Argenteuil, situated not far from the city, where she was educated to such a pitch of Hebrew and classical learning that she became renowned throughout the schools. Peter the Venerable, abbot of Cluny (1092–1156), the first translator of the Qur'ān, would one day write to her: 'I had scarcely passed from boyhood to maturity when I first heard of your name and reputation. You have surpassed all women and gone further than almost all men.' Such a tribute from such a man speaks eloquently for the scholarship offered by unknown Benedictine nuns in the Paris that had displaced Rome as the *patria* of the human mind.

At seventeen years of age, Heloise's beauty of body and mind attracted the attention of one of the mightiest scholars of Europe, Master of the Schools of Paris — the forty-year-old Pierre de Pallet (*c*.1079–1142), known to posterity as Peter Abelard, a 'Goliath with the club of Hercules', to quote his contemporary biographer, 'flashing from philosophy to poetry, from poetry to wild jesting'. Their passionate love, secret marriage, the birth of a son, Abelard's mutilation at the hands of Fulbert's thugs, the entrance of husband and wife into the monastic cloister — she into the Argenteuil of her childhood, he into the Abbey of St-Denis — their perpetual separation and undying loyalty, have stamped themselves upon the imagination and become the stuff of legend. Literature has dealt penetratingly enough with their drama, but has had to rely for evidence solely on the protagonists concerned. This is contained in Abelard's *Historia Calamitatum* and the subsequent interchange of letters of self-analysis on her side, and spiritual direction on his. While a historian such as Dom David Knowles considers the account of Abelard's misfortunes 'a work of the highest value for its historical, psychological and human interest', the authenticity of the so-called 'personal letters' has not gone unchallenged. After careful study, Étienne Gilson, most discerning of critics, has stated his conclusion: 'The wisest and most convincing of all hypotheses is that Heloise is still the author of the letters of Heloise and Abelard of those of Abelard.' As a Benedictine monk assured Gilson in the manuscript room of the Bibliothèque Nationale: 'It is impossible for that correspondence to be unauthentic. It is too beautiful.'

A knowledge of their background is essential to the evaluation of these letters. Abelard and Heloise had lived and loved for only eighteen months before tragedy struck. When about 1120 Abelard entered the Abbey of St-Denis even before his wound was healed, Heloise had already taken the veil at Argenteuil, uttering a passionate cry as she did so, drawn not from the Bible as one might expect, but from Lucan's *Pharsalia*: 'O my bridegroom, cursed am I who have proved your undoing.' In spite of all her later protestations, her monastic life was so exemplary that it met the demands of the severest critics of all, namely, her own community; she was very soon raised to the important office of prioress. Abelard was not so fortunate. Beset by the hostility of the dissolute abbot Adam of St-Denis, he fled in search of freedom and solitude. After several shifts of fortune, he found what body and soul craved when he acquired a piece of land in Troyes, on the bank of the river Ardusson, near Nogent-sur-Seine. Here he built an oratory from reeds and thatch, dedicated it to the Holy Trinity but called it familiarly 'the Paraclete' as being a gift from God, a name that stuck to it. In this remote spot he lived content in utmost poverty until news of his whereabouts spread, and his former students from Paris came flocking to sit in lively disputation at their Master's feet. Buildings in wood and stone soon replaced ramshackle huts, a stately church rose to hold the ever-increasing influx of disciples, and while they gladly provided for Abelard's needs, they shattered his hard-won peace. To the burden of wild and undisciplined students were added calumnies and false charges. Suddenly relief offered — news reached him that the monks of the Abbey of St Gildas de Rhuys in Brittany had unanimously elected him as their abbot. Slipping away from his cherished abode and the intellectual labour he loved, he escaped one danger only to rush into another: he found himself responsible for a community of incorrigible rogues.

It happened that in 1122 Suger, a monk of St-Denis, powerful in Church and State, a man in the forefront of monastic reform, was elected abbot in succession to the unworthy Adam. Research into the deeds of foundation of St-Denis (since proved to be forgeries), convinced Suger that the Abbey of Argenteuil belonged by ancient right to his own monastery and, in 1129, without more ado, he evicted the nuns in a body, making no provision whatever for their future. Their sad plight reached Abelard's ears; he immediately left Brittany to seek out Heloise and the band of nuns who had refused to desert their prioress. It was ten years since husband and wife had seen one another. She gratefully accepted his offer of the Paraclete, and he made over to her the gift of buildings and land, a deed later confirmed by Pope Innocent II. Possibly Abelard hoped to emulate the example of the abbey of Fontevrault, founded in 1106 as a double monastery of monks and nuns for, with a few like-minded friends, he planned to minister to the nuns' temporal and spiritual needs, and so find a refuge and security. The dream was soon broken. Human malice pursued him and drove him back, first to Brittany and then, after searing trials involving the condemnation of his theological tenets, into the compassionate arms of Peter the Venerable who gave him welcome, shelter, honour and veneration, finally sending him for the sake of his health to the Cluniac priory of Chalon-sur-Saône, where he died on 21 April 1142, at the age of sixty-three.

During his second sojourn in Brittany, after leaving the Paraclete and before returning to Paris to resume his teaching, Abelard wrote his autobiographical *Historia Calamitatum*, ostensibly to a friend but obviously meant for circulation. In 1132 a copy fell into the hands of Heloise, abbess now of the Paraclete for some three years. She there read the heart-rending account of his misfortunes for which she largely blamed herself, its perusal made even more harrowing by her husband's reference to herself as one who had found such favour with God that all who knew her — laity, nuns, bishops, all alike — acclaimed her holiness, wisdom, gentleness and patience. Understandably, her reaction was violent. The self-control that had ruled her every action for a dozen years or more broke down. She wrote him a letter initiating a correspondence that has fascinated readers and plagued critics ever since: 'To her lord, no, her father; her husband, no, her brother; his maidservant, no, his daughter; his wife, no, his sister — to Abelard, Heloise.' Passionate and defiant, she will deny or regret nothing of the past, indeed, she still holds to it: 'I want nothing whatever of you but yourself.' He had owned himself blind, weak, lustful, one who in his pride ran along precipices that inevitably led to fall and ruin; yet punishment had brought salvation and, as a monk, he is now wholly given over to God's love and service. Not so, Heloise. For God she has little but reproach on account of the cruel blow dealt to the man she so loved, and her own unfulfilled desire for him. Abelard's tempered reply evokes an even more iconoclastic outburst of erotic self-intoxication, an open declaration of war between body and spirit.

Abelard had concluded his first letter with a humble petition for prayer to be offered for his safety at the end of each Canonical Hour of the Divine Office, begging Heloise to be especially mindful of him in Christ. In no uncertain terms, she forthwith rejects his plea for her prayers: he is mistaking hypocrisy for piety, she has never willingly accepted monastic life: its chains are as much an enslavement as the bonds of wedlock to which she had objected. Was her love for Abelard a sin? 'How can I be guilty since my conscience reproves me with nothing?' Her rigorous self-analysis with its exposition of emotional and spiritual torture lays bare her woman's heart and soul in a manner rare in literature.

Is Heloise telling the whole truth or is she protesting too much? Having taken the monastic habit at nineteen, she had lived at Argenteuil first as a simple nun and then, at an unusually early age, been appointed prioress, a mark of singular trust and esteem on the part of a very observant community. At the time of writing to Abelard, she was in her mid-thirties, abbess of the Paraclete for some years, a figure of arresting beauty, dynamic and intelligent, wielding authority over a house of growing influence and importance both in Church and State, the recipient of homage and affection on all sides. The strict religious spirit of the monastery attracted so many vocations that within twenty years Heloise was to found no fewer than six other houses and establish 'The Order of the Paraclete'. All these young recruits necessarily passed through the abbess's hands. In his admonition to the abbot concerning newcomers, St Benedict in his Rule quotes the Evangelist's 'Try the spirits, if they be of God'; in her *Life*, Teresa of Avila was to point out to superiors, 'Many are mistaken if they think they can learn to discern spirits without being spiritual themselves', and with her usual dry

humour, she elsewhere observes that any who fancy the religious
life to be a haven of quiet pleasure, where no storms come and
a few lilies blow, should try it for a week or so. Heloise's first
two letters to Abelard, filled as they are with beauty and pathos,
express her undying love for him on a purely natural level —
she is ready, she says, to go to hell for him. *Sic et non*, to quote
the title of Abelard's collection of seeming contradictions in the
Bible, viz., common sense and experience argue that no young
woman of her calibre could ever have borne the yoke of monastic discipline, expulsion from Argenteuil, the dereliction and
poverty of the early days of the Paraclete, the heavy responsibility of high office for years, and remained sane, selfless in the
service of others, filled with sincere zeal, courtesy, and a true
daughter of the Church, without a special call from God and
his supporting grace to meet every contingency. She could not
but have known it, yet she represents her fifteen years of monastic life as an adder coiled about her heart's delight. Was the
sadness of her sadness as bad as she made it out to be? Was
she truly dragging out an arid and joyless existence?

Abelard, who knew her best, thought not. His deliberately
passionless reply to her outburst of reproach and grief is built,
as it were, upon a ground bass of deep tenderness. Addressing
her as his beloved, his inseparable companion, he proceeds to
cut her Penelope-woven web of memories to shreds. If she
persists in brooding over her 'old perpetual complaint against
God for the way in which we both entered upon the religious
life' she will endanger the well-being of both soul and body (he
sounds slightly henpecked). Then very delicately, like a surgeon
probing a nerve with a needle, he puts a question to her. Of
course it has no personal application, he wouldn't for a moment
suspect it of her, but does she remember that flirtatious little
minx Galatea of Virgil's third Eclogue who, to escape pursuit
by her lover flees to the willows in order to attract him the
more surely? In other words, is Heloise adopting a pose? In spite
of her unsurpassed intellectual power, her exuberant vitality, her
practical ability, is the abbess of the Paraclete in danger of
becoming a bore?

Reversing his former mode of address, he now salutes her as
a bride of Christ, reproving her for complaints that are far

removed from the true depths of love: 'It was God who truly loved you, not I.' She seems to think that love of God should express itself in terms similar to those of human love, that she should feel for God the same passionate desire that she feels for Abelard. But when the language of divine revelation speaks of love it does so not only figuratively of something familiar to all, but of a tremendous reality unknown to human experience. The God against whom she rails is no insubstantial shadow. Christ, crucified for her love, is her true bridegroom. While he, Abelard, remains totally barren, God has given Heloise a multitude of spiritual daughters, seeking in her nothing but herself – a nice twist, this, to her earlier cry for an earthly love. Away then with tears of sadness, lamentation and woe for a seducer; through her heart's sufferings, she will be awarded a martyr's crown as a strong athlete who has kept the rules and, whereas he and she are one in Christ, one flesh according to the law of matrimony, he hopes by her pleading to win God's forgiveness and protection. He concludes by composing a prayer asking a compassionate Redeemer to unite in heaven those parted by his will on earth, and finally bids her: 'Farewell in Christ, bride of Christ; fare forth in Christ, and in Christ live your life. Amen.'

This letter proved so conclusive in raising their relationship to an altogether higher plane, that much critical discussion has centred upon whether Heloise underwent a real or merely apparent conversion. But was any conversion necessary? Heloise was certainly acquainted with the writings of the 'Pseudo-Dionysius' whose identification with St Paul's convert at Athens (Acts 17:34) Abelard had been bold enough to call in question and, in consequence, had been hounded out of the monastery of St-Denis. *The Cloud of Unknowing*, so deeply indebted to John Scotus Erigena's translation of these writings supposedly of apostolic authority, and *The Dark Night of the Soul* of St John of the Cross, works which form as it were the charter of Christian mysticism to this day, were hidden in the future, but the *Mystical Theology* of Pseudo-Dionysius, which deals with the ascent of the soul to union with God, expresses in exact terms the condition of Heloise and of many a highly spiritual soul aspiring to a life of prayer. Heloise must have known it from the Irishman's translation into Latin, if not in its original Greek dress. Precisely because her faith was so uncompromising, she saw herself as ungrateful and resentful towards God, lacking in love and sincerity, comfortless in unsatisfied desire (which she often confused with consent) for Abelard, so that her consecrated life was a sham. All the years of fidelity, obedience and sacrifice were obliterated when the vivid recital of his persecution and affliction came her way. In such circumstances, was it not perfectly natural that pent-up emotion should sweep her along on a flood of grief, re-awakened desire, and bitter reproach? She was still so young. Undated, her two extant letters of passionate outpouring may have been written within a very short time of each other. Frail woman that she was, as her swift pen moved, she was thinking solely with her heart — the peculiar curse of overwrought sensibility. When she turned to speak to God, she was thinking solely in her head — the peculiar curse of searchers after truth in the groves of Academe. The sometime disciple of Peter Abelard, once the unchallenged Master of dialectic and logic in the schools of Paris, must now learn, as he had already done, to think in biblical terms: to think, not *with* the heart, but with the mind *in* the heart, that hard and rare union.

This precept, so essential to a healthy spiritual life, had been clearly enunciated a century earlier by one of the great Byzantine doctors of prayer, St Simeon (949–1022), a monk steeped in the lore of the desert fathers and, like Abelard, acquainted with persecution from the brethren:

The mind should be in the heart. You must observe three things before all else: freedom from care; a clear conscience; and complete absence of any passionate attachment. Keep your attention within yourself, not in your head, but in your heart.

Heloise's capitulation was complete and characteristic. She signified it by a quotation, not from the gospels, but from the satirical poet Persius (AD 34–62), a disciple of Horace: *Nec te quaesiveris extra* — 'Don't search outside yourself.' Never again would she revert to the past. Like wax in a flame, the storm and mutiny of her first two letters dissolved and vanished: her love for Abelard, sublimated and controlled, would become a union of spirit to spirit within the containing Spirit of God. Behind the powerful liturgical hymn for Good Friday that Abelard was to write for the community of the Paraclete, there lies a whole world of bitter human experience:

> This is that night of tears, the three days' space,
> Sorrow abiding of the eventide,
> Until the day break with the risen Christ,
> And hearts that sorrowed shall be satisfied.

Heloise opens her third and last personal letter with a statement of logic, originating with Aristotle and translated into Latin by Boethius: Nothing is less under our control than the heart; since we cannot govern it, we must obey it. Then, practical as always, she dismisses old heartaches, accepts Abelard's decision, at the same time informing him that if memory of the past is to be put aside, then the future must divert her thought and command her heart at least as effectively. He is the founder of the Paraclete: he it was who sowed it with the frail plants who are his daughters; they now look to him for food and cultivation. *Omnes itaque nos Christi ancillae, et in Christo filiae tuae . . . a tua paternitate supplices postulamus* — 'We, Christ's handmaids and your daughters in Christ, one and all humbly ask of your paternity. . .' Having thus formally and firmly established the spiritual relationship, she makes two requests: that he would instruct them in the historical origin of nuns; and meet their specifically feminine needs by drawing up a Rule to cover the whole monastic observance of the Paraclete. The Rule of St Benedict so far followed by women as by men, is clearly written for monks; the necks of bullocks and heifers, she points out, should not be forced to bend under the same yoke. Indeed, as she warms to her subject, she gives proof that the fragile windflower that was Fulbert's niece clinging to the cloister of Notre Dame, Paris, has developed as abbess of the Paraclete not only the brilliant flower, but also the hardiness in root and stem of a mountain cactus.

The intimations of Easter daybreak and laughter in the new collaboration of husband and wife, monk and nun, priest and deaconess (as he constantly calls her), abbot and abbess, supply a human and attractive dimension to this last act in the drama of their lives. Raised to the plane of the sacred, the partners are now back to their old Parisian game of intellectual skirmish and dispute. In cast of mind and style, Helose belongs to the new university tradition interacting on monastic usage, exemplified most clearly by Rupert of Deutz (1075–1129). When she buttresses an appeal to St Gregory the Great's *Cura Pastoralis* with a quotation from — of all things — Ovid's *Ars Amatoria*, her partner retaliates with a volley from Virgil, Horace, Ovid, Lucan and Juvenal. But the submissive, feminine writer of the third letter to Abelard undergoes a transformation midway: she shifts her argument from the needs of women unfitted by nature to bear the burden of a masculine Rule, to the universal weakness of all living creatures, men and women alike, who daily fall beneath the weight of endless legal prescriptions. In attacking formalism — regulations regarding inessentials such as eating meat or wearing linen — she comes dangerously near to destroying form, and seems to dismiss St Benedict's Rule with uncompromising iconoclasm as a mere collection of trivia, instead of the masterly summary of gospel teaching that it is. Every century produces its dissident idealists intent on a quest for the primitive apostolic life, and all end up, as did Heloise, by remaining very much a product of their own time.

True Christians, she observes, are totally occupied with the primacy of the interior life and personal perfection. With lack of logic, she moves from a request to be given a Rule that provides for a poorer, simpler life, a longer noviciate, spiritual training, and a suitable liturgy, to derision of all who would outdo the gospel. Soon she drops all distinctions of sex to weigh the freedom of the gospel against the oppression of law. In providing a Rule for the Paraclete, let the foundation, walls, beams and roof of God's dwelling-place be constructed of prayer, whether public in the liturgy, or secret in the heart. Her arguments reflect the current debate between Black Monks and White Cistercians, and anticipate the evangelical movement of the friars. 'It should be enough for our infirmity', Heloise concludes, 'if nuns' lives are spent in purity and poverty, wholly occupied with the *Opus Dei.*'

Abelard's reply, filling over thirty columns of Migne's Latin Patrology, displays a wealth of reading. He moves with ease among the Desert and Church Fathers: Macarius, Arsenius and Mark of the *Vitae Patrum* rub shoulders with Ambrose, Augustine, John Chrysostom, Gregory the Great and Bede, but over all stands the commanding figure of Jerome, whom Abelard obviously regards as his model. Jerome's close friendship with Paula, descendant of Agamemnon and wife to a descendant of Aeneas, together with her son and four daughters, is one of the romances of Church history. Without Paula, her friend Marcella, and the circle of nobly born and highly intellectual women leading a life of asceticism on the Aventine in Rome (they sang the Psalms in their original Hebrew), there might never have been a Vulgate translation of the Bible. The important part played by the women is almost always overlooked. Jerome's letters to Eustochium, Paula's daughter, are among the classical treatises of the Church's treasury, and Abelard drew freely upon them in his provisions for the nuns of the Paraclete. But he is guilty of a strange omission. He fails to challenge Heloise's complaint about the non-existence of a Rule written specifically for women. Neither of them seems ever to have heard of the monk of Lérins, St Caesarius of Arles (470–542), born in Chalons-sur-Saône where Abelard was to die, author of a famous *Regula ad Virgines*. His early biographer saluted him as 'another Noah, who built an ark to shelter his daughters against the perils of the times'. Having established a monastery adjoining his cathedral to house two hundred virgins and widows, their welfare became one of the main preoccupations of his episcopal office. He entrusted the government to his own sister, Caesaria, wrote a Rule that emphasized stability and enclosure, insisted that all should be literate, enjoined two hours' study a day, and took library and librarian for granted. Just before his death, Caesarius had himself carried on a chair to console his nuns who were unable to eat or sleep at the prospect of losing him. They wept during the psalms and replaced every alleluia with a groan. He spoke to them, said a prayer, blessed them, bade them goodbye, and returned to his cathedral to die among his presbyters and deacons. Since it was the Rule of St Caesarius that Radegund adopted in Poitiers after separation from her husband Clothaire I, a story reminiscent of Abelard and Heloise, the omission is the more remarkable.

Master Peter's next letter sets out his Rule for the nuns of his foundation. Occupying no fewer than sixty-seven columns of Migne's Patrology, it leaves a twentieth-century Benedictine nun filled with gratitude and content for the *Sancti Benedicti Regula*. After a lofty and lengthy spiritual preamble, Abelard descends to practical details of organization and observance. In view of the movement since the Second Vatican Council to restore the permanent diaconate to women as well as men, it is interesting to find Abelard most often speaking of the abbess as *diaconissa*. The argument frequently voiced today that the office of woman-deacon had died out in the West by the fifth or sixth century is very much open to question. The Crusades had opened up to Europe the spiritual and artistic wealth of the East, as is clearly shown in the work of the renowned school of illumination flourishing in the Irish Benedictine house of Regensburg on the Danube, the possessor of the famous Vienna Codex of St Paul with Latin and Irish glosses. Byzantine influence on monastic technique is clear in the illumination of an abbess wearing a stole held at the throat by a brooch, her hand raised in a preaching posture, surrounded by nuns. To this day Carthusian nuns on the day of their *Consecratio Virginum* are given the diaconal stole, sing the Lesson at Mass, and if no priest is present at the Office of Vigils, the Superior sings the Gospel. St Bruno (1032–1101), the founder of their eremitical way of life, was Abelard's contemporary. The legislator for the Paraclete considers that seven officials should suffice to supervise the administration: portress, cellarer, habit-maker, infirmarian, chantress, sacristan, and if necessity demands, the abbess or deacon, to whom all owe obedience: officials are, so to speak, her consuls. At this point he quotes 1 Timothy 5:9–11, a passage wholly concerned with widows. The nun-reader may be forgiven her broad smile, but the smile may possibly turn to consternation at the list of official duties. The cellarer is responsible for foodstocks, cellars, refectory, kitchen, mill, fishpond, vegetable gardens, ploughshare, herds and flocks; she is sternly warned against withholding goods from the community by a reminder of the fearful fate of Judas, Ananias and Sapphira. The needle-woman must not only procure the wool and linen necessary to clothe the nuns, but must shear the sheep, supply hides, and answer for a sufficiency of beds, sheets and towelling in well-ordered dormitories. Should a group of monks form part of the monastic body, the nuns must make provision for their food and laundry, transferring to them any monies over and above their own needs. In so doing they will obey that teaching of the apostle (1 Corinthians 11:3) whereby the head of the woman is the man, the head of the man is Christ, and the head of Christ is God. Cold comfort for feminists.

One prescription of Abelard's Rule calls for extended comment. It ordains that all should communicate at least three times a year, at Easter, Pentecost and Christmas, preparing to do so by a three days' fast and reception of the Sacrament of Penance. Should any wish to receive the Holy Eucharist oftener, the deacon and subdeacon are dismissed, and a priest of mature age appointed to give Holy Communion after Mass. In support of such a prescription, Abelard appeals to Church Councils: *sicut a patribus est institutum de saecularibus etiam hominibus* ('as the Fathers of the Church ordained concerning people in the world even men'). It is true that this Conciliar decree, originating with the Council of Agde in 506, was reiterated until the Fourth Lateran Council of 1215 substituted the annual Easter Communion. But this, like the Easter Communion today, was a minimum requirement. In 1073, only fifty years earlier, the fiery reformer Hildebrand had initiated a thoroughgoing spiritual renewal of the Church on his election to the papacy as Gregory VII. Abelard must have been about six when the Pope died. Not even Pope Pius X with his famous decree of 1905 on Frequent Communion could outdo Gregory VII in his apostolic zeal to promote daily reception of the Eucharist. 'The most powerful weapon to use against the prince of this world is the frequent reception of the Body of our Lord', he wrote to Matilda, a woman of the world. 'If it is daily bread, why do you receive it only at the end of the year, after the Greek custom in the East? A wound calls for a remedy: the wound is our slavery to sin. And the remedy? The heavenly and adorable sacrament' (*PL* 148, col. 326). He cites to great effect St Ambrose *On the Sacraments*, Gregory the Great's *Dialogues*, and John Chrysostom's address *To the Neophytes*. 'Daughter, it is our duty to have recourse to this unique sacrament, to seize upon this unique remedy. This is the treasure, these the gifts — not gold or precious stones — that your soul asks of me for love of the Prince of heaven.' Unlike Abelard who quotes a prohibition that applies *etiam hominibus* — 'even to men' — it never seems to have entered the head of Pope St Gregory VII that his 'beloved daughter in Christ, Matilda', was a mere woman.

Abelard stood in no such danger: to the end, he was master, Heloise disciple. No further letters, as far as is known, passed between the two, except for her formal setting out of biblical queries for his considered replies. Under the heading: *Heloissae Paraclitensis Diaconissae Problemata cum Petri Abaelardi Solutionibus* ('The Queries of Heloise, Deaconess of the Paraclete, together with Peter Abelard's Solutions') are grouped forty-two questions, twenty-six of them from the Gospels, mainly St Matthew; ten from the Old Testament, seven of them from Kings; and four from Apostolic letters. The two prove themselves abreast of the times by adopting a method of exegesis similar to the fashionable *Sententiae* of Peter Lombard (1100–60) who was teaching in the schools of Paris when Thomas Becket's future secretary, the young and hungry John of Salisbury, sat enthralled, forgetting his poverty in the bliss of listening to the voice of Master Peter Abelard in 1136. Heloise's last question submitted to her husband is unbearably poignant: *Utrum aliquis in eo quod facit a Domino sibi concessum, vel etiam iussum, peccare possit quaerimus* — 'Can one sin when doing what is either allowed by our Lord, or positively enjoined?'

Although there is no evidence of Abelard's ever having revisited the Paraclete, he continued to lavish on the community his intellectual gifts and guidance. At the outset of their spiritual collaboration, Heloise had demanded that prayers should form the foundation, walls, beams and roof of this House of God and, in a concerted action possibly unparalleled in Church history, husband and wife set about constructing a worthy liturgy for daily celebration. Abelard contributed one hundred and thirty-three Latin hymns and sequences, a few exquisite biblical laments, thirty-four short sermons, and a commentary on the Days of Creation. There only remains to mention some two hundred and sixty-seven lines of verse, preserved in an English manuscript, of his *Admonition to Astralabe*, his son. Brought up probably by Abelard's sister, the child can have experienced little parental love or tenderness; it is well to find him addressed as *vitae paterna dulcedo paternae* – 'the sweetness of his father's life'. One of the last acts recorded of Heloise is her request that Peter the Venerable should secure for him a prebend from the Bishop of Paris.

Abelard was to die in 1142 with a reputation for holiness, 'servant and true philosopher of Christ', as Peter, abbot of Cluny, called him. In November 1143 this loyal friend of Abelard secretly bore his body to the Paraclete for burial. Twenty years later, upon the death of the abbess of the monastery, her body was laid alongside his in the little oratory built so many years earlier by Abelard's young admirers to replace his makeshift hermitage of reeds and thatch:

> Low in thy grave with thee
> Happy to lie,
> Since there's no greater thing left Love to do.

Peter the Venerable, abbot of Cluny, humanly one of the most attractive saints in the calendar, gave Heloise an obviously sincere assurance that she had always occupied a large place in his heart. Aware of her past history, he yet felt certain that it was God himself who had called her to exchange her secular studies for the divine Scriptures: for logic, the gospel; for physics, the Apostle; for Plato, Christ; for the university, the monastic cloister. His letter then proceeds to liken her to Penthesilea, queen of the Amazons, who fought side by side with men in the Trojan War, and to Deborah in the Book of Judges. All the same, notwithstanding the romance and glamour, as an historical figure she passes from the stage of life an enigma, yielding yet inflexible, candid yet inscrutable, simple yet subtle, a Frenchwoman to the very last millimetre of her shadow, as an American critic has put it.

Not so the Franconian Hildegard. She would never seek a crown of victory by absolute obedience to any man. Her sole Master from birth to death was the 'Living Light' of the Godhead. Theologian and visionary, poet and musician, physicist and doctor, her day might begin with a sublime heavenly vision and end in prescribing a cure for a child's toothache. *Ego paupercula feminea forma, et humano magisterio indocta* — 'I, a poor little untaught Nobody of a woman' — was to prove a fearless foe to any who ruptured by sin the mystery and grandeur of God's revelation of himself in this universe of ours. When need arose, she would reprove a dilatory Pope Eugene III, castigate the awesome Emperor Frederick Barbarossa, support St Bernard's mistaken Second Crusade, flatly refuse to be bullied by the abbot of Disibodo, make perfectly sure that her newly-built monastery at Rupertsberg was fitted with adequate plumbing and piped-in water — and all the time, in spite of being grounded in earth and earthiness, she was gazing uninterruptedly into the Godhead and seeing the whole world embraced by the Creator's kiss. After eight hundred and fifty years, her voice is ringing out with compelling force to warn, comfort, exhort and command our contemporary world. For this reason she must be given a small decorative panel, perhaps of a flowering vine, to balance and counterbalance Heloise's fleur-de-lys in the general pattern.

According to Trithemius (1462–1516), Abbot of Sponheim, Hildegard's parents, the German knight Hildebert and his wife Matilda, were attached to the court of their kinsman, Meginhard, Count of Sponheim. Their tenth and youngest child, Hildegard, was born in 1098 in the castle of Boeckelheim on the river Nahe, a fortress perched on a rock high above ravines and rapids, hills and valleys, woods and meadowland: fit setting for a poet, musician and visionary. (Other authorities would claim that the saint was born in Bermersheim, south-west of Mainz.) Her father and mother dedicated their child to God from infancy, and gave her at the age of eight into the keeping of the Count of Sponheim's sister, Jutta, a recluse, who lived in a 'cell' so-called, attached to the monastery of St Disibode, one of those wandering Irish scholars of the early seventh century who travelled through Europe evangelizing, and founding monasteries. Jutta's cell consisted of several rooms: kitchen, workroom, refectory, bedrooms, and oratory, this latter looking into the monks' choir. When, later on, the complex was enlarged to house the increasing number of aspirants, it became almost

automatically a separate nunnery. To remove a small child from
the felt love of parents and the company of brothers and sisters
shocks a modern mind, yet not only did such action follow
noble biblical precedent but, to judge from Bede, Boniface,
Lioba and Hildegard herself, in a monastic context it could
produce astonishing results. About the age of eighteen, Hildegard formally received the monastic habit and made Benedictine
vows. She soon became a magnet that attracted other young
recruits, to form a double monastery of monks and nuns, loosely
connected and each autonomous, yet able to give mutual assistance.

There is no account beyond her own of Hildegard's early
years. From babyhood she was sickly and often confined to bed,
a pattern of life to be hers to the end of her days: today we
should probably label her illness psychosomatic. The unvar-
nished simplicity of her autobiography startles and challenges.
The stolid Briton reacts with the reproach of the March Hare:
'You should say what you mean', only to meet with Alice's
response, 'I do — at least — at least I mean what I say, that's the
same thing you know.' As if it were nothing unusual, Hildegard
relates that before birth, God's fashioning hand had set his seal
on her soul in a power of seeing known to her alone — like the
implant of a lens to pierce the veil of mortality:

When I was first formed, and God awoke me with the breath of life
in my mother's womb, he imprinted this vision on my soul. In the
third year of my life, I saw such a great light that my soul trembled,
but because I was so young, I could not put it into words.
    From my fifth year, I have experienced the power and mystery of
wonderful, hidden revelation.

Neither asleep nor in a trance of any kind, she was perfectly
aware of the life around her, acted in a normal way, yet was
being initiated into a supra-normal world of unseen reality. A
parallel might be drawn with the nineteenth-century St John
Bosco, subject from the age of nine to prophetic dreams,
guarded by a mysterious dog that came and went, a worker of
prodigies, a God-inspired prophet of future events, who suffered
anguish similar to Hildegard's when the fabric of the vision had
dissolved: 'My legs were so swollen and painful, I could not

remain on my feet and next day was utterly exhausted.' Prophets and dreamers of dreams are called to a sublime office that few would envy.

Until her fifteenth year, Hildegard spoke freely about the strange things she saw, assuming that they were visible to every one else, but when she discovered that her companions listened with a tolerant smile to what they judged to be sheer romance, she grew nervous and too frightened to open her mouth. Bereft of all courage she confided in no one, retreated within herself, suffered from violent migraines, was shaken with sudden fits of weeping, and bade fair to become a victim of deep pathological disturbance, her wonderful gifts of music, poetry, creativity and spiritual intuition all repressed. Jutta had believed that she was an extraordinary child and had listened to her outpourings, but could give no effectual help or advice, and in 1136 Jutta died. The little band of nuns then took an extraordinary step: they elected Hildegard abbess. The trust thus shown put heart into her. Four years later an inner voice bade her write down what she saw and heard; the abbot of St Disibode, to whom she opened her mind, gave credence to her word, appointed one of his finest monks, Volmar, to act as her secretary, obey her dictation and when necessary correct any faults in her Latin grammar, and so at the age of forty-two she attained to her full spiritual awakening.

It took her ten years to set down in order the thoughts that had been gestating for half a century. She called her work *Scivias* — 'Know the Ways' — and from that time became, to quote a thirteenth-century writer, 'Hildegard, the most renowned prophetess of the New Dispensation, with whom God spoke intimately and revealed heavenly secrets'. But a prophet does not necessarily foretell the future: predictions, always related to historical circumstances, may often be explained as the result of close observation and insight into the religious and moral situation; Hildegard rarely foretold the future. But in a truly prophetic manner, she encourages and castigates in order to bring about the establishment of God's kingdom on earth. Divided into three books, *Scivias* reveals and reflects upon twenty-six visions, each summed up in a mandala closely supervised if not actually executed by the saint herself.

Besides some hundreds of letters, she was to add a dozen or so treatises, of which her *De Operatione Dei* is the chief and, as if that were not enough, seventy-seven Latin hymns and sequences set to music, completed for good measure by a liturgical morality play, *Ordo Virtutum*. What is so striking about all her work, whether in prose, poetry, or iconography, is its rich biblical and doctrinal content. *Scivias* had attracted the attention of Pope Eugene III and his prickly companion, Bernard of Clairvaux, a man unlikely to be over-partial to a she-theologian; both however gave Hildegard's writings a cautious approbation. After all, had not Origen declared: 'It is no small comfort to the female sex and it encourages them not to despair because of the weakness of their sex, that they are capable of the gift of prophecy'?

The voice of papal approbation was a trumpet that resounded throughout all Europe. Overnight as it were Hildegard became a bright star in the twelfth-century firmament. John of Salisbury, whom John Henry Newman was to include in his list of English saints, would one day write to his friend Girardus Pucelle: 'Send me the visions and oracles of that blessed and celebrated Hildegard which are in your possession, because Pope Eugenius embraced her as a familiar friend, with the affection of a special love.' Strong words for a man of such unemotional sincerity! As a result of her growing reputation, the community rapidly increased; it soon became obvious that they must leave their cramped quarters and strike out on their own. Abbot Kuno of St Disibode opposed the separation with all the power at his command. Hildegard openly defied him and about 1151 moved her nuns — now about fifty in number — to St Rupertsberg near Bingen. Here she built a monastery according to her own design, here she lived for the rest of her life, and here she died. Wilbert of Gembloux, a guest in the house during her last three years, wrote to Bovo, a fellow-monk, of the love that bound abbess to nuns, of their service of reverence and obedience, and of their daily round. On feastdays the community sat in spacious cloisters, reading or singing; on workdays they wove cloth, embroidered, copied books, practised all manner of crafts and household skills. 'All the rooms are large, beautiful and monastic', he reported. 'All the workshops have running water and are well-equipped.' Hildegard whose gaze was fixed on the heavens was clearly a woman who walked with feet fixed firmly on the ground.

It can serve no useful purpose either to dismiss her astonishing visions as 'scintillating scotoma', a form of migraine, or to exaggerate her self-styled ignorance and non-importance. The writings of this poor little untaught Nobody, as she liked to call herself, fill 1384 columns of microscopic type of Volume 197 of Migne's *Latin Patrology*. Her work, virtually unknown for eight centuries beyond the confines of a few German monasteries, is today being increasingly published, studied, translated, her mandalas and illuminations reproduced, her prophecies interpreted, her music performed; indeed, she promises to become one of the towering influences of the immediate future in Europe and the Americas. She epitomizes in her person the century which brought the medieval world to birth, an age that like our own was marked by profound racial, political, social, economic and intellectual change. Hildegard looks two ways: backwards, to the traditional *discretio* of St Benedict's Rule, that balance which sees no dualism between soul and body, prayer and work, silence and speech, solitude and communal life; but when she breaks into apocalyptic imagery, mandala drawing, poetry, music, drama, she looks forward to the divine intoxication of Mechtild of Magdeburg (1210–80), Gertrude the Great (1256–1302), Meister Eckhart (*c.* 1260–1327), Dante (1265–1321), Julian of Norwich (*c.* 1342–*c.* 1413), Nicholas of Cusa (1401–64) — all of whom might never have been what they were but for her.

It was an exciting time to live in: Chartres Cathedral, that miracle of beauty with its stained glass lancets and rediscovery in stone of the dignity of the human body, was then rising from the cornfields of France; Bernard of Clairvaux and the newly-founded Cistercian Order were pressing home the monastic and Church reform of Gregory VII; John of Salisbury, to become one day Bishop of Chartres after seeing his master, Thomas Becket, butchered in his own Cathedral church of Canterbury, was sitting spellbound at the feet of Master Peter Abelard in Paris; Peter the Venerable (1092–1156), abbot of Cluny, was opening up to the West the treasures of the Qur'ān in translation; during the Council of Trier in 1147, the *De Mundi Universitate* of Bernard Sylvestris on the beauty and abiding value of all that the senses perceive had been accorded a papal accolade along with Hildegard's *Scivias*. She must have known this strange mixture of meditation and dream, art, philosophy and morals, seasoned with geography, astronomy, materia medica, and a lively zoo, the whole not at all unlike Hildegard's own work. Scholars, mystics, poets looked upon the vast universe as one being, one entity, interdependent and interconnected, a cosmos of mystery and spirit, the proper and only true context for the trinity of art, science and religion. 'The earth', Hildegard exclaimed,

is mother of all that is natural, all that is human. Men and women are sprung from the earth which gave substance to the incarnation of the Son of God. Every being is holy, every being is beautiful, every being is radiant, every being shares a spark of the divine fire. To be a creature is to be brilliant and on fire with the heavenly flame. Holy people draw to themselves all that is earthly. They become a flowering orchard.

No factual description or portrait of Hildegard exists, either in word-painting or in art beyond the stylized illumination *Die Seherin* — the Visionary — which stands at the head of the thirty-five miniatures of the Rupertsberg codex. It depicts her in black veil and flowing cowl, feet resting on a scarlet footstool, the stylus in her right hand actively checking Volmar's text, as he sits anxiously awaiting her verdict. Pentecostal fiery tongues, her 'living Light', descend to pierce her mind; all attention is focused on the vision, not the visionary. She has gone out of herself completely: life is simply obedience to the message. What was that message? How can a twelfth-century nun immured from babyhood in the cloister possibly communicate with our death-dealing world of industrial decline and social violence, peopled for the most part by machine-minded human beings woefully alienated from the mysterious forces of earth, sea and sky?

One can only form a true estimate of Hildegard and her message if one looks at what she was — a Benedictine. For over seventy years she lived within a monastic enclosure following the unbroken round of Mass and the liturgical Hours, all sung in what is now known as Gregorian Chant and, with receptive mind, devoting a greater part of the day to *lectio divina* as prescribed by St Benedict's Rule, together with the commentaries of the early Fathers on the Bible. The monastic life aims at formation, not information; at the integration of the personality, not at feeding facts into the computer of the human brain. It may be profitable to examine the furniture of Hildegard's mind. Monasteries both past and present have proved to be a Republic of Letters. Either directly or by repute Hildegard was brought into contact with outstanding scholars of her age, and when she came to write her seventy-six hymns, she must have already known the unrivalled verse-forms of Hildebert of Lavardin (1056–1133) whom the judicious John of Salisbury accorded a place among the classics, and the one hundred and thirty-three liturgical hymns of Peter Abelard (1079–1147) who inaugurated a new period of great Christian hymnody. In addition, she had at her disposal an intellectual feast in the immense corpus of scriptural theology that today crams the 217 volumes of Migne's *Latin Patrology*, from Ambrose of Milan to Pope Innocent III, her own contemporary. She is steeped in the language of the Bible, especially of the prophets and Wisdom books; she quotes Gregory the Great by name, and when she declares that the whole universe has been embraced by the Creator's kiss, her twentieth-century descendant smiles and murmurs: 'Ah, Jutta must have given you St Ambrose's *De Isaac et Anima* to read during Lent, as my novice-mistress gave me.' It would be difficult to overestimate the effect of liturgical prayer and study on the mind of a spiritual genius such as hers. The Roman Mass and monastic breviary that fed her soul had been drawn up and imposed upon his whole Empire in the eighth century by Charlemagne, through Alcuin, his right-hand man from Spurnhead in Yorkshire; both books persisted with minor additions or alterations until the Second Vatican Council, and only those who have experienced listening to Latin as a living language in the lessons at Vigils drawn from the Fathers, can know the delight of distinguishing between a homily by Augustine of Hippo delivered in words that shimmer like silk beneath an African sun, one by Ambrose, embroidered and intricate as a Milanese Cathedral cope, or Bede's Northumbrian hard-wearing homespun.

Hildegard is in the direct line of biblical commentators: her material is the biblical account of Paradise, Paradise Lost, Paradise Regained, and the eschatalogical fulfilment when time ceases to be. But there is a difference. She is perhaps the first Christian woman-theologian: her whole approach is feminine although it is none the less intellectual for all that, but the change — dare one say it? — is refreshing. The opening chapter of Genesis makes the poet and musician burst into praise: 'The Creator is a living light, the Son a flash of light, the Holy Spirit fire. O Trinity, you are music, you are life!' Creation is a song of exultation, joy, thanksgiving. Cosmos and music exist in partnership. She was to call her hymns 'Symphony of the Harmony of the Heavenly Revelations', and to end *Scivias* with the trumpet, lute, harp, timbrel, cymbal and dance of Psalm 150 that she sang every morning at Lauds. In her *Symphonia virginum*, Christ places on his mother's lips: 'God who created me, and planted in my womb all manner of music in all the blossoms of melody'; while the voice of the first Adam in Eden 'rang with the sound of all harmony, and the sweetness of the whole art of music'. In no way however does Hildegard ignore or minimize the result of the Fall and man's combat with evil. The story of Paradise Lost (Genesis 2–3) is the touchstone of all her meditation on human relationships with God, the devil and one another. Adam and Eve stand at the centre of cosmic history as a sequel to the fall of Lucifer — the light-bearer with all the sparks of his retinue now extinguished to become black charred wood — and prelude to the New Adam, who is to preserve and recycle Lucifer's glory, and give it to the mud of the earth formed in God's image and likeness. Victory will not be achieved until battle has been engaged with the five beasts of the powerful apocalyptic vision in *Scivias*, a dog, a lion, a horse, a pig and a wolf, each of which holds in his mouth a piece of black rope, symbol of darkness and chaos, to undo creation and unravel the closely-woven web of cosmic order. The breaking of right relationships — love of war, luxury, uncleanness, robbery, injustice, to which we in our times could add the dumping of

toxic chemical and industrial waste on tiny African states —
ruptures the cosmos. The air belches out these loathsome animals and this filthy pollution to wither life and destroy fruit
meant to feed mankind: 'Nothing can hide from me the eyes of
the poor who weep, because they lack life's necessities.' God's
warning rings loud in twentieth- as well as twelfth-century ears.

It goes without saying that Genesis also provides Hildegard
with the pattern of sexual relations, the theology of marriage,
and the place of virginity. Like our own, the twelfth century
saw a growing awareness of the incarnational, and the story of
Eve's creation aroused lively debate. Was she formed *ad
imaginem Dei* like Adam, or simply *ad similitudinem* (Genesis
1:26)? The Benedictines for the most part supported the image,
Abelard and the Cistercians the likeness. In her own downright
fashion, Hildegard strongly supports the equality of man and
woman: 'Man cannot be called man without woman, neither
can woman be called woman without man.' Biologically and
essentially different, they are equal in partnership, a balance
between hierarchy and complementarity. The man, she holds,
represents Christ's divinity, the woman his humanity, and the
two are inseparable. Sexuality has a value quite apart from
marriage; it forms the spiritual being of man, so that each sex
is given a specific task in the human community in general.
When she searches for a figure to express God's supreme love
for all he has made, she can find none nobler than the union of
man and woman in marriage: 'I compare the great love of Creator and creature to the same love and fidelity with which God
binds man and woman together to make them creatively fruitful.' Virginity, a denial of natural values, is the special sign of
Christ's suffering flesh, but also a reflection of a paradisal state.

Hildegard's iconography is rich in doctrinal content. Broadly
speaking, three points of light —God, man, the cosmos — bring
her visions into focus, but these three are not juxtaposed, they
are inseparably one. Divinity, she says, is aimed at humanity.
We are encircled, one and all, by the motherly, loving and
deeply compassionate arms of the God of mystery, who reveals
his compassion supremely in the cosmic Christ. A strikingly
beautiful illumination in *Scivias* depicts Calvary in the upper
half, and the wedding-feast of the Eucharist in the lower, with

Ecclesia, the golden bond, standing between the two. Above, the Bride holds a chalice to catch the stream of blood from the pierced side; below, in a priestly gesture, Ecclesia raises eyes and hands to heaven. Suspended on the tree, the cosmic tree of life and axis of the world, the Saviour holds the universe in balance and tension. Likewise, Hildegard declares, true Christians, and more especially contemplative nuns, must suffer as living, burning offerings on the altar of God, a counterpoise to the sin and evil in the world. When we realize that our universe is filled with mystery and grandeur, beauty and healing, that humanity is the consummation of the work of wholeness, interaction, of macrocosm and microcosm, then every one and every thing will become a temple and an altar. For we live in a sacramental universe filled with God.

It is worth noting that although Mary, the Virgin-Mother of God, is here, there and everywhere in Hildegard's visions, nowhere is she seen as priest. On the contrary, the saint teaches, the priest should be like Mary for, just as the Holy Spirit brought Christ to mankind by overshadowing the Virgin of Nazareth, so the same Holy Spirit brings Christ to his own by overshadowing the baptismal waters and the Eucharistic bread. That is why in several illuminations, a blue mandala of water symbolizes Mary's womb, living source of those who thirst for God. The central point is always Christ incarnate: in a strangely contemporary twentieth-century fashion, however glorious her place in the cosmos, Mary is a redeemed member of Ecclesia, the translucent substance through which the Word of God acts. In her many lovely poems to Our Lady, Hildegard plays with obvious delight on the words *vir, virgo, virga, viriditas* — man, maiden, a flowering branch, the power to grow green — this last, a key concept of hers.

To take but a tiny example: a poem *De Sancta Maria*, filled with flowers, scents, birds, feasting and joy, opens with the verse:

O viridissima virga, ave,	Greenest of green boughs, I greet you,

quae in ventoso flabro sciscitationis
    sanctorum
prodisti.
	whom questing saints of old
	    in whispering winds,
	first descried.

Living as we do on a planet severely damaged by radiation, blast, fall-out, and threatened by nuclear destruction, we need to return with songs of exultation, joy and thanksgiving to God's gift in creation of this earth of fire, air, stars, sky, flowers, grasses, water, for ever bathed in divine glory by the incarnation of the Son of Man. 'In the beginning', Hildegard says,

the shoots of all created things sprang green; they blossomed in a flowery meadow until the Greening Power himself came down. The Word, through which all things were made, fell upon Israel when God's Only-Begotten descended into the fruitful greenness of the Virgin.

Mary has given us the living vine that will never be drained dry, but brings moisture, life, healing and creativity to the shrivelled and barren. Hildegard could speak from her bitter experience in young womanhood of the unfruitful spiritual withering caused by incomprehension and dull inertia! When abbess, she redressed the balance.

As a young superior she fell into a common trap: she tried too hard, demanded too much, and a few of her subjects revolted to her lasting grief. She mellowed and, having founded another monastery across the Rhine at Eibingen for thirty nuns, devoted herself with motherly care to the fifty under her charge. Was it for them that she wrote her hymns? It is difficult to know what she means when she declares that she learnt neither musical notation nor any kind of singing. In their critical edition of the melody and text of her songs, the nuns of Eibingen have reproduced (1956) two hymns straight from the composer's hand, as they are found in the manuscript sent originally by Hildegard herself as a gift to the Cistercians of Villers in Brabant in 1175; this precious original is now in the monastery of Dendermonde in Belgium. She must have studied liturgical chant from her entrance into religious life; it took ten years to train a cantor, and the repertory was known by heart. Latin came to her as readily as her mother tongue, and she had a first-class musical ear. Her music is written on a four-line stave, pretty well a new discovery in the twelfth century, but her soaring neumes defy all boundaries and fly in all directions. Some listeners may be attracted to it as being 'Gothic'; others will compare it to its disadvantage with the traditional melodies, so often derived from the Jewish synagogue. But in its self-revelation, her music is truly Hildegardian and perfectly singable.

At some point during her rule, the abbess became dissatisfied with the unchanging appearance of her 'sober, steadfast and demure' black-veiled community. She considered that, as virgins, they should be visibly adorned with some emblem to denote the bridal splendour of the primeval Eve in paradise: *O feminea forma, quam gloriosa es*! She accordingly ruled that on high festivals, her nuns should wear white veils bound by a form of *mitra*, the headband that distinguished the consecrated virgins of the early Church; these she embellished with mystical symbols — the Lamb of God, angels, and a human being, a trinity of the divine, the angelic and the human. In her vision of the celestial Sion in *Scivias*, there they all are, crowned with circlets, singing their new song of praise against a backcloth of bishops, priests, monks and nuns. The twelfth century was about to pass into the age of romance, chivalrous love, and the songs of the troubadours. Obviously Hildegard the visionary was not proof against the spirit of the age: in some ways, she anticipated what was to come, yet neither age nor infirmity curtailed the activity of this contemplative nun. Her abbey of St Rupertsberg, free from rules of rigid enclosure — the Council of Trent lay in the dim future — became the headquarters from whence she travelled over the Empire and beyond — as far south as Constance in Switzerland, as far west as Tours and Paris. The Rhineland was little more to her than an extended enclosure. She occupied the cathedral pulpits of Bamberg, Trier, Würzburg, Ingelstadt, Cologne, delivering her message of encouragement, exhortation, reproof, in the presence of archbishops, canons and immense congregations. No castigation of ecclesiastical abuses can be so blistering as that which issues from the lips of saints, and Hildegard did not mince her words. Simony on the part of bishops, impurity of priests became her special target. Prelates who buy and sell what is not for sale, she told her audience, contaminate Christ's wounds by their greed and ambition; priests who deface Christ's Bride by handling his sacred Body and Blood in the filth of fornication, are wallowing in mire like a child in a pigsty.

Hildegard may have been a great woman and a great saint as she stood in cathedral pulpits in all her twelfth-century abbatial regalia of white robes and crosier, to put her ecclesiastical audience in their proper place, but the common man, subjected to the scrutiny of eyes that literally saw through him, cannot have found her an exactly comfortable or comforting companion. What those eyes of hers discovered, she has related in the sixth vision of *Scivias*:

The communicants were divided into five kinds:

1. Those with dazzling bodily beauty and souls on fire with the Spirit — after resurrection they will appear in heaven.
2. Those with pale bodies and dark souls — not yet hardened sinners, but reluctant to yield to the Spirit.
3. Those with unkempt bodies and filthy souls — these live shamelessly yet dare to approach the Sacrament.
4. Those with bodies hedged round with piercing thorns, and with leprous souls — thorns in their hearts of anger, hatred and jealousy: they harm themselves grievously by communicating.
5. Those with bodies stained with blood, and souls like decaying corpses — those who by bloodshed cause division among men, are cruel and perverse, and devoid of fear of God.

It is well to provide a counterbalance to the Cassandra-like figure predicting calamity: there was about her a most human attractiveness, evident in her letters to friends and fellow-religious. Monks treated her as an oracle of wisdom and holiness, frequently asking her to leave them directives on the Holy Rule. Some of her replies evoke a broad smile. Does St Benedict restrict the diet of his sons to vegetables and fruit? With motherly kindness one imagines her surveying the splendid physique of her young compatriots:

> Breathing out leeks and ardour,
> Great friendly souls, with appetites
> Much bigger than your larder —

as the fifth-century patrician Sidonius once described them, and then applying with the deft touch of a first-class physician the necessary remedies.

The Rule of St Benedict explicitly forbids only the flesh of four-footed beasts, except for the sick who may eat it until they regain their strength. It ordains that there shall be two cooked dishes for each meal, with the addition of fruit or *fresh* vegetables. Bread, cheese, cereals, olives, figs, dates and raw greens are all taken for granted, to say nothing of the psalmist's fowl of the air and fish of the sea.

Not a starvation diet. Hesitation vanishes in the face of such comforting assurance and common sense.

The tone could change abruptly, and become the voice of the Sibyl of the Rhine, moulding and taming, warning and even scolding. The monks of the abbey of St Matthias at Trier, an ancient foundation dating from AD 500 which later adopted the Benedictine Rule, wrote and asked for her words of counsel. The oracle replied:

God remembered man, and through a woman he crushed the head of the serpent when the Word was made flesh. Then Mount Sion came into being, where God dwells in humility — in other words, the Son who rests in the Father's heart. Pay attention now, you who are gathered in community, that you may be Mount Sion, grafted by the Father into his Word.

The living Light says to this community: 'You are the walls of the temple founded by the early Church. If so, flee vanity, pride, and constant stormy upheavals. Be vigorous and vigilant in God!'

For in a true showing, I saw some members of this community shining like dawn, others sparkling like sapphires, others twinkling like stars. The first with fear of the Lord joyfully observe the Rule; the second from love of God willingly do penance when they sin; the third are warmhearted and do not quarrel with their companions.

But I saw some others dimly through smoke, embittered and obstinate, keeping tight hold on worldly possessions. They find no joy in a spiritual life; not only that, but they frequently and violently oppose those who are living virtuously. And I heard a voice from heaven cry out: 'As long as this community bears the stamp of these three virtues, God will not abandon it.'

God has kept his covenant. The ancient monastery of Trier still stands, its monks still bear the stamp of the three virtues. The whole community is strikingly flexible and open, especially sensitive to the ecumenical dimension of the spiritual life, and to the crying social needs of our day. A long and close association in their work with the Benedictine nuns of Dinklage was shiningly illustrated in the late 1970s. Moved by the desperate plight of the poor surrounding them, the monks handed over a plot of land to a building firm for the erection of one hundred interconnected units for the homeless, the deprived and the handicapped. The new tenants took possession in December 1979 whereupon, as the monks required women's help to cope with urgent domestic problems, they appealed to Dinklage and received a response that was both immediate and generous.

The prophecy of Hildegard, the poor little untaught Nobody of the twelfth century, has been verified in the twentieth.

Superficially it might seem as if Abbess Hildegard rode in triumph, a regal and revered figure, along the path leading from earth to the heaven of her Living Light. But St Benedict's warning that his disciples must expect to meet harsh treatment, humiliation, hardship and trial was verified beyond all doubt when the year before her death brought grievous suffering — was it perhaps a reprisal? Hildegard and her nuns were placed under interdict by her diocesan superior — the archbishop was absent — for having given burial to a rebel declared excommunicate. This Hildegard denied. The young man, she explained, had received absolution, reconciliation, and the Holy Eucharist on his deathbed. Fearing that the body would be exhumed, the abbess at once had the whole burial-ground levelled so that the graves should be indistinguishable one from another. The spirited woman who had defied in youth the abbot of St Disibode had not altered overmuch with the years. For a time, the choral office of praise and thanksgiving was silenced, but the interdict was mercifully lifted in time for the aged abbess to die on the date she had foretold, 17 September 1179. Her death was characterized by the same selflessness that had marked her life. Her biographer's account is laconic in its brevity: 'Labouring in her infirmity, in the eighty-second year of her life, she completed her sojourn on earth in a joyful passover to her heavenly bridegroom. Her daughters, to whom she had been delight and solace, wept bitterly at her burial.'

Hildegard's final illumination in *Scivias* is concentrated on the Cosmic Symphony of the Communion of Saints, a concept demanding music of every kind. 'O Trinity, you are music, you are life!' was an exclamation constantly on her lips: jubilation and joy were unerring signs of the Holy Spirit. She had seen herself as the lyre and harp of God's tenderness and compassion, from which the divine plectrum plucked and drew forth a canticle of glory, benediction and thanks for all the amazing things wrought by God in this cosmos of ours. Her singing will never be done.

In tympano et choro, in chordis et organo
(PSALM 150)

I praise thee, Lord!

I praise thee with the organ — with the roll
Of thunderous chords, with the lilting flute,
In rhythm and measure, in the ebb and flow
Of murmuring tides and wave on mounting wave
Through infinite diversity of sound,
And in the healing depths of silence.

I praise thee, Lord!

I praise thee with the elemental powers
Of air and lightning, harnessed to perform
The will of one frail mortal and evoke
Majestic music 'neath my human hand.
I praise thee, Lord, through these material things —
Symbolic tithe of thy creation, each
Bearing due part in thy concerted praise —
Timber and metal, Indian ivory,
And homely leather; through you, giant pine
Whose summit, rocked by many a roaring gale,
O'erfrowned a forest half a world away,
Through moulded lead and tongues of vibrant brass.
I praise thee, Lord, through thud of echoing axe,
Through chiming forge and busy workshop's din.

I praise thee through the love of lovely sound
Implanted in man's breast, that not content
With voice alone, must search his universe
And haply find or fashion some device,
To enhance his joys and woes with rhythmic strains
Of ampler range and richer resonance,
Yet ever dreams of music fairer far
Than mind may grasp, or venturing art express.

I praise thee with an immemorial lore
Perfected through the centuries, since first
That flash of God-given insight long ago
Discerned the music latent in the reed
Cut from the river's bank. Not in one day
Nor from one master-mind alone, could spring
Full-formed so vast a concept. Man by man
Obscurely toiling, in the intricacy
Wrought for the worship of the living God.

I praise thee with the treasure-hoard bequeathed
By masters from of old. Wondering I roam
Through palaces of sound their hands have reared,
Built in three dimensions, tense and strong;
Make trial of their wealth, half-apprehend
Once and again, tentative utterances
Of thought that slips through language and escapes
Snatches of angel-song, elusive hints
Of blissful colloquy 'twixt God and man —
Intent, lest aught of conscious hindrance mar
The fine response of hand and hearing, due
To thine own gift of genius that can catch
Some whisperings of thy spirit, can recall
The authentic accent, can perpetuate
The transient grace for heedful ears to hear . . .
Let not thy message fail through fault of mine!

D. SCHOLASTICA HEBGIN †1973

6

Leading Captivity Captive

1949–52

The nineteenth century saw a powerful resurgence of monastic life. In France, Germany and Italy, three important Confederations rose pheonix-like from the ashes of revolution and anti-religious laws: Solesmes, Beuron and Subiaco. In the political sphere, colonial expansion frequently went hand in hand with Christian missionary activity, and the monks of St Benedict who had moulded Europe, now went further afield to the southern hemisphere and the East. In 1883–4 Dom Andrew Amrheim, a Beuronese monk, founded two German missionary Congregations, that of St Ottilien for monks, and its feminine counterpart, known far and wide as the Tutzing Sisters. An uninterrupted flow of worthy recruits has made the two Congregations among the most numerous and influential in the entire monastic family. 'Blessed are you when men hate you, reject you, abuse and calumniate you on account of the Son of Man.' This summit of the beatitudes is well exemplified in the account that follows* of the heroism of a group of our own contemporaries.

In May 1949 sixty-seven German Benedictine missionaries — Ottilien monks and Tutzing sisters, all working in North Korea — were arrested and imprisoned at Pyengyang. Eighteen monks were crowded into one cell. At night there was only just room for each to lie on his side; during the day they were made to squat in silence on the floor. The sisters were housed five in a cell and, as they managed to communicate with each other from cell to cell, and eventually even softened the hearts of the

---

* Translated from German by Dame Frideswide Sandeman

wardresses, they fared better. Prisoners were fed three times a day with a mash of millet and beans, and soup consisting of warm salted water with potato peelings or a few vegetable leaves sometimes floating about in it. Thirst was one of the worst torments the monks endured; three or four ladlefuls of water at each meal had to be divided amongst the eighteen inmates of their cell.

Naturally various forms of illness broke out, but it was only with great reluctance and when there was already danger of death that the guards consented to transfer patients to a separate cell. The elderly abbot had been in another cell with one of the monks since their arrival and his condition rapidly deteriorated. It was especially hard for the community to know how much he was suffering and to be unable to do anything for him.

Though days seemed endless their time was not wasted: they prayed in silence most of the day, but when they were sure that the guards were at a safe distance, they would whisper a rosary together or make the stations of the cross. On Sundays when they heard the Mass-bell sounding from a nearby mission station they risked defying prison orders and celebrated a whispered dry Mass — sermon and all — while one of them stood guard at the slit in the door, watching for the approach of a warder.

At first the captives had no idea what their ultimate fate was to be: were they going to be shot or would they be sent home? In June it became clear that they were to be transported to a labour camp. The brothers were separated from the priests and sent ahead to construct living quarters for captives and guards. Finally in August came the day for general transportation. They had longed for it as a means of release at least from prison, but actually it brought a great sorrow with it: their abbot and seven of the monks were to be retained as 'criminals'. Several years later they learnt that the abbot and one of the fathers had eventually succumbed to their afflictions in prison. Of the other six no definite information could ever be obtained but it is presumed that they were shot in October 1950.

Transportation to the labour camp was a secretive business. Curtains were hung round the lorry which conveyed the monks to the station, driving so close up to the train that they could get in without being seen. To their surprise and mutual joy they found the sisters already installed in the carriage.

Shortly after midday on 6 August they arrived at their destination and were given orders to run straight down the railway embankment and lie flat in the long grass in case anyone else in the train should see them. There was a long, steep climb before them up a narrow pass. Police went ahead to make sure that no one saw the European captives; soldiers marched in front and behind. Two of the missionaries whose hearts were giving out had to ride on ox-back. At about 4 p.m. they caught the first glimpse of the camp and soon some of the brothers were hurrying down to welcome them. Once again there was sad news to temper the joy of their reunion: two of the brothers had already collapsed and died from exhaustion, undernourishment and heat. Oksadok, the site of the camp, lay in a natural hollow high up in the hills. To the north it was bordered by virgin forest and otherwise, apart from the narrow defile leading down to the plain, closed in by steep, rocky cliffs. A mountain stream traversed the site. On the first evening after dusk they gathered together out of doors for Compline followed by a German hymn to our Lady.

The next day was Sunday and the former prior, now their superior, celebrated their first Mass for three months, while the rest squatted on straw in the hut. In stirring words Father Prior reminded them of the previous day's feast, the Transfiguration: they had now mounted up their own Tabor where through suffering, renunciation and exile they were to win through to transformation.

On the following day work began in good earnest. There was still a considerable amount of building to be done before winter came on — beams to be salvaged from abandoned huts, whole rocks to be rolled away, loamy soil to be found, sieved and kneaded, then smeared over walls of plaited twigs.

The sisters' prioress, Sr Gertrud Link, played an outstanding part in maintaining a supernatural outlook amongst monks and sisters alike right through the weary years of their captivity. Musically gifted and something of a poet, she composed about eighty songs for them to sing. When they were finally released they were not allowed to take away a single scrap of paper with anything written on it, and many of the songs would have been lost, had they not hit on the plan of dividing them up among them and learning them off by heart. Forty-one of them have since been published and a few of these are given here in translation; the metre and rhyme scheme of the originals have been retained as far as possible.

It was intended that the prisoners should earn their own living by agricultural labour. Police conducted them to the so-called fields — patches of stony ground amid rocks and tree-stumps. They had to follow the plough with boxes or bags of seed and manure on their backs, stooping to sow the seed and fill in the earth. Working in this bent position for hours — days — weeks on end proved torture.

Ploughing song

The plough tears furrows in the soil,
  Black stony ground gapes wide;
Backs doubled up, along we toil
  To scatter seed inside.

While hunger gnaws and grief reminds
  Of fair fields, once our hope,
Exhaustion from forced labour binds
  Our limbs as though with rope.

The driver goads, the plough's shafts groan,
  And we in God's name move;
With prayer on lips — no curse or moan —
  We sow seed in the groove.

Our eyes perceive in distant light
  God's harvest thrive indeed,
Where now the red plough plies with might,
  And we are scattered seed.

Missionary enthusiasm had brought them to Korea. At the liturgical ceremony on the eve of their departure for the missions, they had all declared themselves ready to give their life's blood for the faith. It had sounded abstract enough then, but now they were faced with the reality.

Mission oath

We made to you
A promise true,
Our life was our oblation;
We longed to serve
Without reserve
In joyful self-donation.

You often gave
What we did crave,
With joy you did requite us;
But pain and need,
Shame, death indeed,
To these you now invite us.

So help us now
To keep our vow,
Your grace alone availing;
In serfdom sad
Or freedom glad,
Your will be all prevailing.

Within a year six of the inmates of the camp were dead, and
the next year six more followed them. Seventeen of them died
in all. Another song celebrates a twofold harvest:

Harvest oblation

From what were once but barren fields
    Stream blessings for us all;
Your mercy still this bounty yields,
    Despite oppression's pall.

The choicest harvest crowns a mound,
    Six golden sheaves this year;
Six sheaves, which Death itself has bound,
    Without a blemished ear.

Six graves have opened up the sward
    For those Death reaped for you;
Accept this sacrifice, O Lord,
    As harvest tithe your due.

A still worse nightmare was in store for them. One morning

in October 1950 they were suddenly informed that they must leave the camp that day. A couple of days later after travelling partly on foot and partly by train but always under cover of dark, the missionaries arrived at the small frontier town of Manpo where they spent two nights in prison. After that they were again moved on. Three days and three nights had to be spent motionless on the ground out of doors at a railway station. By morning they were covered with thick, white frost. They had practically nothing to eat and were exposed to the taunts of the crowds around. It was a relief to find themselves back for a time in the Manpo prison, though it meant that the sisters had to work in the kitchen from 3 a.m. to 10 p.m. Yet another of the fathers collapsed and died. Korean prisoners carried his body away and it was impossible to find out where he was buried. Not long afterwards the prison went up in flames during an air-raid. The missionaries were next housed for a month in a cold dark shed with a leaking roof. Three more of the brethren died there. This time some of the monks were allowed out under police escort to bury the bodies but the ground was so hard that they could only cover them over with snow.

After this the survivors first spent a night in a two-storey dug-out in the ground. It was warm enough but stifling; on the next day they were taken back but given a shed with a more adequate roof and some sort of heating. There were fifty of them crowded together; at least they kept each other warm.

On Christmas Eve they begged the guard on duty to let them hum a few carols; they kindled a few chips of wood, sat round the fire and sang 'Silent Night' and other favourites. As soon as a ray of morning light shone through the paper window, Fr Prior sat down on the floor in front of their Mass-box, put a stole on under his jacket, and began to celebrate Mass. The sisters working in the kitchen missed Mass but were not deprived of Holy Communion. One of the fathers who always had to be present when food was doled out, took some consecrated hosts with him to the kitchen, and as he stood in a corner, each sister in turn left whatever she was doing, received Holy Communion and quickly returned to her work. None of the police spotted what was happening. It was truly a wonderful Christmas.

Again and again the missionaries begged their captors to allow them to return to the camp at Oksadok and at last their petition was granted. On the evening of 17 January 1951, they climbed up the pass to their mountain home. It was a relief to be back but their possessions had of course been rifled, and the provisions they had stored up were partly consumed and partly spoilt by frost. Worst of all was the reign of terror inaugurated by a new commandant who was to remain in charge of the camp for three and a half years. From their first arrival daily Mass had been the sustaining joy of the exiled Benedictines. They had managed to bring some wheat with them which they ground into flour for very small hosts. To their delight they were able to find wild grapes growing in the neighbourhood; they squeezed these out by hand, left the juice to ferment and then used just a few drops at each Mass. Not even the commandant dared to forbid them their Mass outright, for religious freedom was officially upheld. They had already had to reduce their daily Mass to two or three times a week because their store of wheat had vanished in their absence; their only hope was a plot of ground they had sown before their departure. But such a poor crop began to appear that the commandant gave orders that the whole area should be ploughed up and planted with maize. The brother who carried out the order worked with great care, leaving tufts of wheat here and there to survive amongst the maize. The ears they gleaned tided them over the critical period, and later they managed to sow hidden lines of wheat between the rows of maize. Never during all their time at Oksadok were they deprived of the sacramental presence of their Lord.

Trust

And if
  each single cherished hope
Should disappear like dew,
My heart would still not lose its calm,
Because I trust in you.

And if
  we are exposed to all that scorn and hate can do —

There's comfort left within the thought
My God, that I love you.

And if
    your presence too must go,
I'll weep not nor repine,
Because I know your love for me
Is lasting and divine.

Every winter they begged that the priests and brothers might
at least be spared the exhausting and dangerous work involved
in charcoal burning, but they were always told that it was
necessary to make charcoal in order to buy oil and meat. So
every winter they made charcoal, but they never saw the oil or
meat. In the winter of 1952/3 the wood had to be taken from
a deep, frozen ravine, and the workmen were all the time in
peril of their lives. Added to that, they had nothing on but
padded rags, and only straw sandals on their feet. Sister Gertrud
helped them that year with

Charcoal-burners

Brothers in the iced ravine
    Clinging to the rocks,
How I feared what might have been,
    Hearing crashing stocks.

Saw you later, bathed in sweat,
    Stir the crackling coals,
Then in hissing ice you'd let
    Cool your glowing poles.

Harsh the work, yet full of cheer
    What you had to tell;
Smiling you would volunteer:
    'This time all's gone well!'

Brothers, this your strength explains:
    You with faith behold
How your sweated labour gains
    Increase for God's own fold.

One of the sisters was a doctor; she worked and pleaded
valiantly for the sick. It was heart-breaking to watch them

fading away when she knew that, given the necessary remedies, she could save their lives. The guards were relentless in insisting that her invalids should go out to work — they were only shamming. If they could not go, their rations were reduced. It was pitiful too when they had to leave a dying monk alone, first banking him up with sweet-smelling shrubs, and not knowing whether they would find him dead or alive when they got back from work in the evening. So things continued at Oksadok until autumn 1952 when conditions immediately began to improve: the guards behaved like human beings, better clothing was provided and even a few medicinal supplies appeared. But the hard work still went on. The final change of fortune came in November 1953 when an important official arrived to inform them that, though they had had to endure a hard time, they were now to be honoured guests and were invited to Pyengyang. Four days later they celebrated a Mass of thanksgiving with a heartfelt *Te Deum*, then processed up to the cemetery to take leave of their beloved dead. There they sang the *Libera* and everyone of them sprinkled each grave with holy water. They also prayed for those buried at Manpo. In the afternoon they sang the prayers for travellers and then started down to the valley. From Pyengyang they were sent on to a rehabilitation camp, where everything imaginable was provided for their material comfort — plentiful food, a doctor and two nurses to care for them, a barber to attend to hair and beards, twenty cigarettes per day per man, films, newspapers and gramophone records. Clearly rumour had reached the outside world, in spite of all precautions, that these religious were being detained; protests had proved effective and international reputation was at stake. Monastic life could be lived more fully in the rehabilitation camp: Mass was of course celebrated daily and, except for Matins, the whole office was said in common. So the weeks went by until in January everything was arranged for their transportation back to Germany by rail. With what mixed feelings they left can be gathered from this final poem.

Farewell

One step on the way — just a short one —
   And then we are free and released;
Oppression, sly cunning and lying,
   They all at long last will have ceased.

One step on the way — but a sad one —
   Which heavily weighs on the heart;
No one who has not tasted exile
   Can guess what it costs to depart.

One step on the way — what a hard one —
   Which tortures a sensitive nerve:
We have to abandon the people
   Whom love has allowed us to serve.

One step on the way — with a last look,
   Tears scarcely permit to discern;
Korea, you land of our mission,
   O when will you bid us return?

Never in all their lives had God seemed so near to them as in
the years of their captivity.

PART TWO · THE WEFT

7
What Christ Means to Me*

Dear Mother Mary Clare,
During your recent visit to Stanbrook, you engaged me just outside your cell in a conversation that went something like this:

'Would you contribute an article to *Word & Spirit* on your own personal Christology?'

'Please, Mother, would you define "Christology" in words of one syllable?'

'Yes. Will you write an article on what Christ means to you?'

'Good gracious, how can I possibly say what Christ means to me? He's the very air I breathe, and you don't stop to define or analyse breath, do you, apart from the fact that it is necessary to life?'

'Exactly. Say so, will you? Ten to twelve typewritten pages. You needn't feel bound to a deadline, so long as I can have it before January. Thank you!'

The voice would obviously refuse to take No for an answer. Nothing for it but to trust in God's help and go straight ahead. Yet I feel wholly inadequate. Incapable of abstract thought, I have no knowledge whatever of philosophy or metaphysics, and today's theological dialectic leaves me, as Sam Weller said, 'what the Italians call reg'larly flummoxed'. Not for me to discourse of 'existential proclivities', to explore a 'Jesus decisive for self-understanding', or to 'vindicate political and social reform as a proper implication of the Christian understanding of freedom' (I quote from the *Times Literary Supplement* of 24 September 1982). To me, none of this spells Christ, Lord and Saviour. Well, what does? you may ask.

---

* Letter from F.C. to the Prioress of the Benedictine nuns of Petersham, USA.

A lapidary phrase of St Augustine sums up my attitude: 'This is my life: to praise Thee.' It goes hand in hand with my favourite psalm-verse: *Quid enim mihi est in coelo, et a te quid volui super terram? Defecit caro mea et cor meum, Deus cordis mei, et pars mea Deus in aeternum* ('Whom have I in heaven but thee? And there is nothing upon earth that I desire besides thee. My flesh and my heart may fail, but God is the strength of my heart and my portion for ever' [Ps. 72:25–6]). He is the Christ and God of the Bible, not of the textbook of dogmatic theology. If the best part of Shakespeare's best plays is the vast and serene personality of Shakespeare himself, then infinitely truer is it that the best part of the Scriptures, from the first pages of Genesis to the last of the Apocalypse, is the Word of God in Person. When he came to earth clothed in flesh, he spoke words outwardly plain even to the dullest, but they are words which conceal enigmas and mysteries, to be interpreted throughout a lifetime by those to whom the Holy Spirit gives the key to spiritual realities. For God's word is no mere vibration of air forming consonants and vowels: it calls for an answering resonance in the heart of the listener. Our Lord uses the common things of everyday life: he speaks of bride and bridegroom, father, mother, son, daughter, rich, poor, bread, wine, fire, cloud, thunder, lightning, stone, fish, mountains, birds, flowers, the four points of the compass — and all the time, he is talking in parable and riddle, as if deliberately to veil his own divine glory as God and Creator. *Lectio divina*, as we call it in monastic usage, demands courage, for we walk deliberately into the Divine Unknown, aware that many hard things may be required of us to whom so much is given. But only a foolish reader would imagine he comprehended fully the seemingly clearest statement.

This is where the liturgy comes to one's aid, for the breviary, missal, sacraments, are inexhaustible storehouses of teachings and interpretation. The opposition of psalms, scriptural readings, commentaries, prayers, possibly unrelated at first sight, coalesce to form a unity, filled with a common meaning and significance, all converging on the Christ of revelation. So I am content to admire from a distance the parterre gardens laid out by theologians in neat rectangular flower-beds of analysis and synthesis, and prefer to blaze my own trail through the thickets of the liturgical ground with its profusion of symbol, parable and metaphor, all powerfully communicating divine truth without subjecting me to fact-grinding or logical method. No human insight, of course, can be other than partial so, quelling my feelings of despair, I shall try to put something down, even though words of their very nature obscure and blunt the edge of the very truth one is trying to express.

In retrospect, the central ideas moulding my approach to Christ our Lord have been with me since childhood. From infancy, 'our blessed Lord' was cognate with God, the God who made me, and 'made me to know, love and serve him in this world, and be happy with him for ever in the next'. The words came tripping off my tongue, for Penny Catechism drill went with the baby's bath and its unchanging lullaby, 'I'll sing a hymn to Mary, the Mother of my God.' Truth was absolute and as plain as a pikestaff. At three or four years of age, my greatest treasure was a holy picture of our Lord, framed in crystal glass. Night prayers said, I stood before it 'to learn him off by heart'. This was immensely important: I must recognize him the moment I saw him. He had a thin face with red-gold hair that led to a beard terminating in two curious curls, and he was dressed 'a little bit funny' in a pale-green tunic and pink cloak spangled with golden stars. Of course he was God, and that's how they dressed in heaven. I closed my eyes tight to stamp him indelibly on my mind. Yes, when I died, I'd recognize him all right. So I climbed into bed, knelt facing the pillows, draped the top sheet over my head, clasped it firmly under my chin to make a veil, plopped down, played nuns, held my breath — why wait to die? — gasped, and fell asleep murmuring happily, 'for ever . . . and ever . . . and ever'. It was a sad day when reason asserted its claims. So strong was my reaction that when my picture lost all charm, I became apophatic for the rest of my life. When I stopped playing at nuns and became one, I found myself completely at home with *The Cloud of Unknowing*, 'for a naked intent directed unto God, without any other cause than himself, sufficeth wholly.' I have referred always to 'our Lord', yet that does not seem the current usage either in England or America. Here I face a problem which I propose to set out: What name to give to him whom the author of *The Cloud* calls 'our lovely Lord Jesus Christ, King of kings and Lord of lords who, among all the sheep of his pasture graciously would choose me to be one of his specials, and set me in this place of pasture'?

In his *Hymn to God*, St. Gregory of Nazianzen asks:

> Bearer of all names, how shall I name you —
> You alone, the Unnameable?
> You who are beyond, beyond all! —
> No other name befits you.

God's own arresting revelation to Moses on Mount Horeb, I AM WHO AM, later particularized in Isaiah's '. . . his name will be called Wonderful Counsellor, Mighty God, Everlasting Father, Prince of Peace', was finally etched in sharp relief by St Matthew's '. . . you shall call his name Jesus'. It is significant that whereas the evangelists speak simply of 'Jesus', the historical figure who they learned by slow degrees was the Messiah and recognized to be God only after his resurrection, St Paul, who knew none but the risen Lord, uses very different terms. He can scarcely mention Christ Jesus, or Christ crucified, or our Lord Jesus Christ, without breaking into ecstatic praise of him who is the Power and Wisdom of God. Why, then, during the last two or three decades, have so many reverted to the use of the plain name 'Jesus' in exegesis, theology and sermon? Half a century ago such a manner of speech, at least in England, would have stamped the speaker as a Low Church disciple of John Wesley. I am not sufficiently familiar with American practice: Wesley personally appointed his superintendents to New York, and left over 43,000 Methodists in the USA at his death, but I don't know how powerful their influence over the language was. Does it greatly matter how we refer to Christ our Lord? I think it does. *Lex orandi lex credendi* [The law of prayer is the law of belief]. May there not be an element of real danger in the exclusive use of the simple historical name? May I argue it out for a few minutes, simply because it disturbs me so?

There would seem to be valid reasons for a departure from tradition just at present. The Second Vatican Council reaffirmed a fact largely ignored for centuries, namely, that truth must be felt and experienced before it can be really apprehended. So the post-Conciliar stress is on a God incarnate, a God capable of being known and loved, a God who twice in the gospels declared the rapture of his union with humanity: *Hic est Filius meus dilectus in quo mihi bene complacui* [This is my beloved Son in whom I am well pleased]. In the mysterious words of our Lord, quoted by Matthew and Luke, 'Where the body is, there the eagles are gathered together' (Matthew 24:28; Luke 17:37), God is not merely a spirit endowed with certain attributes. Christianity is concerned with a Being of flesh and blood, a God-Man who took his body from a human mother. Many Christians of today therefore would rather think of the risen body than of the immortal soul of Christ our Brother, kith and kin, rather than *Rex et Judex Justus* ['King and Just Judge'].

> In a flash, at a trumpet crash,
> I am all at once what Christ is, since he was what I am, and
> This Jack, joke, poor potsherd, patch, matchwood, immortal
> > diamond,
> is immortal diamond.

Yes, there are valid reasons for the use of the holy Name pure and simple. I am not of course treating here of private prayer, for to any true Christian the name Jesus is a magnet. The incarnation is not a mere historical event, it is renewed in the body of every one who receives the Holy Eucharist: 'My heart and my flesh have rejoiced in the living God.'

Having admitted all that, it is worth recalling that even the term 'our Lord' applied solely to Jesus Christ dates no further back than the Book of Common Prayer and the Authorized Version of the Bible. By thus narrowing its association, the reformers forfeited a deep theological insight. Fisher, More, and the Rheims translators follow Walter Hilton and the medieval writers in rendering the Vulgate *Dominus* or even *Deus* (without any possessive pronoun) as 'our Lord' or more often 'our Blessed Lord', even in translation from the Old Testament. *Spiritus ante faciem nostram christus dominus* (Lamentations 4:20) which literally refers to Zedechiah who, as anointed King, was 'the breath of our nostrils' is translated by Hilton: 'Our Lord Christ is a spirit before our face.' Even in such a highly personal outpouring as Richard Rolle's *Song of Love-longing to Jesus* he never departs from this tradition:

> Jhesu, God sonn, Lord of majeste . . .
> Jhesu, my God, Jhesu my keyng . . .
> Swete Lord Jhesu Cryst . . .

The treatment of our Lord's suffering in the eighth-century *Dream of the Rood* is typically English:

> Then I saw Man's Lord
> Hasten with great courage, intent on climbing me . . .
> Then the young warrior — it was God Almighty —
> Stalwart, resolute, stripped himself; climbed the high gallows.

The Ruler, the Lord of heaven, the Son of God, *Christus Miles, Imperator* — it is the tone and temper of the greatest processional hymn of all time, the sixth-century *Vexilla regis*. This tradition, with its determined contemplation of the Divine Person in whom the fullness of Godhead dwells bodily, has persisted from Bede and Cynewulf to the mid twentieth century. Their whole attitude is crystallized most strikingly in Julian of Norwich's vision of 'our courteous Lord God' in his Passion. She sees the red blood running down beneath the garland of thorns, but hastens to add: 'And in the same shewing, suddenly the Trinity fulfilled my heart most of joy . . . For the Trinity is God. God is the Trinity, the Trinity is our Maker, the Trinity is our Keeper, the Trinity is our endless joy and bliss, by our Lord Jesus Christ and in our Lord Jesus Christ. For when Jesus appeareth, the Blessed Trinity is understood as unto my sight.'

Once, as a novice, I noticed the deep distress of my novice-mistress, a contemplative of the first rank. Brash young thing that I was, I knocked and entered her cell without more ado. She was sitting in tears, an open breviary on her lap, and at sight of the unwelcome intruder said coldly that she was saying her Office and did not wish to be disturbed. Nothing abashed, with my eyes on the breviary, I countered: 'You are not saying your Office. You are saying the 21st psalm. Please, Mother, tell me, what's the matter?' At this, all annoyance vanished, her voice changed, and she replied: 'To think that all during the Passion, there was not a ripple over the surface of the Blessed Trinity.' Could anything be more directly in the line of the fourteenth-century Julian? Mention of Dame Joanna Hopkins has brought me to my own entry into the monastic life and the land of vision.

I pass on to the liturgical year through which our Lord reveals himself in his mysteries. To me, it takes the form of a triangle of three pivotal points: at the summit, Easter, supported by two feasts at the base, that of the Mother of God on January 1, when our nine foundresses made their Solemn Profession at Cambrai in 1625; and the annual commemoration of the Dedication of our monastic church under the title of Our Lady of Consolation on 6 September 1871. All three are closely interwoven, but each has its own special magic. So much has been written about the centrality of the Paschal triduum that one hesitates to add anything further. But in our house Maundy Thursday, a day of pure agape, sees the thirteenth chapter of St John in action — Christ in our midst, and we celebrating the birthday of the chalice and of all priests throughout the world, whose hands are empowered to consecrate it anew: *Potestas enim erat in manibus Christi.* (Carmelites are not the only nuns who pray for priests!) The abbess, holding the place of Christ as the Rule ordains, washes the feet of twelve of her nuns, and then moves down the ranks in the refectory to serve each with a portion of food garlanded with tiny nosegays of violets, wild anemones, blue borage, primroses, golden celandines, all the wealth of spring glory. The climax however is reached, naturally enough, in the evening Sacrifice of the Mass. Never do I feel the power of consecrated virginity at the heart of the Church as on Holy Thursday, that power already evident at the Last Supper in the virginal John, leaning on Jesus' bosom. In his *Expositio in Lucam* II, 87–8, St Ambrose writes:

Veniat ergo Deus, aedificet mulierem, illam quidem adjutricem Adae, hanc vero Christi . . . Veni, Domine Deus, aedifica mulierem istam, aedifica civitatem. Ecce mulier omnium mater, ecce domus spiritalis . . . haec diligitur a Christo quasi gloriosa, sancta, immaculata . . . Haec enim est spes Ecclesiae — 'Let God then come, let him build woman, one woman Adam's helpmate, but this one Christ's. Come, Lord God, build such a woman, build the city of God. See her now, this woman who is mother of all; see her, the abode of the Spirit;

see her, Christ's beloved, a glorious bride, holy and spotless. This woman is the hope of the Church.'

One of the tragedies of our day has been the almost incredible defection of so many nuns, unparalleled surely in the history of the Church.

At this point and although not directly connected with the subject under discussion, I am tempted to digress for a few moments, turn to the question of clerical celibacy, and ask: Why is the priesthood so often conceived of today in terms of office rather than of consecration? A young nun with whom I had discussed the topic recently put into my hand this note:

I have just read in Anscar Vonier's *A Key to the Doctrine of the Eucharist* this argument against over-spiritualizing the Incarnation. 'The sacrifice of the Cross', he writes, 'is not primarily definable in terms of spirit but in terms of the body; it is not the heroic fortitude of Christ on the Cross which constitutes the sacrifice, but the material fact — we need not hesitate to use the word — of the pouring out of the Blood. There is in the sacrifice of the Cross, as well as in the ancient sacrifices, an element of absolute stability, the body of the victim . . . Everything that constitutes the sanctity and the holiness of the victim is a direct addition to the value of the sacrifice.' He then summarizes Thomas Aquinas — that the holiness of the victim consists in (i) a flesh without blemish, without sin; (ii) the charity of the one offering his flesh. The celebrant at Mass is so intimately linked with the offering of Christ that he stands *in persona Christi*, doesn't he? And that seems to entail a fundamental share in the same offering, 'This is my Body, which is given for you.' I am not convinced by arguments for priestly celibacy based on freedom from worldly cares (1 Corinthians 7:32–4), or on a simple reflection in the material realm of spiritual *puritas cordis*, but Vonier's words suddenly presented a *priestly* reason that seems very much more telling.

The Blessed Eucharist, the priesthood, our Lady, the human soul — they are all facets of the same mystery, but before leaving the Mass there is one small point I'd like to make. Hebrews has always been my favourite Epistle. I love the open- ing fanfare of trumpets: 'God who, at sundry times and in divers manners, spoke in times past to the fathers by the prophets, in these days has spoken to us by his Son . . . called by God, a high priest according to the order of Melchisedech.' Melchise- dech, that mysterious priest of El-Elyon, King of justice, King of peace (Hebrews 7:2) is a fascinating figure. With his symbolic prophetic offering of bread and wine he stands alongside Abel holding in his arms the sacrificial lamb in the Canon of the Mass, to show forth that the Lamb, the 'I am before Abraham was' has been 'slain from the beginning'. Since the Council, we have become much more aware of the spiritual experiences of millions who have never known or accepted the Judaeo-Christian revelation, and in the two figures of Abel and Melchisedech, the Christian priesthood with their 'merciful and faithful high priest', build a bridge that unites cosmic religion and Catholic worship so that, from the eternal standpoint, temples, sacred groves, pagan priests and worshippers are all drawn into the orbit of the Mass and find in it their fulfilment.

It is but a short step from the Bethlehem, the 'House of Bread' of the Mass to the Mother of the Lamb of God, the Word made flesh, and I find that the Vesper antiphons of January 1 pretty well sum up my whole unashamedly feminine attitude:

> For, ah, who can express
> How full of bonds and simpleness
> Is God,
> How narrow is He,
> And how the wide, waste field of possibility
> Is only trod
> Straight to his homestead in the human heart,
> And all his art
> Is as the babe's that wins his Mother to repeat
> Her little song so sweet.
>
> Patmore: *Legem tuam dilexi*

If the book of Proverbs proclaims that from the foundation of the earth Divine Wisdom was at play in God's presence, at play everywhere in the world, delighting to be with the sons of men, the gospels show him playing in his Mother's presence and finding a special delight in the daughters of men. Have you noticed — yes, of course you have — the sparkling freshness that our Lady, in figure and substance, brings to the story of our Lord's incarnation and birth? The antiphons of January 1 are saturated with it. She becomes poetry personified. Hers is the bridal bed and mystic marriage; her divine fruitfulness the flowering of Aaron's rod and the heavenly bedewing of Gideon's fleece; her virginity the sealed fountain, the enclosed garden; she is cedar, rose, honeycomb, perfume, spices. By extension the women in the gospels introduce at once an atmosphere of joyful relaxation: their children play with our Lord, and they give him not only physical but spiritual comfort as well. Their feminine instinct responds to him with an insight that is subtle, quick, spirited, and unfaltering in the very faith he had come on earth to seek. How many poets have told the story of King Cophetua and the beggar-maid? . . . Shakespeare, Ben Johnson, Tennyson, Patmore, all retell the legend of the King who looked through his window and fell in love with the beggar-maid and married her. I'm not sure that it isn't the story of every nun's vocation:

> Bare-footed came the beggar maid
> Before the king Cophetua.

The incident is reflected in all our Lord's dealings with women: the Creator craves to become captive as it were to his creature, to the small, the truly humble, the insignificant — our Lady, Martha and Mary, the women he healed, the prostitutes who were, so St Matthew tells us, among the first to believe in him. My favourite episode is the dialogue between our Lord and the Sidonian woman (Matthew 15:22) which has so much in common with our Lady at Cana. Our Lord's relationship with them reveals that he is really fully human, he can tease, say outrageous things with a poker face and twinkling eye in order to provoke his partner to go one better, and I'm quite sure that it all ended in delighted laughter. I think that the Sidonian woman, who was no lady, probably wagged her finger at him. Both she and our Lady were so unafraid of the Infinite God that they could daringly ignore him and go over his head: each knew perfectly well that he couldn't refuse, and each got exactly what she wanted.

My special love of the Sidonian woman may perhaps derive from a childhood experience. I was five, and for months had watched my baby sister scream from the pain of a line of abscesses open from throat to ear — 'My daughter is grievously troubled'. One day the family doctor said very gently to my mother: 'Your baby is dying. Be kind to her. Don't move her.

Let her die.' No sooner was he gone than children's clothes were being hurled into a travelling-bag and in a flash my elder sister, younger brother, and the year-old child in my mother's arms, were entrained along with me en route for Holywell in North Wales and its famous shrine of St Winefride, with the wonder-working spring of . . . 'pale water, frail water, wild rash and reeling water' which, until the advent of cheap air travel to Lourdes, had been thronged with pilgrims from as early as the twelfth century:

> And not from purple Wales only nor from elmy England,
> But from beyond seas, Erin, France and Flanders, everywhere,
> Pilgrims, still pilgrims, more pilgrims, still more poor pilgrims.

As his poem shows, Gerard Manley Hopkins loved the place. Dr Johnson who visited it with Mrs Thrale in 1774 was shocked to find 'The bath is completely and indecently open. A woman bathed while we all looked on', he thundered. There was no bathing when my pilgrim group reached the shrine in the late afternoon. It stood, nestling in a deep valley encircled by hills, a gem of late Perpendicular architecture open to the skies and populous with praying pilgrims. A small stout man sat at the turnstile to receive the trifling entrance fee. 'Please, will you take my baby and bathe her in the Well, now, immediately? She's dying', said my mother's urgent voice. 'No, Madam. No bathing is allowed in the afternoon. The times for bathing are men at 7.30 and woman and children at 9 o'clock every morning.' 'But the baby's *dying*. Please put her in the water', she pleaded. Further rebuff. 'No, I can't accept the responsibility.' 'But of course not. I accept the responsibility. I'm her mother. My baby's dying. Please take her into the bath!' With a gesture of mock despair, he capitulated and soon appeared in a bathing suit. With Christlike tenderness he clasped the screaming mite and plunged her three times in honour of the Blessed Trinity into the ice-cold pale green water — it never exceeds 52 degrees and never freezes. 'She came and adored him saying, Lord, help me.' Pilgrims dotted everywhere prayed aloud to God, to our Lady, to St Winefride, until the attendant handed the child back to my mother. No further dressing was ever applied to the wound. It merely healed within a few days as if naturally, and

we returned home as though it were the most normal thing in
the world:

> on heels of air departing,
> Or they go rich as roseleaves hence that loathsome came hither!

' "O woman, great is your faith. Be it done as you desire." And
her daughter was instantly healed.' That daughter was to make
a happy marriage and become the joyful mother of children.
In his poem on St Winefride, Hopkins goes on to speak of
gifts greater than physical healing,

> Those dearer, more divine boons whose haven the heart is.

After that, I became very much aware of suffering children. At
six, I made my first Holy Communion and with a child's quick
eye noticed a mentally-retarded girl clinging to her mother's
arm each Sunday at Mass. Now why, I asked myself, had our
Lord made her like that and me like this? After studying her
through laced fingers, I went home to practise in secret being
blind and deaf and witless, asking myself at each point: 'Why
can I see and hear and think? Our Lord has given me my eyes
and ears and he could take them away at any time.' This sense
of absolute dependence on God has followed me all my life,
deepened as I went along by the specific text of Romans 11:33.
This formed the *leit-motif* of a highly edifying novel, *Via Dolorosa*, by a North Country curate, picked up at a parish fair
when I was eight. How I rolled those cadences round my tongue
and savoured the list of genitives: 'Oh the depth of the riches
of the wisdom and of the knowledge of God. How incompre-
hensible are his judgements and how unsearchable his ways' —
and with what joy as hebdomadarian I sang those words in
euphonious Latin at Vespers years afterwards!
Perhaps love of Wisdom Incarnate drew me to Blessed Henry
Suso's *The Little Book of Eternal Wisdom* during my novitate.
'The sharp dart of love' of *The Cloud* had brought the conscious
discovery of the pure prayer of the will as being the only means
to reach God as he is. As with many novices, my prayer became
the be-all and end-all of life; I foolishly imagined that I'd soon
arrive at the glorious summit of the Godhead. Not for me to
have to climb into the cleft of the rock covered by God's hand

and unable to see his face: leave that to Moses. Needless to add, the Ascent of the Great Above was all of a sudden changed into the Descent of the Great Below, and Divine Wisdom's warning to Henry Suso of light turning to darkness, barrenness of heart, and suffering of mind and body, sounded a very personal note: 'You will never arrive at my naked Divinity except by breaking through my suffering humanity.' And this brings me naturally to the feast of the Dedication of the Church, symbol of the building and adornment of the temple of one's own soul. We sing in the Vesper hymn:

> Tunsionibus pressuris
> Expoliti lapides.

Only with the cutting edge and hard blows of chisel and mallet, and the jointing and cement of prayer are the living stones cut, polished, and built into the spiritual house to 'be a holy priesthood and offer spiritual sacrifices acceptable to God through Jesus Christ' (1 Peter 2:5).

The contemplative life is not, and is not meant to be, a primrose path of dalliance; it is a *Via dolorosa* even though, to keep a correct balance, one freely admits the truth of Blake's

> Joy and Woe are woven fine
> A Clothing for the Soul divine;
> Under every grief and pine
> Runs a joy with silken twine.

On the very eve of his Passion, our Lord spoke of his abounding joy: the two are by no means incompatible. He was moving by painful steps to Gethsemane and the final crux of obedience. Experience teaches that sooner or later every monk and nun will have to face this acid test of obedience to the Father's will. More and more have I realized that obedience was the one bitter lesson that our Lord as Man had to learn. Of all the translations of Hebrews 5:8 I like best R. A. Knox's: 'Son of God though he was, he learned obedience in the school of suffering.' Poverty in the sense of destitution is pretty well non-existent in monastic life; deprivation of family joys demanded by virginity often goes almost unnoticed; but — obedience? Whatever the trial, however, God is there all the time, and so often it is the liturgy which supplies the antidote to the bitterness that can be overwhelming on the natural plane. My favourite Collect, now allotted to the ninth Sunday of the Year, has proved a life-line: *Deus, cujus providentia in sui dispositione non fallitur* . . . whatever his ordinances, God's providence never makes a mistake. The theme is closely linked to the depth of the riches of the wisdom and of the knowledge of God. May I conclude by making the vision of Julian of Norwich my own:

See! I am God: see! I am in all things: see! I do all things: see! I lift never mine hands off my works, nor ever shall, without end: see! I lead all things to the end I ordained it to from without beginning, by the same Might, Wisdom and Love whereby I made it. How should any thing be amiss?

8

A Bunch of Liturgical Wild Flowers

The Tabernacle

EARTH speaks:
  Oldest of things created, lo, I bring
  This precious metal, hard and glittering,
  Hewn from my secret stores with toil and stress,
  Tempered and forged to strength and comeliness —
  I bring
  My richest gift to build thy house, O King.

CEDAR-TREE speaks:
  Proudest of things created, lo, I bring
  Smooth fragrant timber, planed for panelling;
  Ringed by a thousand years of sun and snow
  I soared in splendour, now for thee laid low —
  I bring
  My noblest gift to pave thy house, O King.

SILKWORM speaks:
  Puniest of things created, lo, I bring
  My fine-spun threadwork, soft and shimmering,
  In woven substance exquisitely wrought
  For use and beauty — though myself am naught —
  I bring
  My loveliest gift to veil thy house, O King.

MAN speaks:
  Regent of thy creation, lo, I bring
  Tribute from forest, mine, and living thing,
  My strength, my skill to fashion and design,
  My labour, love, and worship; all are thine —
  I bring
  My heart to be thy dwelling-place, O King.

Mother of the Living
(for Advent)

Not yet the flower is seen;
  Only the fresh young green
Spurts upward, fountain-wise, from sombre mould;
  Soon shall the bud unfold,
    The lily blue
    Burst radiant through,
Full in the light for all men to behold.

As the Flower of the Field
(for Christmas)

The fleeting lovely flowers of May
  Have faded into lifeless hay,
  Ripened, and mown, and stored away.
'All flesh is grass', the Prophet saith.
  In wintry chill when God's lamb lay
  Becradled in poor bed of hay,
  Dreamed he then of flowery May?
The Word made Flesh hath vanquished Death!

Lenten Triolet

  Lent has been long
And I'm weary of praying;
    Is it really so wrong?
  Lent has been long
And I'm weary of praying,
And the blackbird's new song
Sets my thoughts all a-straying —
  Lent has been long
And I'm weary of praying!

Song for an Easter Profession of Vows

The Son of God hangs on a tree
Between two thieves for all to see,

I heard his voice say, 'Follow Me!'
Et nunc sequor.

What daylight will this grey dawn bring?
'The Lord's!' I heard a blackbird sing:
'Lo, he is risen, Christ your King!'
Et nunc sequor.

Then by the gleaming water-side
The Master's hands were opened wide:
'Children, come and dine', he cried,
Et nunc sequor.

Lord, on this joyous Easter day,
Take thou my heart and soul I pray,
Thou art my Life, my Truth, my Way,
Et nunc sequor.

Feast of Easter

Yesterday I was crucified with Christ, to-day I am glorified with him. Yesterday I was buried with him, to-day I rise again with him. Let us therefore sacrifice to him, who suffered and rose again for us. Perhaps you think I shall speak of sacrificing gold or silver or woven stuffs or gleaming gems of great prize, frail and transitory substance of earth, earthly in its very nature. Nay rather let us offer to God our most precious possession, the one most our own — let us offer him ourselves. Let us render to the type what is becoming to it, and acknowledge our own dignity. Let us be like Christ, since Christ also is like unto us. Let us become gods for his sake, since he became man for ours. He took upon himself what is lower, that he might give us what is higher. He became poor, that by his poverty we might be rich. He took the form of a servant, that we might recover our freedom. He came down, that we might be raised up. He was tempted, that we might overcome. He was despised, that we might be glorified. He died, that he might bring us salvation. Nothing else that any one can give will be so great as if he gives himself properly understanding the nature of this mystery, and becoming for his sake whatsoever he became for ours.

(From St Gregory Nazianzen, 'Upon the Holy Pasch')

Feast of the Ascension

To whom was it said, 'Be thou exalted above the heavens, O God'? to whom was it said? Would 'Be thou exalted' be said to God the Father, who never humbled himself? be THOU exalted: Thou who wast made flesh of her whom Thyself hadst made; thou who didst lie in a manger; thou who, made flesh indeed, didst as a little one feed at her breast; thou who bearest the world, yet wast borne by a mother; thou whom the old man Simeon saw as a little one and praised as the Great One; thou whom the widow Anna saw as a babe at the breast and recognized as the Lord Almighty; thou who didst hunger and thirst for our sake, and for our sake wast wearied (is it for the Bread to hunger, or for the Fountain to thirst, or for the Way to grow weary?); thou who didst endure all this for our sake; thou who didst slumber, yet sleepest not, keeping watch over Israel; and lastly, thou whom Judas sold, whom the Jews bought but never possessed; thou who wast seized, bound, scourged, crowned with thorns, hung on the cross, pierced with the lance; thyself who wast dead, buried — be then exalted above the heavens, O God!

From St Augustine, *Serme* CCLXII *de Tempore*

Two hymns of Corpus Christi

Praise God for the life in the germ of wheat,
For the furrowed earth and the raindrops kind,
For the marvel of root and leaf new-sprung,
For the green field rippling 'neath sun and wind.

Praise God for the well-filled ripening ear,
For the rhythmic stroke of the reaper's blade,
For mellow sunlight and harvest-song,
For the sheaf well carried, the stack well made.

Praise God for the strength of man and beast,
For the trusty sinew, the willing heart,
For horse and waggon and iron tool,
For the wheelwright's craft and the thatcher's art.

Praise God for the thresher's whirling wheel,
For its cheerful hum through the frosty morn,
For timber and metal, coal and steam,
For the swelling sacks of golden corn.

Praise God for the mill by the harnessed stream,
For the hard stone quarried and hewn aright,
For the pitiless grinding, smoothly slow,
For the flour perfected, pure and white.

Praise God for the mighty forces set
In earth and water, in air and fire,
For the power of mind that can plumb their worth
And bid them labour for man's desire.

Praise God for the yeast that spreads unseen
Through the formless mass of the rising dough,
For skilful kneading and cleanly care,
For the bakehouse fire with its homely glow.

Praise God for the life his love has given,
By whom all living things are fed,
For seed and harvest, for plough and mill —
Praise God for his gift of our daily bread.

II

Ere the third day of that first week was ended
Wherein he fashioned earth and star and sun,
Ere man, his guest, of slime and spirit blended,
    His course had yet begun,
    The master would prepare
With eager joy and all-embracing care
Board and provision for that marriage-feast
To which he calls alike the greatest and the least.

Seeing what should befall
In the clear noon of his eternal day,
How man would scorn his bounty, and repay
The proffered gift with vinegar and gall —
Yea, seeing all —
He would give freely Very Life, no less,
To those that heed his call,
And trusting to his promise, enter in.
Shall not God's love be wider than man's sin,
His boundless mercy still surpass man's wretchedness?

Behold, a sign!
Nothing in all earth's paradise that grows
Shall be more fair to see,
Than from the stark black branches of that tree
Grey downy buds unfolding, tipped with rose,
To leaf and tendril's twine,
Perfect in tint and line,
Whilst golden flowers to rounded clusters shape,
That slowly ripening reach
Their consummation in the empurpled grape.
— Its Maker's seal on each
Created thing is set; but, for a sign,
Surely his finger-prints are traced upon the vine.

Speedwell

Speedwell in the spinach bed,
Lifting up your dainty head
From the earth, an inch or less,
Perfect in your loveliness;
Mirror clear of heaven above,
Small shrill voice of praise and love,
Joy's own smile — was ever hue
Lovelier than your living blue?

Now the garden must be freed
Clean and bare from every weed,
Groundsel, bindweed, shepherd's purse,
Goosefoot, thistle, dock and worse,

All are doomed; but, Speedwell, must
Must I wrench that mirrored sky
From its foothold in the dust?
Must I mar that radiant gaze,
Quench that rapturous song of praise?
Heaven forgive us, no, not I.
Live and thrive, fear naught from me —
Sure, you're far too small to see!

9
Monastic Miscellany

A LETTER-BOX EXCHANGE

Rule of St Benedict Chapter 54

On no account may a monk exchange letters, tokens or small gifts of any kind, with his parents or anyone else, or with a fellow-monk, unless the abbot gives permission.

Exposition of the Rule by Dom Augustine Baker
Chapter 4

To help & succour those that are in tribulation & affliction, that is, so far as we be able & our state of life will permit & howsoever to have a good will to help in such a case. And this Instrument tendeth to the removing or lessening of our neighbours affliction so far as we can, & our condition of life will permit.

To comfort those that be sad & sorrowfull. This tendeth to remove, if we can, or to lessen in our neighbour sorrow or other distress of mind by our counsell or otherwise the best we can. And for this there may be the frequent occasions even in Monasteries.

To estrange our selves altogether from worldly actions. This among other points would have us not to love conversation at the Grate, nor correspondences by letters without meer necessity. Also it forbiddeth all solicitude of getting or retaining the loves or favours of others, especially of those that are without doors, & all vain complying with them or distracting our selves by occasion of them, so far as we may avoid those occasions.

I am astonished at those prelates who follow the Rule of St Benedict so superstitiously that they keep their subjects away from letter-writing as though from a brothel. Is not this the quickest way to keep good literature from their monks? What saints they think themselves when they command this, and thunder about the virtue of obedience! We ought to obey God rather than man, (Acts 5.20), and He said: 'Increase and multiply' (Gen. 1.28), and this applies to good arts and virtues, as well as to natural propagation. It is wrong to bury literary talent in the earth.

ROBERT JOSEPH, monk of Evesham,
to John Cadecraft, monk of Pershore, 1530

F. C. to Mari Aida
(oblate of Stanbrook
sometime Japanese Buddhist)   1 December 1983

A letter of yours crossed with mine, and now I have to thank you for the loveliest postcard of the approach to a temple — which? All the characters are Japanese, so I have to guess. Kyoto? Right? Wrong? A picture of the steps to the temple made me wonder whether you ever recited — or better, sang — the Gradual psalms as you ascended them. The 'Gradual psalms', as you know, are Pss 119–127, sung by the Israelites as they approached the Temple of Jerusalem. I have been very much occupied in mind of late with the universalism of salvation: our Lord has redeemed the whole human race. When my sister Anne died, her Muslim son-in-law wrote from Tunisia to tell me 'of the deep sorrow caused by the death of my mother'. He went on to say that his family had slaughtered a lamb on her behalf at the sacred shrine of Marabout on the morning of her death, and that he would always remember her in his prayers. When I went to Mass that morning, the sacrifice of Abel and the Paschal Lamb took on a new significance, as I wondered whether Christ the Priest would extend a warm greeting to the priests of so-called pagan or heathen cults for, like their Christian brethren in the priesthood, they also have sacrificed the symbolic Lamb of God in union with every Mass offered on the Christian altar throughout the world and throughout all time. I love to dwell on the 'cosmic priesthood' of Christ. The Canon of the Mass speaks of Abel and Melchisedech, priest of El-Elyon a Canaanite deity; neither were Jews or members of the priestly tribe of Levi. When we reach the further shore, it will be exciting to see the reversal of values, won't it?

By the way, have you any access to Newman's works in Tokyo? If so, do get hold of Volume I of *Parochial and Plain Sermons*, and read the one on the resurrection of the body. Newman was two centuries ahead of his time. He dares to suggest that actually the body itself does not die: only the accidents visible to human senses disappear, the substance persists. So God is the God of Abraham, Isaac and Jacob exactly as he said he was — not merely of their souls, but of the living men. It puts death into an entirely new perspective, and links it up with the Consecration at Mass, doesn't it?

F. C. to Margaret Alexander
(scribe and illuminator)   *12 January 1967*

Such a lot to thank you for — an argosy of good things: your letter, the splendid quotations (what quick, even thrilling response a passage of Belloc's prose evokes), and the Monte Cassino verse, touching especially to a Benedictine. Do you know the Gaelic Rune of Hospitality?

> I saw a stranger yestreen —
> I put food in the eating place,
> Drink in the drinking place,
> Music in the listening place;
> And in the sacred name of the Triune,
> He blessed myself and my house,
> My cattle and my dear ones.
> And the lark said in her song:
>> Often, often, often,
>> Goes the Christ in the stranger's guise.

As for *God's Grace in History*, I find neither Desmond Fisher nor Rosemary Haughton devastating, you know. With all their journalism and theology, they haven't the remotest conception of 'the Church'. They talk glibly of 'the institutional Church' and that causes them to wring their hands and beat upon a wailing-wall. What of the Church who feeds them with Christ's own Body, forgives their sins, reconciles them, saves them, glorifies them? Like the journalistic scribes and the theological pharisees of our Lord's own time, they are scandalized by the all too-too human face of Christ in the form of a slave. There is no comeliness in that Face that they should esteem it — we have heard it all before.

If the Church sometimes seems to treat her sons harshly, how did the Father treat his Only-Begotten Son? These people have lost all sense of the tremendous mystery and paradox of the Christian life. Yves Congar, Père Teilhard de Chardin *grew* immeasurably, became great and powerful because, like their Master, they learned obedience in the school of suffering, as Hebrews puts it.

. . . The deaconess article arouses much interest, and brought a letter from our local Dean. I replied: 'Father, the day may yet come when you will have to pray for "Amabelle, our Bishop", and what will happen in Barchester when the Bishop dies, and Mrs Proudie, the last of the Neros, puts his mitre on her own head — doesn't bear thinking about.' I hope my letter left him chuckling.

F. C. to Margaret Alexander   *10 September, 1967*

'Every man hath his proper gift from God' — but what a wonderful and enviable gift is yours. The beautiful bookmarker is a treasure. I love your script, its delicacy, rhythm and perfect set-out. It will mark my daily Vespers and remind me to keep you in my cowl-sleeve. Before I forget. How do you interpret this week's Collect? We agreed, didn't we, that the Mass Collect provides the key to the Church's liturgical treasures each week, we should get to know them by heart, be soaked in them. This week's, the 27th of the year, prays: *ut dimittas quae conscientia metuit, et adicias quod oratio non praesumit*. It asks God to forgive the wrongs we know we are guilty of, and grant what prayer doesn't dare to ask. And what is that? Is it a bold request for the grace of pure contemplation? — no imaginative scenes, no intellectual concepts, no emotional aspirations, but plain God AS HE IS, as our Lord's infinite gaze comprehends him.

That is why it is good to climb into our Lord's side and see with his eyes, adore with his mind and soul, love with his heart. It will be sightless seeing, wordless praise and adoration, *per Ipsum et cum Ipso and in Ipso*.

That is by the way. Dear S. S. died from an abdominal cancer, swiftly and painlessly, without agony. He ceased as a susurration on eternity (he loved the soft sibilants of his name, Siegfried Sassoon) on Friday night with none of his own near him. He had his best-loved Lady and his guardian angel at his side, as he had had them both as companions throughout the ten years of his Catholic life, when his angel often gave him visible proof of his presence at midnight prayer. Mother Margaret was kneeling before the Blessed Sacrament exposed; I, knowing nothing, made the Stations of the Cross at 7 o'clock, and prayed for the dying.

F. C. to Margaret Alexander   *October 1972*

I am hoping that you will settle down in your studio to something worthy of your gifts, which only Margaret Alexander under God can do. A gift such as yours is in itself companionable surely? I know that when I am concentrating, I don't want any human interference. Don't you agree that as one gets older, one ceases more and more to look *around*; sometimes one takes a backward glance, but that is pointless unless there is someone near who actually shared the experience. More often one's eye travels upward. Heaven and Hope! After all, from one point of view there are only two people in all the world who matter — God and myself. *Abyssus abyssum invocat*; the abyss of our nothingness cries aloud to the abyss of God's infinity, and they meet in a kiss. No one on earth can enter that inner sanctum of God and the soul, and that is all that matters.

Yesterday two teachers from a state school in Worcester brought forty or so backward teenage boys and girls for talks in the parlour. They specially asked to end with an organ recital. I slipped into the parlour beforehand and explained to them that I'd play three items. In the first, a Pastorale on the horn, they were to go to Bethlehem to see the Babe with the shepherds, and notice how one little shepherd was so excited that he kept going flat (the melody employed a flat rather cunningly and unexpectedly), but the Baby liked it; the second item was a conversation between them and our Lord. He wanted them to gather round and talk to him very quietly — and at the end, they would tell him they loved him and he would bless them; and lastly, I'd play a piece that described his dreadful suffering on the cross and his death, but that wasn't the end — if they waited, they'd hear the music break out into a glorious hymn of victory, because Christ rose from the dead to live for ever, as they all would one day.

The result was interesting. Boisterous, noisy, extroverted, irreverent, they trooped into church to an accompaniment of Sh — sh! from their teachers. The horn Pastorale captivated most, but not all. It was the hushed solo dialogue of the second — a movement from Mendelssohn's First Organ Sonata — that completely subdued them. There wasn't a flutter. They were caught up in its magic, and I think their angels were busy; it was the feast of the Guardian Angels. The final piece went superbly, and I followed it with *God save the Queen.* They stood up and sang with all their hearts. Then — was it at the bidding of a teacher? — they all knelt down, and one could see nothing but bowed heads in an *absolute* silence. It lasted for a mere minute or two, then they rose, walked on tip-toe, spoke in whispers, looked at the sanctuary and the statue of St Benedict until, with smiling faces, they found their way out of church. There were no Catholics among them, and a good many foreign faces, Indian some of them, so I have no idea how much religion they professed.

I am so glad that Noel was able to get to Oxford and receive an accolade for his study of Dora's drawings. But don't worry overmuch about his seeming lack of faith. Faith is rather more than the theological definition, and frequently the agnostic has far more true faith because a more sincere search for the Unknown God, than has the 'pious' Catholic.

F. C. to Margaret Alexander   10 *June* 1974

Your Stanbrook visit is fast approaching. I hope that Woodpile
Meadow will still shelter its flock of goldfinches, that the Felicitas climbing-rose will be in full blossom, and the pink campion
spreading everywhere in its friendly fashion may remind you
of your delightful Tudor cottage named after the St Edmund
Campion, whose wit and brilliant sallies so delighted the heart
of his Queen, Elizabeth I. Why, oh why, did she let him go to
such a death? Yet the tale of heroic suffering for conscience'
sake is told in our own day, and we have recently listened to
the most inspiring account of modern martyrdom from the lips
of Mrs Richard Wurmbrand, wife of the famous Rumanian
Pastor Richard Wurmbrand, who has spent fourteen years in
Soviet prisons, three of them in solitary confinement in a cell
thirty feet below ground in Bucharest. His wife, Sabina, spent
at least four years in prison under terrible conditions. She
reminded me very much of another heroine of mine, Dorothy
Day: there was the same serenity, the same poverty both of
body and spirit, the same spiritual radiance, a joy that flowed
out like electric currents charging all her hearers with vitality,
courage and strength. She is a woman in her early sixties, I
think. Once a Jewess, intellectual and wealthy and thoroughly
materialistic in outlook, she married the Jewish Richard and
together they planned to have a pleasurable existence — until
God erupted into their lives, challenged them, and conquered.
He came in the guise of a German carpenter under the Hitler
regime. All that can be found in their published biographies in
cheap paperbacks. What cannot be found is the smile on
Sabina's face as she says:

God is full of surprises! The Bible is full of surprises! Take Acts 12
and study it for surprises and you'll see. There's Peter condemned to
death. He should be worried and fearful and all nerves. Is he? He's
fast asleep, perfectly content, with the happiness of a child. That's the
first surprise. And then the second — the people who should be asleep
in the middle of the night are all awake. The Church, we are told,
was praying for Peter. So one who should be awake is asleep, and
those who should be asleep are awake and praying. And the third
surprise? With the head condemned to death and the Church hounded

to death, the Church should have died — but [with a laugh full of delight] look at us all here. Here we are, all alive STILL! Yes, God is full of surprises. Someone said to my husband: 'When you were in prison, did you see any miracles?' Richard answered: 'No, I didn't *see* any miracles. I *am* a living miracle of God.'

Mrs W. had been imprisoned with 1,000 women, some of them society women who only possessed the evening dress they were wearing at the time of their sudden arrest. She had stories only to be equalled in the annals of the early Christians, and listening to her I was transported to the past, to the times of St Cyprian and my own Felicitas and I began to realize something of the intense veneration felt for heroic confessors of the faith, for my instinct was to kneel and kiss Mrs Wurmbrand's feet. She told of the nuns in her filthy overcrowded barrack-room, who in the face of all threats, calmly went on singing psalms and praising God. Their captors finally decided to make an exhibition of them. Summoning the whole camp as witnesses, they ordered them on to the frozen lake in bare feet and scant clothing. They should have died of exposure and frost bite. Instead, their song grew louder and sweeter. So the dogs — great specially-trained brutes of terrifying ferocity — were set on them to tear them to pieces. The camp set up a wail and begged for pity — in vain. The dogs hurtled themselves on to the ice, ran in circles round the nuns, and then sat down quietly without a growl or menace. In angry frustration, the warders ordered everyone back to their cells, sent for a doctor, and asked for an examination of the prisoners after their exposure. Not a single sign of injury. The nuns sang on. The tale of their trial and victory very much resembles that of the Forty Martyrs of Sebaste which the higher critics would dismiss as myth — here it is a history in our own day. This, I felt, is where true ecumenism is to be found: no barriers whatever of confessional faiths. Only tribulations, anguish, persecutions, hunger, dangers, the sword, in fact the entire list given by St Paul in Romans — and over all, the joy of any man's inability to separate his own from Christ. We gave Mrs Wurmbrand a Stanbrook tea — those who have sampled it will know our recipe. She ate the crisps and macaroons with appreciation and then produced a bag to collect the overs with: 'I must let Richard taste these delicious cakes.

May I take these home?' She lives in America for six months of the year and for the remainder travels about Europe directing an anti-Soviet underground movement, largely financed by her and her husband's books, I surmise. It was an inspiration to see this very human saint, and especially moving when she asked Lady Abbess to allow her to kiss her. One again thought of St Paul's: 'Salute one another with a holy kiss.'

F. C. to Margaret Alexander   26 *September* 1982

Tomorrow the usual appeal will go up for apple-pickers and the place will be swarming with nuns perched on ladders like goddesses on pedestals, swaying among the apples and nestling in a house of fruit (I have been reading Paul Claudel). Beneath the trees, like so many rapacious harpies, Jasper, the magnificent Welsummer cock, Victor in French silver and black plumage with his Maran Parisian belles, Isidore the pragmatist with the pickaxe voice, a mere White Dorset, with their hosts of meek-eyed adoring wives will be darting hither and thither snatching at all the more precious varieties wondrous ripe, rejecting with unerring instinct any goodly apples rotten like falsehood at the heart. And I, who no longer climb ladders, will stand afar off, keep perfectly still, and wait for an apple to fall from time to time like a weighty and ripe thought.

Do you remember the medieval carol: 'Adam lay y-boundyn in a bond, / Fowre thousand wynter thowt he not too long: / and al was for an appil, an appil that he tok, / As clerkis fyndin wretyn in here book'? That apple accepted from Eve by her husband, provided a guest of ours with a very weighty and ripe thought indeed. But first let me introduce her. She is an endearing little Japanese Sister of the Australian Institute of the Good Samaritan — usually abbreviated to 'the Good Sams' — founded in 1857 by Archbishop Polding, a monk of Downside. As every one knows, the Japanese social revolution during the latter half of this century is without precedent in the history of mankind. After the Second World War, the Bishop of Nagasaki (territory made holy by St Francis Xavier and the Japanese martyrs of the seventeenth century) appealed to Australia for help, and the nuns responded by going out and founding schools — they set up in Nagasaki itself a kindergarten, middle and high school. Education is the primary goal of ninety million Japanese, and schools run by religious stand high in public estimation. English Sacred Heart nuns from Roehampton had already established a school for girls in Tokyo to which a small Japanese pupil was sent to be educated. There, in addition to her studies, the highly-intelligent child heard of the Christian God. A fortnight ago, she spoke here at Stanbrook on Luke 9: 1–6 in which our Lord bids his apostles take nothing on their missionary journey — no staff, haversack, bread or money. 'This cannot be taken literally: the apostles were not told to hitch-hike', said the foreign voice with an amazing command of English. She went on to speak of the primary importance of prayer since the Holy Spirit alone can bring the salvific gift to the people. By way of illustration, she asked to tell her own story. As a fervent Buddhist, she found no difficulty in accepting God the Father — she already in a very real sense loved and adored him. But Christ, God and Man, was an altogether different proposition. She had asked one of the nuns to instruct her in Christianity, and both found themselves at a dead standstill. Painfully through months of darkness, both of them prayed for light. 'Then one day God's silent but gentle word took root deeply in my heart: "This is my son: listen to him." ' From that moment there was no doubt or hesitation. With glad conviction, her tutor remarked: 'Some unknown person must have been praying for you.' With that, she turned to us, an enclosed community, whose task it is to supply the vital element in all missionary activity. But my introduction has taken me away from the apple. Let me return. She was the first Japanese to ask entrance into the Good Sams — a step that required courage, for the Australians had been so recently enemies of Japan. Among her many accomplishments, Sister Maria Regina arranges flowers as I (who have always been similarly interested) have never seen them arranged. Her arrangements give a marvellous insight into the beauty of God and Nature: every line, every curve, every angle is thought out, and one of her loveliest, full of rich and ingenious design, was a brightly-coloured apple nestling among pines in a low white bowl that led the eye further up to a simple arrangement of roses, terminating needless to say in the statue of our Lady of Consolation in cedar wood that is the principal shrine in our cloister. I feel, I scent, I disentangle, I track down the connections, the associations, the harmony. I asked Sr Maria Regina why she so often chose pine for her arrangements; the apple was obvious: once the old Eve, now symbol of the New, foreseen in the Song of Solomon. She replied that the Japanese pine is strong and supple, made to resist fierce storms, able to draw sustenance from dry and stony ground, an evergreen with a harmonious capricious framework of branches — like life itself. Therein of course lies the moral. The lines and colours, by defining and delimiting one another, speak an authentic language to one who will look and let the eye listen, and the pungent scent speaks to the heart. One day in Chapter, Sr M. R. gave the assembled community a talk on monastic life compared to the Japanese Tea Ceremony. She grouped her points under four headings: 1. *Simplicity*: a minimum of need, no cushions, no furniture, one or two flowers in a vase, not more than two small cakes on a tiny white paper. 2. *Reverence*: accepting the guest with a profound bow (how like the Holy Rule!), careful of one's posture. 3. *Silence*: No background music, few words spoken with sincerity from the heart; sense of companionship in silence. 4. *Ritual*: how to walk, sit, pour water in the bowl, how to drink and express appreciation simply in order that all should be permeated with peace and serenity — almost with sacredness. 'So much akin', said she, 'to the spirit of monastic set-up!' Then she spoke of the *haiku*, their extreme concision with a central image that sets up resonances in the mind, like a tiny pebble thrown into water destined to spread immense concentric circles. And while she was speaking to me of my first chapter of Helen Waddell's biography, set in Tokyo, she was rapidly making notes on a sheet of paper in Japanese calligraphy, all vertical, decorative and suggestive — quite fascinating. She has promised me all kinds of postcards as possible illustrations for the biography. My first sentence reads: '25 Nakano-cho, Azabu, Tokyo, a large charming house built after the Japanese fashion entirely of wood raised on piles a couple of feet above floor-level, stood apart on rising ground, concealed behind a high bamboo fence.' It was heartening to see Sr Maria Regina's reaction: with many smiles and many bows she said: 'Ah yes; Azabu is still the residential quarter of the legations and foreign missionaries.' Next time I met her, she had made a list of the legations at present to be found there! Besides a Japanese sister, we have also had a Korean with us for some months, and one day at recreation two dainty figures in pale grey habits with blue flowered pinafores, the picture of feminine elegance, stood behind a table on which stood layers of spam, dishes of grated carrot, spinach and mounds of rice, and proceeded to show us how to make *Nori maki* — in other words, a seaweed roll, to be eaten with chopsticks, deep red and handsomely carved. Each did her own *osushi* — held up a rectangle of dark green seaweed and then filled it with layers of food with due attention to colour and density and the rest, rolled it and cut the roll into thickish little slices laid on a silver salver with an invitation to lift a morsel between the chopsticks — they did it with such ease. You may imagine the scrum and amusement. Curiosity made me taste . . . In splendid poetry, the prophet Jonah exclaims: 'The seaweed was wrapped round my head at the root of the mountains.' That seaweed was wrapped round my innards, not my head, and would it disappear? I longed for a few drops of Lea and Perrins' Worcester Sauce but no one would give to me. *Osushi* is decidedly an acquired taste.

. . . I wonder how many saw the photographs of nineteen glowing faces under huge straw hats at jaunty angles over black and white veils, with arms up-raised in enthusiastic love and farewell to the departing plane of Pope John Paul at Coventry: the fetching picture found its way into many newspapers including the *Illustrated London News*. Know that they were the faces of 19 Dames of Comfort of Stanbrook Abbey, Callow End, who had immediately caught the eye of umpteen photographers. One up for black-and-white? I wish I could enclose one of the spider's webs glittering with dewdrops that adorn the yew hedge. 'Give beauty back, back to God, beauty's self and beauty's giver.'

F. C. to an unknown correspondent, whose friend, a poet and convicted murderer, had recently died in prison.

In answer to your letter of this morning, may I preface my remarks by saying how sorry I am that your task of editing the poems must involve personal pain? To quote another poet, 'The felicity of the angels and glorified saints and of God himself', writes Coventry Patmore, 'would not be perfect without the edge of pathos, which it receives from the fall and reconciliation of man. Sin, says St Augustine, is the necessary shadow of heaven; and pardon, the highest light of its beatitude.'

In the broadcast of May 9th last year, I quoted from Francis Thompson's prose essay *Health and Holiness* — or rather, I didn't directly quote. I summarized an argument of his thus: Siegfried Sassoon had seen while at prayer at midnight 'an almost life-sized, short-haired seraph, with arms outstretched — quite clear, and lovelier than anything I could have pictured. What is your attitude to such experiences?' he asked me. Here is my reply:

What is my attitude? If it isn't perilous to tease you, can you recall how Francis Thompson lumps together saint, poet and murderer? He shows that before their sudden burst of achievement, they suffer birth-pangs which leave their bodies devitalized and spent. It is precisely then, when nerves are worn thin and sensitivity is at its highest, that they experience — what shall I call them? Supernatural visions, or hallucinations? St Ignatius Loyola steps out victorious from the cave of Manresa, and promptly sees a green serpent coiled round a wayside cross; Francis Thompson emerges from a period of darkness into light, strolls down the garden, and meets a minute white-stoled child cupped in an arum lily; Macbeth in his castle-court clutches wildly at an air-drawn dagger. You, in your solitude at Heytesbury, incubate a poem in which you are to 'ask your Angel — ask that vigilant voice'; and, hey, presto! the seraph stands before you and illumines your midnight prayer. Well what about it? Being a nun, and therefore a rationalist and sceptic, I want to know what you mean by a life-sized seraph with arms. Aren't you simply adopting the iconography of Christian art? Can a mighty spirit be so circumscribed? Has an angel *got* arms? . . .

I hope that this passage, taken from the BBC script, is what you want and will help?

F. C. to Sydney C. Cockerell   *19 June 1957*

Thank you for the loan of Edith Finch's biography of Wilfrid Scawen Blunt, and for your diary of 1900. Of the two, your diary scores points every time, even from the W.S.B. angle. (Edith Finch is Bertrand Russell's wife, isn't she?)

I have been trying to collect my impressions of the book — a decidedly weighty volume if 400 odd pages go for anything. I cannot help wondering what Miss Finch's aim was? She writes good well-knit prose which does a thoroughly business-like job well, she can marshal facts and present them in an orderly manner, she can wend her way through the tortuous labyrinths of the *Who's Who* without notable error, in a way which must have given an American immense satisfaction. But beyond that?

Broadly speaking I missed three things.

(I) Blunt, the real man, as he was in his own home, as he was to live with, never appears at all except in half-hints and innuendoes. If family veto, discretion, and inability to quote sources make a biography impracticable, why attempt it?

(II) What might have been done has not been done. There are very long political chapters — Egypt, India, Ireland — by far the greater part of the book. Dare I describe them as tedious? Place names are given as in an atlas, journeys may be traced as on a map, names figure such as one would find in any school history book. . . . But life, adventure, colour, landscape? What Freya Stark would have made of some of the travel routes! Instead the biographer can't get away from the petty intrigues of 'high society'. And there is not the slightest attempt at any creative, critical appraisement of Blunt's efforts to secure justice for the small nations. I have been startled time after time to find how prophetic was Blunt's vision — 'the insane convenant' of the Cyprus lease from Turkey, for instance, in 1878; or the manager of *The Times* in 1882: 'English people had only two interests in Egypt, the Suez Canal and their bonds. . . . Beyond this they did not care for the truth.' But there was no attempt at an integration of the political scene with what had gone before, and what has happened since. Whether W.S.B. was no hero to his biographer I do not know, but she constantly comments upon his seeming altruism in terms such as . . . 'of course the position of intermediary . . . satisfied both his pride and his imagination' — (p. 136). He was 'the beneficent lord and master' who, in order to confute political opponents collected stories of their social failure or unhappy literary attempts. Not an attractive portrait. One gets the impression that fighting and intrigue were loved for their own sake, and that he espoused the cause of the underdog *de haut en bas*. He was aristocratic by conviction as well as by birth.

(III) Blunt was a poet, and if he lives at all he will live as a poet. Surely one chapter should have been devoted wholly to W.S.B. the thinker and poet; to a discussion of his philosophy and style, to his place in English letters? I wondered throughout the book why there is so little direct quotation when there was such an abundance of matter to choose from. We are told of the 'Secret History Series' and they are described but never quoted. The account of his childhood and youth should have been given in his own words as far as possible. He is hardly ever allowed to speak for himself in the whole 400 pages.

What worried me most in the book was the biographer's unwillingness to let facts unfold and speak for themselves. The reader is never left in that condition of suspense so essential to dramatic interest. A classic example of the failure of the biography occurs in the opening lines of Chapter 3, page 53. Poor Lady Anne is given no chance to make her own impact on the reader. We are warned, even before it takes place, that her marriage was a failure, and we are given her epitaph before we have realized she has been born. Thus the reader progresses with a growing sense of bewilderment throughout the hundreds of pages which follow. Far from disagreement with W.S.B. his wife is at his side in every crisis and adventure, ready to defend him with her life if necessary, putting her fortune at his disposal, and displaying a charm and power which rather dwarfs her husband. The same thing happens over Judith and her children. Instead of winning the reader's sympathy by allowing the story to take its natural course, by letting us see the father rejoicing in his brilliant daughter, happy in her marriage, delighted with his grandchildren — as he was from your Diaries — the biographer steps in from the outset and sums up at the beginning, long before the tale is told! And of course one simply LONGS

to know of the vision which led Lady Anne to the Catholic
Church. It is referred to THREE times and nothing whatever
said of it further. I shall not bother to comment on the lamen-
table ignorance the biographer displays when dealing with any
question of Catholic doctrine or practice. But two pages stick
out in my mind and move me with the *lachrymae rerum*. Pages
37–39 deal with Blunt's close friendship with Schomberg Kerr
in a way which suggests at first sight (but not on close analysis)
that S.K. was of the same temper and mind as W.S.B. Nothing
could be further from the truth. Schomberg Kerr was Dame
Francis Kenyon's uncle and an excellent biography of him exists.
Far from opposing his sister's entrance at Roehampton he supported her and was her great friend, the more so as he was
himself contemplating becoming a Jesuit. He did in fact enter
the Society of Jesus of which he became an illustrious member.
As I read W.S.B.'s biography, I see Kerr as Blunt's higher self,
what he might have been, the embodiment of all that was
noblest in him.

The second thing which caused me an intense pang as I read
it was the account of Blunt's reaction to his wife's diaries after
her death. They 'made very painful reading for him. Why, he
asked, did she give them to me?' His egocentricity was only
conscious of his own pain, not of the unspeakable pain he had
brought upon her. She wasn't trying to wound him for the
perverted pleasure such an act might offer. She was far too
heroic for that, it seems to me. She was using cautery and knife
as a surgeon does, to heal. She hoped to bring him to his senses.
And she failed. He was merely filled with self-pity.

So much for the biography. Yet, I like W.S.B. better because
I understand him better. His childhood was a nightmare and
the poor litle fellow never had a chance. He needed a father's
strong influence morally, and a home life and mother's love
spiritually. Instead of which he lost both parents at an early age
and was whipped from pillar to post. I read into his early life
a kind of Esau–Jacob parable. Stonyhurst might have made him
what he really longed to be, but he was only there for a few
months. What an indelible mark it left on him all the same! It
comforts me that he never denied that he was a Catholic; indeed
he always proclaimed that he was one, and that in spite of

everything. He had much to pull him in the direction he took, and lacked his brother's guts. This I say in the teeth of Lady Russell who seems to equate religion with spineless ineptitude. Yet I admit that I am conscious of having been hard on her work; our outlooks are so different and I am perhaps impatient at her inability to get under Blunt's skin. But as a piece of research the book is excellent, and I hope I have not proved myself a carping critic.

Diary (24 hours — no, even less)

June 21st: Determined after Vespers to slip down to the library to look up the Life of Henry Schomberg Kerr to verify references. Found it. Yes, born 1838; elder brother of Mother Henrietta Kerr of Roehampton Sacred Heart Convent. When Henrietta was five she was very distressed at being set on one side by the birth of a sister. Her brothers teased her unmercifully and once, having crept into hiding to cry, she was discovered by Schomberg who made her climb with him to the top of a hayrick, and there solemnly promised her he would always be her friend and champion. She in return promised to adopt the same career in life as he. He replied they ought to take an oath on it but neither knew how to set about it. So they joined hands and said they wished to make a pact as Abraham and Isaac had done. (Neither were Catholics at the time.) In 1863 Henrietta entered the Sacred Heart Order. Schomberg was ordained as a Jesuit in 1875. I shouldn't imagine he could be any other than W.S.B.'s friend? Certainly Mother Henrietta Kerr is *the* famous figure at Roehampton. Two of her nieces, Mother Margaret Kerr and a sister Monica became Sacred Heart nuns.

8.30 p.m. We were peacefully reciting the psalms at Matins when there came a whirr of wings and a crescendo of exultant cries as Martlet accompanied by Martlette, his wife, whom he had obviously invited out for a game of high jinks, swept into choir through the usual window. They proceeded to give a wonderful display of aeronautics — circling, skimming, looping the loop and making figure eights among myriads of blazing candles and huge bowls of pink poppies and larkspurs surrounding the high altar where the Blessed Sacrament was exposed. It was *such* a distraction as one felt they must knock a candle over and cause some dreadful catastrophe. Not a bit of it. They revelled in the game, and added to our *Te Deum* their profuse strains of unpremeditated art which sounded something like Jip-jip! Pr-pr-pri! Hip hip hurrah! Finally with a rapturous Goodnight away they sped. And so to bed.

June 22nd. 3.40 a.m. Rose, washed and dressed in order to be in church at 4 a.m. for my hour's allotted 'watch' before the Blessed Sacrament. Everything grey and silent, but as I neared choir I felt again that atmosphere of intensity and life lived at its very centre which always seems to mark Quarant Ore. As the clock struck four, I took my place on the prie-dieu. Points of flame everywhere, flowers, and in the centre of everything, the glittering disc of the white Host enthroned in the monstrance. Was it fancy, a mere illusion, or was the Host penetrated with a light of its own, was it a kind of window through which I could look straight into the heavens, a mirror of God's faultless and transcendent beauty? At twenty minutes past four a rustle and flutter, a cheep, a tiny musical phrase, the diffident testing of a scale, and then as if in response to the baton of some angelic conductor, a glorious symphony of sound, Nature's Lauds and Hymn to the Creator. Then all of a sudden, hurling themselves through the open window in an ecstasy of joy at the dawn of another day, came our two martlets, sweeping, gliding, soaring, singing. The sparkle, the richness, the mastery and the achievement! It somehow seemed exactly right that the court of the Lord at that early hour should consist of tongues of flame, glowing pink poppies, two blue-black singing birds gashed with colour, and two nuns kneeling in silent adoration.

5 a.m. Rising bell. Everyone astir. Prayer at an end. Spell broken.

8.30 a.m. Delivery of letters. A BRILLIANT one from the nineteen-year-old S. who has added Horace to his Ronsard and Shakespeare. Typical of boys of that age to show off. But what marvellous letters he can write. Wonder whether I should tell him so, or would it increase his conceit? Also, a letter from Dr Harrison, Professor of Plainsong and Polyphony at Oxford

University. He thinks I'm clever. Shall send the letter to S. just to show him that I am. And a p.c. from Mr Murray from Fiesole.

10.45 a.m. Rain, soft, penetrating, life-giving — such a relief from 'the bloody sun' — I merely quote the *Ancient Mariner*, but it has slid into my very soul. Haven't slept with the heat for a week or more. Shall sleep tonight.

Now what on earth is the use of writing a diary when nothing ever happens and my great-great-grandchildren will take no interest in it whatever? It is definitely 'no go'. Let Lady Clarke with her 2000 guests embark on one; but you'll agree, won't you, that as far as I'm concerned it is out of the question. I've only done the above to prove to you that it CAN'T BE DONE.

F.C. to Sydney C. Cockerell   *20 March 1959*

Tomorrow is the feast of St Benedict, and for the first time in living memory we shall have no Second Vespers of his feast. According to Pope Pius XII's revision, the Office *de Tempore* takes precedence — ferial Vespers unaccompanied! However we face solemn Matins tonight and then plunge into the Great Week.

By the way, have you any idea why everyone eats eggs at Easter? Is it because eggs were forbidden by the medieval laws of fasting, or are eggs symbolical of our Lord's resurrection from the tomb? It is interesting to find St Augustine saying, *Restat spes quae, quantum mihi videtur, ovo comparatur. Spes enim nondum pervenit ad rem; et ovum est aliquid, sed nondum est pullus.* ['There remains hope which, it seems to me, may be likened to an egg. Just as hope has not yet attained to reality, so the egg is a something, but not yet a chicken.'] Thus he compares the egg that is not yet a chicken to our hope in our own resurrection. We have been sent two of the most delightful toys I have ever seen. I don't know where they were made, but they are two small monkeys clad in fur, so lifelike that I, who rarely like toys, found myself talking to them and playing with them as though they were alive. They wind up and then perform. One, the he-monkey, delivers himself over to an ecstatic frenzy of cymbal clashing. His whole body trembles and vibrates in sympathy with the movement, and when I inserted a finger between the cymbals and remonstrated with him for giving himself over so completely to such barbaric music, he turned luminous hazel eyes upon me, and resumed the noise more madly and vociferously than ever. Meanwhile his wife squats on her haunches, her whole being a monstrous personification of brutish gluttony, engrossed in a huge cone of strawberry ice-cream. Forth flicks her long scarlet tongue and into the luscious mountain of froth it plunges until satiety forces her to rest awhile. We have laughed quite immoderately over their antics.

John Betjeman? Have you made any further headway with his poems? I found that so long as I approached him looking for affinities with Wordsworth or Pope or the Metaphysicals, I got nowhere. But when I dropped all my preconceived notions of what a poet should say, and approached him with a receptive mind to discover what he actually was saying, I began to see light, even though the light was fluorescent and streaming from a concrete standard in Camden Town. One should not pay too much attention perhaps to his beefy tennis-players and suburban bathrooms and tinned foods. What he is hammering home to a contemporary world deaf to the theologians is the fact of sin (which he does not hesitate to call by its 14th century names), and the necessity of Redemption. Because he says it all in a semi-humorous fashion — although sometimes he can be literally terrifying and terrible — one cannot escape the main theme:

> Not my vegetarian dinner, not my lime-juice minus gin,
> Quite can drown a faint conviction that we may be born in sin.

... Dame Hildelith wonders whether you received copies of *The Monotype Recorder* devoted to the work of Eric Gill? Also, can you give me any idea how much Joan Hassall would charge for illustrating a book? And in my last letter, I said I should try to get hold of the text of the novices' Ophelia parody. It is too long to send, so I only send you these snippets. Polonius warns Ophelia:

> How now, Ophelia, dost dream of Hamlet still?
> But thou must be obedient to my will.

That Fellow's good for naught, dishonest, too,
I fear that to his vows he'll prove untrue.

To which Ophelia replies:

. . . But if I spurn him, maybe he'll be bowed
With sorrow, and perhaps he may go mad,
Or be a Jesuit, which is just as bad.

(Song: When a wooer goes a-wooing)

Hamlet enters unobserved.

Ophelia (aside):

He little knows I want to be a nun
And all my love for Hamlet's only done
To hide the truth because full well I know
If he suspected, he'd not let me go.

Hamlet (aside):

They little dream I want to be a monk
And yet I'm really in a dreadful funk,
I know Ophelia really loves me so,
If she heard this, she'd drown herself for woe.

Exeunt Ophelia and Polonius.

Hamlet:

To go or not to go, that is the question
I've worried o'er till I've got indigestion.
Whether it is nobler in the mind to bear
The heartaches and the dreadful wear and tear
Of worldly life, or leave it all behind
And live in cloister with a quiet mind.
To pray and spend one's time in quiet oration
Indeed methinks this is a consummation
Devoutly to be wished. I must not shirk
The issue of to pray perchance to work.
To work; aye, there's the rub that gives me pause,
For who knows what may lie beyond those doors?

And once they've got me in, I dread to think
What I may have to do at kitchen sink,
Sorting potatoes, picking apple trees,
Or cleaning dirty floors on hands and knees,
For who would fardels bear, a novice be

When he might smoke and drink and watch TV?
Thus fancy doth make cowards of us all
Some leap within and some without the wall.

(Song):   Is life a boon
             If so it must befall
             That voice whene'er it call
             Calls not too soon.
             Though we be young and gay
               We'll give it all away
               Our silver spoon.

             What reason for delay
             Why wait another day,
             Why enter in July
             And not in June?
             Why wait another day
             Why enter in the eve
             And not at dawn?

So it goes on for pages and ends with the final chorus:

             I have a song to sing — o!
             Sing me your song — o!
             It is sung to the swell
             Of a pealing bell
             And a joyful peal, ding dong — o!
             It's the song of maidens free from care
             Who may be young and who may be fair,
             Who left the world and who laughed aloud
             Avoiding the pitfalls of the proud,
             And instead lived humbly and full of mirth
             In one of the happiest spots on earth
             Where of Consolations there is no dearth
             For they live with the love of Our Lady
             Heighdy, heighdy,
             Happy are we, happy to be
             In a place where everyone can say
             That she lives with the love of Our Lady.

Perhaps I ought to have quoted Hamlet's:

             Get thee to a nunnery, deceiving maid,
             Too long with my affections have you played.
             A convent's just the place for girls like you,
             They'll teach you to behave, and how to do

What's right and proper. Truly I have heard
That Stanbrook's a fine place and oh my word!
They train you very thoroughly indeed.
They'll make you mend your ways so you take heed
Of what I say. Your faithlessness confess.
To Stanbrook hie thee in a short black dress.

Have you wrinkled your nose in disdain — or have you
enjoyed the nonsense? Anyway, I know you'd love Polonius,
the Beefeater. His face is marvellous, so are his scarlet hat and
gold uniform, and the calves of his legs.

Sydney C. Cockerell to F.C.   *21 March 1960*

I have been thinking of the average memoirs which give a false
picture of their subjects by dwelling on their merits and omitting
their shortcomings and defects. This led me to wonder what
sort of picture of myself would be given by any one who might
take it into his head to write my biography. My three children
would be asked to. They know nothing whatever about me,
and there is nobody that I can think of who would give at all
an accurate account of my aims and aspirations during my all
but 30 years as Director of the Fitzwilliam Museum — by far
the most fruitful period of my life. ????

F.C. to Wilfrid Blunt
(Curator of the Watts Gallery,
author of *Cockerell*, 1964)   *30 August 1964*

Once begun, it was impossible to lay your biography down
until I had finished it: since then, however, I have found it
necessary to pause a little in order to allow my thoughts to
settle into some coherent pattern. I am now about to set down
a few observations. They will be frank and sincere — I owe
you no less than that. I trust that nothing I say will wound or
offend: nothing could be further from my desire, but you would
not wish me to dismiss your book with a medley of polite
nothings, would you?

As a piece of writing, your work is first-class. It is alive from the word 'Go', and the interest never falters: the uncompromising Sydney C. Cockerell is there with all his vitality, truculent honesty, and selfish generosity. True to himself, he refuses to draw his last breath until the last word is written. He surely would have approved the format? With its good type, generous margins, fine illustrations (the end-papers are specially attractive), the appearance of the biography is as imposing and solid as a Webb table or a Morris chair. The plan is well constructed, the prose has directness and bite, and you have obviously striven to mirror the man as you saw him, without conscious bias or distortion. Yet it will be part of the thesis of this letter to point out that your study has not gone deep enough to depict the whole man; the portrait is therefore unintentionally falsified. S.C.C.'s instructions to paint him warts and all have led you unwittingly to view him with jaundiced eye through green spectacles, so that he has been able to do nothing right. He himself gave you your commission and you have fulfilled it only too literally.

May I first run quickly through the book, noting my comments as I read? Some are mere trifles, others may be of more importance:

p. 15 Was an annuity of £500 for ten years granted to S.C.C.'s widowed mother 'little enough' to suggest poverty? Many women in England at the time were bringing up six children quite respectably on less than £50 a year, let alone £500.

p. 18 Carlie's pay — ten shillings a week — 'was meagre'. He was 17½, and his diary for that year adds, if I am not mistaken, that he was given three months holiday with lots of money for good lunches, £20 for having written a letter which pleased Grandfather Cockerell, and £1,000 shares in the family business. Was that bad going for a youngster who had no expenses of upkeep? Poverty?

p. 19 'But Carlie could not accept God.' Is that correct? He could not accept an incarnate God: he certainly accepted a Supreme Spirit who, according to his quaint notion, created the universe and promptly forgot all about it, as being beneath notice. In the chapter on Bernard Shaw in *In a Great Tradition*, I had to withdraw at S.C.C.'s hurt request a passage in which

G.B.S. referred to him as an atheist who cared no more about a reliquary than about a football cup. During his last years there were times when he showed a yearning for spiritual reassurance — hence his gravitation towards priests and nuns and Catholics as a whole. 'Are you a Catholic?' became the first question with which he greeted a stranger, and disappointment was written large if the unfortunate had to answer No.

p. 50 A welcome tribute to the essential goodness and integrity of the man. He showed an equal generosity and equity to the end of his life. I mentioned once a young Vietnamese priest's past sufferings and present poverty. With exquisite tact S.C. wrote to ask whether the priest could supply him with a few stamps for his collection. In return, he 'bought' them for £10, the price, as he well knew, of some warm winter underclothing. He acted likewise towards our Italian POW, offering to head a subscription list with £40 to bring him back from Canada where he was not too happy. Instances like these could be multiplied indefinitely.

p. 104 G. K. Chesterton was never a friend. S.C. heard him speak only once, I think, and disliked him on the spot because he laughed at his own jokes and criticized scarlet pillar-boxes. G.K.C.'s genius and humility were beyond S.C.'s comprehension.

p. 167 I found this and kindred chapters on his family relations painful reading, the more so as S.C. himself possessed to an eminent degree that virtue of *pietas* so prized by the ancients. He never discussed either wife or children, never indulged in criticism, never 'pulled to pieces'; what he disapproved of, he consigned to oblivion, and when others made charges, he offered excuses. That was a remarkable trait in his character. There is a saying that if you want to know a man's faults, you should ask his friends. They will know them, but they will not tell you them. I am sufficient of a Bible Christian to believe that the story of Noah and his sons is valid for all time — one would not willingly inherit the curse of Ham. And in the final analysis, precisely what was S.C.'s crime? Many a father fails to understand his children yet is loving and devoted for all that; many a man does not look after his wife as he ought, yet is no worse a husband than some of the best of men. I feel that in this matter especially you have lacked the dispassionateness necessary for a cool assessment, and in allowing yourself to be unduly influenced by a possibly irrational sympathy, have shown yourself a little less than just. For a man like S.C. the burden of an invalid wife within a few years of marriage was a grievous trial, yet his diaries prove how he supported it and made the best of it. He might have left the search for day and night nurses, for instance, to the Kingsford sisters or his own daughters, yet it was he who hunted high and low and found them. You say he rarely mentioned his wife as time went on. Then you have never read his unbroken correspondence with Dame Laurentia, where she is brought in increasingly as the years go by. He gave no dinner parties? No; a man needs his wife at his side if he is to entertain, and she must feel equal to it. For a woman who could have carried anything off with her artistic sense and handsome presence, dress was a minor consideration, and there seems no evidence that he was stingy. May it not have been that an invalid wife rendered lavish entertainment impossible, and so made the Fellowship of a College more desirable from a purely practical point of view?

As for Katharine's sixteen-year-old letter (how it haunts the memory!), one would like to know what her parents thought of the proposal. They may very well have discussed it and dismissed it for some excellent reason unknown to the teenager. Her mother was then in sight of her sixties, she was a bad sailor, and was an invalid dependent upon others. The prospect of a Mediterranean cruise may well have daunted one who shunned society at the best of times. Moreover her father may have considered that Katharine was too much tied to her mother's bathchair as it was, and that she needed a complete holiday. I suggest these considerations to show that you have possibly painted only one side of the picture. The book nowhere points out that there was unfortunately a wide gap in age between the children and their mother as well as their father. Was it bridged any more successfully? Perhaps her son understood her? Did she understand him? Were mother and daughters on terms of mutual understanding and sympathy? I think not. Do you remember how S.C. took Katharine out from school, sat in a field with her and ate red currants, learned of her misery at the prospect of exams, returned with her, interviewed the headmistress, arranged that she should be exempt, and departed leaving a much happier little daughter. (And one has to bear in mind that he was a Victorian, and did not belong to the 'Darling Daddy' Age.) And how he took her to Newbuildings to show off his pretty child? And went to concerts in Cambridge with Margaret constantly at his side? ('We're rather fond of her', he told Dame Laurentia.) And after Margaret married, wrote in high spirits to tell Dame Laurentia that he was now a grandfather — 'to think that my little Margaret has given birth to the bonniest baby-boy in the Middlesex Hospital!' And when Katharine's longed-for child died, how her father sat by her side talking her out of her grief, and was not satisfied until she had dried her tears and smiled for him? This S.C.C. never appears in your pages. But it is at least as true an S.C.C. as the one who does. Let me go further. Muirhead Bone spoke a profound truth when he told S.C. (*The Best of Friends*, p. 122): 'Artists are always taking as persons, I'm afraid, and only in the vague impersonal way of their art, giving.' Florence K. Kingsford was not a giver in the human way. Her face, even before her marriage, was marked by a deep brooding melancholy. She was an out-and-out artist. Would any one have made her happy? She was not cut out for the role of wife or mother. Her life was bounded by her love of physical beauty. Had she been a spiritual woman, had she shown any sense of religion, her whole household, including her agnostic husband, would have been the better and the happier for it. If the atmosphere of the home was academic, cold, and sterile, then the fault may largely lie with the woman who should have been the heart of the family, and the humanizing and spiritualizing element in it.

p. 187 I have not read Anthony Lytton's account of his grandfather, but I have ploughed through Edith Finch's 'labour of love', and a duller story or one that tasted so strongly of warm flat-irons has never come my way. Wilfrid Scawen Blunt is my pet aversion, and I have always regarded him as S.C.'s evil genius. On the whole, your judgements throughout the Blunt chapters seem to me admirably sound, but I can recall offhand three separate charges at suitable intervals levelled against S.C.'s morality: each time the indictment is drawn from the same dubious source, unsupported by proof. Innuendo and half-hints can be far more poisonous than fact; when enough mud is thrown, some of it is bound to stick. If the proof lies in the fact that Cockerell remained a firm friend of Blunt to the end, then I reply that so did Hilaire Belloc and Wilfrid Meynell, men of unquestioned probity both.

p. 289 I don't agree that Neville Lytton's is a valid criticism of *Friends of a Lifetime* or its companion volume. If a letter is up to the usual standard of greatness of a literary man, then its place is almost certainly in his printed works, not in an envelope bearing a penny — or a threepenny — stamp. That's precisely what's wrong with Freya Stark's letters — they are all drafts of passages for her books. Take away the opening gambit and the concluding signature, and you could stick them into any of her published works. So also on

p. 342 I don't consider that you have made any very damaging criticism. The plain truth is that no publisher would have dreamt of accepting letters from unknown women with the dull names of Sara Anderson, Jane Duncan, or Nell Worthington, however good their letters, whereas they'd jump at letters from a G.B.S., a Siegfried Sassoon, or a Freya Stark. I myself witnessed with what courtesy yet with what firmness Mr Rupert Hart-Davies weeded the plot: only flowers of commercial value were retained.

pp. 333–5 These pages are guaranteed to evoke smiles and unprintable observations from the worldly-wise. The quotations have been taken completely out of their context, of course, and I assume that some at least of them are the words of professional women, artists, scholars and experts in their own right, women unlikely to waste precious time or go out of their way at great personal inconvenience to visit S.C.C. merely for the sake of a trivial bribe. (Incidentally the passage on p. 335 about friend-ship needing constant attention is pure nonsense; true friendship stands in need neither of word nor of gift.) It is easy to dismiss or underestimate the trials of the last ten years of S.C.'s life, and the amazing courage with which he bore them. As Pope has observed, we can all bear our neighbours' misfortunes with the most perfect Christian resignation. S.C. had to piece together the broken fragments of an unusually interesting and varied life, and adapt himself to one of complete inaction, hemmed in by four ugly walls and cut off from all his former activities. His physical state during those last years does not bear thinking about. He rose above it by ignoring it and making others ignore it too, and out of very unpromising raw material he fashioned for himself a thoroughly human life again. It was not done easily overnight. When I first came into contact with him, his defences were down — perhaps through the sheer relief of finding a successor to Dame Laurentia whom he felt he could trust. His early letters make almost unbearably poignant reading. He was an old old man, waterlogged and weary of his body, feeling subhuman and 'like a crushed beetle', longing for the angel of death to enter at his door and annihilate him. In the Rule of St Benedict, there is a chapter entitled, 'Of Old Men and Children' which opens: 'Although human nature itself is drawn to pity towards these times of life, that is, towards old men and children . . .'. You have surely overheard the affectionate tones in which nurses address aged patients. Why? Because the old need two things above all: they need to retain their own self-respect, and they need human affection. And having said that, I can only thank God for the middle-aged women who had compassion on S.C.C. in his pathetic state. They played a game which was obviously a game in which both sides knew the rules, and they played it often at the cost of considerable self-sacrifice. Theirs was true friendship.

Now I come to the important chapter that was never written, the chapter which should have redeemed the book from the serious charge of lack of depth and penetration. For it stands to reason that a man who had the power to win the whole-hearted trust and affection of men such as Morris, Lethaby, Shaw and Alec Guinness, and of women with such keen judgement and fine sensitivity as Katie Webb, Dame Laurentia and Viola Meynell, must have had outstanding interior qualities as well as oodles of charm. He had; but they were buried deep. The tragedy was that heredity, the age in which he was born, the people with whom he consorted, his own natural mental laziness, all these militated against their development, so that the final picture is of a man deluded by false values, devoid of any real philosophy of life beyond the pathetic humanist premise that the criterion of conduct is its effect on our own comfort and happiness in this world, a man who had spent a long life concentrating upon sensation as opposed to intellect, on the acquisition of knowledge as opposed to wisdom. After reading of the Sotheby sale, Siegfried Sassoon's satirical muse moved him to this verse:

> Ah, what avails the Worcester Sauce
> Which paid for Dyson Perrins' Missals?
> Sure, 'twould have been a wiser course
> To profit by St Paul's Epistles.
> The Perrins manuscripts are sold
> And Syd's invested in debentures.
> The gift he might have gained was told
> In different letters – Dame Laurentia's!

Walled-in by worldliness, preoccupied with human interests, activities and people all his life, an extrovert in every way, he had developed from youth a tough resistance to all spiritual influences. His tenuous abstractions, his vague respect for 'all great religions' went hand in hand with a total lack of any sense of mystery; not a single word or action gives the slightest hint of any spiritual experience. He presented the spectacle of a medieval scholar with a flair for spotting 12th century missals, or the MSS of a Jerome, Augustine or Gregory, who never in his life pondered a word the missals or MSS contained. He was like an uncomprehending child enjoying a picture-book. He gave no evidence of even the most elementary understanding of the Christian philosophy and doctrine he so glibly denied – he could not distinguish between baptism and confirmation.

But I and others can assure you that during the long vigils of sleepless nights, there were times when the facile generalizations such as that of Renoir which you quote on p. 226 – 'he found it hard to believe that two hundred and fifty million Hindus had been mistaken for four thousand years' – faded before the stark reality of death and the fearful possibility of the truth of Christian revelation. And then he called on Catholics for comfort and reassurance that he would find pardon on the grounds of 'invincible ignorance', a phrase he clung to as to an anchor of hope. But all this, as I have said, belongs to the chapter that was never written.

After reading *Friends of a Lifetime*, I wrote to tell S.C.C. that beneath the nobility of character of his correspondents, their loftiness of humanitarian motive, desire for social reform, and love of fellow-men, there was a negation and a philosophy of despair which made it in essence a most depressing book. I say precisely the same of *Cockerell*, but that is not necessarily any fault of yours. Your unsparing pen has fulfilled its allotted task; it has depicted for all the world to see, the failure of a man possessed of noble and endearing qualities, who tried to satisfy with the husks of hero-worship the hunger of the human soul for God. Who would not be sad?

F.C. to Father J. J. Coyne
(Sometime Professor at Oscott College,
Birmingham) *Easter 1965*

On Tuesday of Holy Week we suffered a painful shock to learn that our beloved chaplain, Abbot Wulstan Knowles, had been found dead. He was well-named for, in addition to being a perfect priest-monk, he was also a Worcestershire man born and bred. I made his acquaintance years before I entered Stanbrook, when I wrote and asked him as Abbot of Fort Augustus to accept one of my choir boys who lacked education and wished to become a priest. He gladly admitted him and gave him the necessary training to fit him for St Edmund's, Ware. One incident stands out in my memory. My protegé fell ill and opened his eyes one morning to find the abbot sitting at his bedside holding a bowl of fruit. 'Alex', an anxious voice said, 'you need a lot of fresh fruit, and the price of citric fruits in Fort Augustus is prohibitive. Would your mother be able to send some from Liverpool?' The abbot knew perfectly well that she could afford it and would be only too willing to comply. But it was the abbot himself, not the infirmarian or the Prefect of Studies who did the asking.

When he was appointed chaplain here a dozen years ago, he found that the departing monk — one of his own brethren of Fort Augustus — among his discarded possessions, had left behind two cast-off habits. Abbot Wulstan seized upon them,

parcelled them up and despatched his treasure to the nuns of
Talacre Abbey to ask if it were possible to make one decent
garment out of two — he thoughtfully enclosed his measure-
ments. They managed it, and this was the habit he wore all the
years he was here, until he was invited to America three years
ago for the Blessing of Dom Alban Boultwood as Abbot of St
Anselm's, Washington, a monastery founded by Abbot Wulstan
himself. Lady Abbess protested that he could not present himself
in patched clothing green with age: he remonstrated. A new
habit would cost more than he could afford. Finally he compro-
mised: he wrote to Fort Augustus to ask if one of the brethren
would make him a new habit of the cheapest stuff at the cheapest price. The abbot replied that they had consulted their files
and discovered that the last new habit had been made for his
ordination; with great pleasure therefore he would make a gift
of the new one for his trip to the U.S.A.! This spirit of poverty
was typical of the man and in no way implied meanness. All
his life he had managed to utilize what others rejected, without
anyone being aware of it. After his death, his little 'housewife'
with needles threaded and a sock in preparation (all the directions for knitting carefully copied in his own hand) came to our
Cellarer who, to my joy, handed me Abbot Wulstan's penknife
as a keepsake. We shall not see his like again: the halcyon years
during which our two abbots, Wulstan Knowles and Bruno
Fehrenbacher, gave such an example of holiness, humility and
simplicity with a strong admixture of commonsense and fun are
over. Abbot Bruno, now almost blind, has returned to his
beloved Buckfast — it is obvious from the letters we receive
that the community realizes what a treasure they possess in him.
Abbot Wulstan's body was taken up to the Fort for burial
among his own monks. *Requiescat.*

I'm in the throes of writing an article on Julian of Norwich
which has had at least one good result — it has sent me to our
collection of rare books and revived forgotten memories. The
first printed edition of Julian's *Revelations* in 1671 was made
by our chaplain from our Cambrai MS, and the two earliest
MSS recently discovered, one in Westminster Cathedral Library,
the other at Upholland College, Lancashire, are in the hand of
our Dame Barbara Constable. A first edition of Fr Augustine

Baker's *Sancta Sophia*, printed in 1657, presented to us by the President of St Edmund's, Ware from their Douai archives, caused Abbess Laurentia at the time immense enjoyment. On the last leaf of the book its original owner, obviously one of our nuns (for it bears the Cambrai press-mark), has transcribed upside-down a prescription for a purgative medicine. The abbess loved the human touch and wondered whether the nun's father was an English apothecary who recommended the mixture when visiting his pale-faced daughter at Cambrai?

F.C. to Father J. J. Coyne   *22 June 1969*

Your continued colds and arthritis call for remedy, and I have been wondering whether a cure could be effected if you went out to Freshfield, climbed that glorious stretch of sand dunes, and followed the prescription propounded by Abbot Feckenham, last Abbot of Westminster under Queen Mary I. It is contained in a 'booke of sovereign medicines against the most common and known diseases both of men and women . . . collected by Mr Doctor Feckenham and that chiefly for the poor who have not at all times the learned phisitions at hand'. As Abbot Feckenham spent the greater part of his life in prison, this must have been his apostolate: his book of prescriptions comes from our monastery of Cambrai, and the text is in his hand and that of our Dame Barbara Constable. On the spine is written: 'Doriti Hoskins her booke 1630'. She was one of our nine foundresses in 1624 — we don't know how the precious pharmacopoeia fell into her hands. Are you prepared to follow this monastic 17th century recipe? Here it is: I guarantee you will be completely cured in the making of it, no need to apply it:

Take lavender, spike, valerian, rosemary tops, strings of vines, french mallows, plantains, walnut leaves, violets, sage, fine Roman wormwood, woodbine, elder-tops, camomile. Beat all together very small, then add 1 quart of Neatsfoot Oyle and let them stand for 10 or 11 days. Then take 24 swallows alive, cutte of y top fethers both of tales and wings, kill them (they must be but newlie killed), putte them in a Mortar, and stampe them gutts, fethers and all. You may add to this, one ox his gaule and beat it amongst the rest as also 50 black snales. Add halfe a pint of good Rose water and halfe a pound of good yellow wax. Boil all in a stone potte for 8 or 10 hours, then strain it and keep it in well-leaded potts for your use.

Does this treatment of live swallows, those most beautiful creatures whose flight is pure ecstasy, cast light upon the butchering of men and women for conscience' sake at Tyburn and Smithfield during that same century? You refuse to try the prescription?

F.C. to Father J. J. Coyne   *8 January 1971*

You are already well-acquainted with the extern sacristy at Stanbrook, yet curious to know what lies on the other side into which you never penetrated. Odd what a fascination the unseen always exercises over the human mind, isn't it? Very well: I'll take you on a conducted tour of the few square yards which constitute my special domain, since I was appointed sacristan for the coming year at the Advent yearly Change of Offices. Ready?

There are three rooms, the main sacristy very large, airy, and well-stocked with handsome cupboards and drawers all built into the wall, and communicating easily with the extern quarters. Parquet flooring adds to its elegance, but the greatest joy of all is its high glass roof through which one can look up at the skies, look at all the fire-folk sitting in the air, the bright boroughs, the circle-citadels there. How can I resist in such a context closing with Hopkins's final lines:

> This piece-bright paling shuts the spouse
> Christ home, Christ and his mother and all his hallows.

A small tiled room called 'Nazareth' opens off from the sacristy. A sink fitted with cold soft water tap and good drainboards and shelves provides for the washing of vessels and storing of flower tins and utensils. Finally down a long flight of steps, one goes from Jerusalem to Jericho. Jericho is hot, very hot, because there are stacked all the hot water apparatus of heating the church above. The great pipes envelop three dark chambers. I am always reminded of Jonah: 'I went down into the countries underneath the earth, to the peoples of the past. The seaweed was wrapped round my head at the roots of the mountains.' I can imagine in a nightmare feeling those pipes intertwined round my body like the snakes about Laocoön and his sons in the Vatican Museum! Trunks containing the junk of a century or more are stored in Jericho, and it is handy for forcing blossom in the early part of the year after a hard winter. This brings me to Christmas decorations. 'What did the novices do?' Almost nothing. The edict went forth this year that as the church had been cleaned and the stonework was so lovely in its simplicity, arches and windows would be spoilt by greenery. All the novice-ship did was to adorn the entrance arch to the choir with holly and a large Alpha and Omega. The sanctuary decoration was the work of . . . the sacristy. Dread and apprehension at offending artistic sensibilities. Luckily for me, one of our chief artists is my aid and she carried out my suggestions of two rows of candles of various thickness and height painted to reflect the colour of the sanctuary tiles, issuing like flowers from greenery. She worked with her palette on the spot under strong electric light in order to catch the shades and tints. Our handyman constructed the double board on which the candles rested — three were almost as thick as the Paschal candle. She adorned the board with delicate feathery cedar and gilded poppy heads and love-in-the-mist seed pods, and hid the base with laurel branches. The effect was quite entrancing when they were lit during Midnight Mass — a kind of Festival of Light. It was also rather amusing because all unwittingly we had constructed what looked exactly like a little German Positif organ with two rows of organ pipes bursting into points of flame. All it needed was a little St Caecilia to sit at the keyboard and an angel or two to blow bellows in the rear.

The flowers beneath the altar consisted of scarlet carnations and tulips and anemones from the florists, with Christmas roses, viburnum, tiny-leaved golden privet and smilax which everyone admired and thought had been terribly expensive. 'Where DID you get the sprays of greenery in the background?' they asked. 'By the old shed up the chicken-run' was the answer. They had all assumed it was some kind of privet and had never given it a second glance. To all this, add a large black bowl of four pink and three tawny-gold chrysanthemums on a pedestal at the side of the tabernacle, so that the sanctuary glowed with colour on Christmas night and *mirabile dictu* every one seemed to approve. Well, have I managed to tell you what you wanted to know? As far as the rest goes, I sat at the organ for many hours over Christmas and thought what a pity it was that organ and sacristy reach their peak points always at the same time. By the time I got to Compline on Christmas Day I was praying the prayer of the Ox in *Prayers from the Ark*: 'Dear God, give me time./Give me time to eat./Give me time to plod./Give me time to sleep./Give me time to think./And give me time to pray!'

F.C. to Father J. J. Coyne   *15 September 1971*

You never forget, nor do I, your coming over from Oscott during the war, accompanied by a deacon gifted with a fine singing voice, to help Dom Maurus Moorat carry out the heavy liturgical programme — and how wonderful is the memory of your three beautiful renderings, high tenor, baritone and bass, of the Mass and Scripture readings. I suspect you of having left part of your heart in the Stanbrook sanctuary, along with Michael Allmand, your boy-server from Ampleforth, who was to be awarded a posthumous V.C. and never become a monk as he hoped. So you want me to send you an account in your Liverpool fastness of the Centenary celebration of our Church. Shall I then begin at the beginning?

The architects employed to re-design the sanctuary and extern chapel had approached their task with nervous trepidation: to give a typical Pugin church a 1971 face might daunt the bravest. We had been rigidly excluded from the building while work was in progress. There is wisdom in the saying, 'Never show a half-done piece of work to children or fools!' Not to see anything in the making saved a lot of time and discussion — and possibly, tempers as well. Had things worked out as they should (do they ever?) we would have taken possession on 31st August, but by then the church was still ankle-deep in stone dust and didn't look as if it would ever be habitable. The organ had been lying about in pieces also, since that too had been cleaned and given a thorough overhaul and repair. Meanwhile unable to get together in choir to practise and rehearse for the Day, we all felt a bit scratchy. It was not until the evening of the 4th that we trooped into church, eager to see the completed work. And when we did, what quiet satisfaction was to be seen on every face. For it is quite lovely. All the clutter has been cleared away and the soaring arches of sanctuary and choir can be seen in all their beauty of line. As someone remarked, the architect has introduced the desert and we find it spiritually comfortable, we can all live in it. When I entered at Stanbrook on this day, we still had the original Pugin altar, a great erection of alabaster flanked with gradines, every available space filled by angels or brass flower-filled hideous vases. The walls were covered with murals depicting the falling-asleep of our Lady, and two mighty statues in stone, one of St Benedict, the other of St Scholastica, stood sentry on either side of the altar, high up on the walls with sheltering canopy. About 1938, the Centenary of our final settling at Stanbrook, Abbess Laurentia replaced the Pugin structure by a dignified stone *mensa* to bring it into line with the liturgical ideas then prevalent. We have now conformed to the contemporary trend once more. *Tempora mutantur, et nos mutamur in illis*. Ah yes; times change and we with them. Everything now is plain and unadorned: all centres on the altar, an almost square structure facing us but raised five steps above the choir. Behind it a kind of shadow in stone — the tabernacle raised another two steps above the altar so that it is visible above it from a distance. And all is light. The rather poor stained glass window of the Extern Chapel has been replaced by plain glass which lights up the hitherto very dark chapel, and the outline of green trees against it renders the whole effect most pleasing. The fine rose window high up on the East wall of the sanctuary depicting our nine foundresses grouped round our Lady of Consolation now glows with colour and can be seen to great advantage. The furniture of the sanctuary is designed to harmonize with the altar and tabernacle: reddish wood which turns crimson in the gules of coloured light thrown at sunset from the stained glass windows in the West wall of the bell tribune, the chairs and chaises longues — or so they seem —

upholstered in black to match the thin black line separating *mensa* from plinth in altar and tabernacle. The Sacred Heart altar which used to adorn the Extern chapel has disappeared and been replaced by the more than life-size statue of St Benedict who has been given a new crozier and looks every inch the Master of the House, as indeed he is. Two more details: the sanctuary has been re-tiled with tiles in three shades of what? rose? pink? terra-cotta? The varying shadows and lights form part of the charm of the scene – all depends on the position of the sun. The lighting has been completely altered also, and we have bulbs hidden in black and silverish sleeves, some throwing light into the vaulting of the arches, others pointed downwards at the stalls. The effect is quite entrancing and gives an impression of soft candle-glow, and no ugly pendant shades obscure the ribbing of the stone. Finally, the handsome wrought-iron and copper grille separating choir from sanctuary has now found a home in a Birmingham Museum. Nothing stands between nuns and altar, but two thin aluminium grilles shut off sanctuary from Extern chapel — yet only between Offices, for they are opened right back during Mass and the Divine Office, once the Community are in choir. It is interesting to notice how this has affected the acoustics: the singing is now very much fuller in tone because there are no heavy curtains and suchlike to absorb the sound.

And now over to 2.30 p.m. September 6th 1971 for the solemn consecration of the new altar. The procession was most imposing: our Archbishop was chief celebrant and entered in full pontificals, golden mitre and crozier and our finest white cope. He was preceded by the Abbots of Downside, Douai, Belmont, Quarr and Prinknash, four other monk-concelebrants, many other monks from here, there, everywhere; three martial Jesuits, always unmistakable from their carriage; and about five of the pastoral clergy. The rite of consecration was unforgettable, especially when the Bishop traced the five crosses with chrism, placed crosses of wax upon them with grains of incense, set fire to them, knelt and invoked the Holy Spirit. How it made the Dedication of Solomon's temple live: 'When Solomon had ended his prayer, fire came down from heaven and consumed the burnt offering and the sacrifices, and the glory of the Lord filled the temple. When all the children of Israel saw the fire come down and the glory of the Lord upon the temple, they bowed down their faces to the earth on the pavement, and worshipped and gave thanks to the Lord, saying, "For he is good, for his steadfast love endures for ever." ' That is exactly how it felt.

The setting of the scene for Mass was resplendent. Perhaps it can best be set forth in the words of T. S. Eliot's Choruses from *The Rock*:

> Now shall you see the Temple completed:
> After much striving, after many obstacles;
> For the work of creation is never without travail;
> The formed stone, the visible crucifix,
> The dressed altar, the lifting light . . .
> We thank Thee who hast moved us to building, to finding . . .
> And when we have built an altar to the invisible Light, we may
>   set thereon the little lights for which our bodily vision is
>   made . . .
> O Light invisible, we give Thee thanks for Thy great glory!

To my own joy, the consecration crosses round the church were wreathed in purple heather from the Scottish Highlands, as on the day I entered, each cross surmounted by its tall white candle in newly-burnished sconce, while on either side of the altar stood three tall ebony and silver stands with three squat candles. The Archbishop preached a first-rate sermon. He had 'learnt his stuff' admirably, and the history of the house rolled off his tongue without a single error either of date or fact. But what was immensely inspiring was his defence of the contemplative life in the face of modern activism. He, a man always on the road as it were, confirming, ordaining, dedicating churches, serving on committees, with the thousand and one cares of a huge diocese, showed an amazing intuition into our life that of itself spoke of his own life as that of a man of God.

In a Mass sung throughout in English there were two — dare I call them oases? — of Latin. One was Credo III sung *con brio* by the entire assembly antiphonally and *can't* monks carry the roof off with a profession of faith! The other was the dismissal. His Grace gave the final blessing in Latin, whereupon our chaplain, Dom Dominic Allen sang — and sang beautifully — the long *Ite, missa est* of Mass VII, that incomparable melody ascribed to the English St Dunstan, who is said to have heard the angels sing it. As I listened to the Latin pieces (in fact I was at the organ accompanying throughout) it seemed to me that a single line of Plainsong expressed more of the numinous than all the rest put together, and I thought of Wilfred Owen's letter to his sister Mary in 1914 after hearing a Requiem Mass in Boulogne for the first time. He, an anti-Catholic Welshman, was forced to admit: 'The solemn voices of the priests was what I had never heard before. The melancholy of a bass voice mourning, now alone, now in company with other voices or with music, was altogether fine; as fine as the Nightingale (bird or poem). And although the chanting was Latin, yet was it more intelligible to the human soul than could be statements distinctly enunciated in the vernacular.'

After Vespers I noticed many lost in the contemplation of the moving shadows across the new sanctuary in the light of the setting sun — it was 6.30. The dome of the silver tabernacle in its white silk veil was throwing an enormous shadow across the East wall, so that it looked exactly like a tent — the tent of meeting of Exodus: 'And Moses erected the court round the tabernacle and the altar, and set up the screen of the gate of the court. Then the cloud covered the tent of meeting, and the glory of the Lord filled the tabernacle. For throughout all their journeys the cloud of the Lord was upon the tabernacle by day, and fire was in it by night, in the sight of all the house of Israel.' I should just place on record the joy it gave us all when the Mother Superior of the Anglican nuns at Malvern was admitted into our choir with her companion and two nuns from Battenhall, to join our own community during the Pontifical Mass. Shall I end by asking with Browning:

> When earth breaks up and heaven expands,
> How will the change strike you and me
> In the house not made with hands?

F.C. to Joy Finzi   *14 January 1979*

In the chapter of St Benedict's Rule entitled 'On the Tools of Good Works' there is one enticingly forbidding, 'Not to embrace delights'. Rarely, you will admit, does the postbag ever tempt one to lay aside such a tool but, when your letter came, I flung the tool over the enclosure wall, and I leave you to answer for my fault at the Day of Judgement. Thank you very much for the *delights*. I have embraced them again and again. All the more so as I had recently been given Helen Thomas's *Time and Again*, so I already knew her account of Ivor Gurney; and Leonard Clark made us a gift of Ivor Gurney's poems with Edmund Blunden's Introduction, as deep as it is calm, in 1973. After digesting your letter, I happened to open a book from my shelf and found it marked by a postcard from Theresa Whistler to Sir Sydney Cockerell. Cockerell, de la Mare, Theresa, Laurence and Rex Whistler, and back to Cockerell and Siegfried, de la Mare, Blunden and Leonard Clark who first spoke to me of Gerald Finzi. Another quite different link, this time with Helen Thomas, comes of my knowing Mary Thomas, George's widow, to whom Helen was kindness personified. As you may not have met it, may I offer you an exchange of gifts if not of delights, in the little biography of George here enclosed? What a beautiful anamnesis that passage of Edward Thomas's prose is, and how much we need to recall that past today. Edward Thomas, David Jones, Helen Waddell all hammer it home to us, and we take no notice. America and the Money Market drown their voices. That sounds as though I have been re-reading Siegfried's post-war satires.

How fascinating to have Blunden and Himself to a tea of strawberries and cream on the anniversary of Passchendael, and what an experience, an embracing of delights for you! With a composer for husband, you must have been better able than most to meet spirits of such intense sensitivity. S.S. used to leave me limp and recreated all in one, and the delight still lives on when I not merely recall, but relive those visits of his, when words poured out in spate. Such trenchant criticism of contemporary poets — he missed nothing and no one behind that shy self-depreciatory facade.

We all share gifts, and yours will give pleasure to the whole community. Laurence Whistler's work is well-known to our artists of course. One of them has made a special study of glass, and his engravings have often been the object of admiration and comment at recreation. So in every one's name as well as my own may I thank you. Thank you especially for writing to tell me that you enjoyed Poet's Pilgrimage.

F.C. to Father Kenneth Gillespie OFM, Llanidloes

6 July 1975

Father Kenneth, son of St Francis and animal-lover, urges this Black Benedictine to send him a contribution for his favourite journal *The Ark*. Animals are not my strong suit, and all I can think of is that man is a poor, bare, forked animal. Will birds do instead? Not the melodious creatures that sing madrigals, but a simple story of the domestic life — possibly a modern parable — of two young Muscovy ducks and a drake who could not even quack; when pleased they wagged their tail feathers like puppies, hissed when annoyed, and made their home on the Stanbrook pond where their handsome white plumage was much admired. Indeed, they were little more than objects of visual delight for they laid no eggs except during the Spring mating season. One day, the word went forth: 'A duck is sitting.' All roads thenceforth led to the pond. The nun in charge rigged up a *bijou* lying-in ward on the path, and surrounded it with tempting tit-bits of cabbage leaves and bread and cheese. And there, cynosure of all eyes, My Lady Duck sat in state on no fewer than eighteen eggs. She sat — yes, she sat. Her husband, the soul of chivalry, stood at her side day and night. She was clearly his favourite wife. The other was a gadabout. She went her independent way. Rumour had it that she had laid an egg and buried it in Woodpile Meadow, and deposited a second in a disused storehouse. We gave her up. She was obviously a difficult teenager and you could do nothing with her — such a contrast to the virtuous Mrs Faithful stay-at-home. We placed all our hopes in her eighteen eggs. Yet it seemed odd. The period of incubation was long past, but on she sat. At last, the eggs were tested. Addled, every one. Nature from her seat gave signs of woe, that all was lost. For days, a white-billed duck with pale pink eyes sat huddled up on the cinder path mournfully surveying the pond, and refusing all food and comfort. During all this time, Mrs Gadabout was nowhere visible. Occasionally she was seen, so it was reported, on the pond, but none took the slightest notice of her. And then one sunny day I was standing at the northern end of the pond when she caught sight of me, evidently gave the word of maternal command, and up she came proudly leading a flotilla of butter-coloured baby ducklings, seventeen in number, not only swimming but actually running on the water. On the verge splashed newly-hatched smoke-blue moor chicks, six of them, quite prepared to play with the ducklings, while two smart black and white water-wagtails hovered and hopped and generally policed the groups. The delight of the whole scene beggars description — it made one cry aloud in songs of praise to the God who thought them out! Mrs Stay-at-Home showed not the slightest interest in her rival, and her husband supported her in her disdain. I christened them Elcana, Anna and Phenenna from the first Book of Kings. For the drake seemed to be asking his poor love: 'Anna, why weepest thou? Am I not better to thee than ten children?' As for that naughty jade Phenenna: 'Her rival also afflicted her and provoked her' — for she had delivered the goods!

I am afraid this is not a very edifying story for *The Ark*. I've got an even more disedifying story of the day when the 'men's yard' as it is called, the large quadrangle (where all the farm machines are kept and the workshops occupied by our workmen are situated) re-echoed with the voice of one of our oldest workmen saying in his broad Worcestershire voice: 'Ee! so 'e's come back to we, as 'e? 'E's finished makin' eyes at 'er an' billin' an' cooin' an' makin' love to 'er. Tired of it, is 'e? So back 'e's come to we, eh?' He was speaking to Tim, the monastery cat. It was the same carpenter, who asked the Cellarer one day whether every one was well — was any nun ill? Touched by his solicitude, she assured him that all was well with the community, and wondered why he asked: 'Oh, I have a nice bit of elm wood', he replied, 'just about enough for a coffin.'

Oh dear, I've wandered from Noah's ark dreadfully. Who

was it said that Time is a river and its current is strong. So it is, and my time's up. Father Kenneth, I'm quite sure this isn't what you had a right to expect, but after all, what did you expect? Franciscans specialize in all manner of wonderful beasts, birds and flowers; we Benedictines have only an old black crow. But perhaps Shakespeare can even redeem the crow: Light thickens; and the crow makes wing to the rooky wood. And so for the present, we leave you.

Rumer Godden, author,
to the Abbess of Stanbrook   *Friday 21 July 1961*

Dear Madame Abbess,
Leonard Clark has, I think, written to you of me as Rumer Godden, but this week I am far more importantly the mother of Jane Murray-Flutter for whom you and your community have prayed with such steadfast kindness.

Almost immediately, the toxaemia that threatened disappeared; and as you will now have heard, on Wednesday morning she had a little daughter almost six pounds (wonderful for a premature baby), perfectly formed and with auburn hair like hers. I go to her on the 24th and, as we drive through Worcester, wonder if we might come for a few minutes to give thanks, either on Sunday evening or Monday morning. There will be no time for an answer so we shall just call, and if you are busy, or a visit would be an interruption, the portress will tell us and we shall understand. You will understand too how much we thank you.

May I tell you how much we admire the beautiful book you have made for Siegfried Sassoon? I am taking a copy to his dear friend and American publisher, B. W. Huebsch, who has not yet seen it.

Yours gratefully,
Rumer Haynes-Dixon

Rumer Godden to F.C. *25 July 1961*

It was, for us both, a wonderful experience to meet you yesterday, and Lady Abbess — it was most good of her to come in. We had thought you might spare us perhaps twenty minutes and lo! it was almost two hours. I hope we didn't encroach too much. I know very well that your lives are filled sometimes to over-brimming, but we were enjoying ourselves too much to count time, and it was more than enjoyment. You perhaps glimpsed some serious difficulties, not only for us, but for Jane and Anthony.

We saw Jane last night looking so well, sparkling and happy, and she was walking about. Surgery goes so fast nowadays. I wish you could have seen her face when she showed us Elizabeth — a very tiny baby fast asleep in her shawl, both hands clenched, a small round head with dark, not red, hair and an unmistakable cleft in her chin. Jane says she has Paula's blue eyes. One wonders what the future holds for this little morsel: perhaps she will be a Stanbrook girl.

We enclose a token gift to buy a few bricks with thanks from Mark and Elizabeth — and us both.

F.C. to Mrs Haynes-Dixon *28 July 1961*

After that pleasurable morning with you both, I was overcome with confusion. 'Why did I stupidly mention the cloister?' my conscience kept asking. 'Sounded as if we couldn't do our job without receiving reward. Simony, plain simony!' Meanwhile, between your visit and your letter, our Secretary of Publications received no fewer than four letters from America. The writers were all admirers of *China Court*, and they wanted to know how and where to get *The Little Breviary*. The jewel of the bunch concludes: 'This letter is just a stab in the dark. I hope that Stanbrook Abbey is not just a pile of ancient ruins, and that there are really sisters still there who might answer this question.' Query: What precisely would an American consider a pile of ancient ruins? 1350, 1850, or even — 1950? (And our librarian has just received a catalogue of 'Spiritual Books for

Nuns' — an horrific delight. Among them is advertised 'Cheer-Up Booklets I and II. Prescriptions for weary souls. When feeling in the dumps, depressed or discouraged, these little books are ideal, and religious are continually asking for them.' The last sentence is not meant to be funny, I'm sure, but I wish the author could have heard the Stanbrook merriment as it was read aloud.)

But to return to my simoniacal conscience. When I heard of the *China Court* appreciations and received your generous gift for the Cloister, everything suddenly turned right-side up. It seemed eminently fitting since Elizabeth means 'House of God' that her 'China' grandmother should erect part of God's House, wherein the Canonical Hours of praise and thanksgiving should rise daily until Stanbrook becomes in truth an ancient ruin. By then, we shall probably have founded a few monasteries in an all-Christian China to carry on the great tradition. So please accept our warmest thanks for the gift of the Mark-Elizabeth arch of the new Cloister.

And I didn't feel really satisfied about the babe and her mother until your very reassuring report came of them both. *Deo gratias!*

I hope to find time to write to Siegfried Sassoon at the week-end to ask him for an invitation to tea. Of course he'll be delighted, but you must be prepared for nerves. He will talk at a *tremendous* rate and leave sentences unfinished, if I am a true prophet.

I came across this naughty verse of Dame Scholastica's on Retreats and thought it might amuse you, Cenacle devotee that you are. Please give my greetings to Mr Haynes-Dixon and to the little family I know, without having met at Tonfanan. I must apologize for not knowing what initial to use in addressing my envelope. Shall I call you 'Mrs D-for-Darling'?

Misnamed

To attack or defend I will do my endeavour,
To advance or explore, I'm as ready as ever,
But you ask me to make *a Retreat* — well, I never!

The thing may be good; you'll agree all the same,

That some kind maiden-uncle was sadly to blame
For giving it such a detestable name.

Perhaps 'twas a foreigner, wanting in tact,
Didn't know how the dull British mind would react
To a hint of white feather — misjudged us, in fact.

Or was he a weakling, a coward confest,
Who honestly thought to turn tail was the best,
And flee from the devil, the world, and the rest?

Whoever he was, it seems useless to wonder
What sort of delusion he could have been under
To make such a strange psychological blunder–

Though if sermons, and silence, and searching of soul
Will knock the Old Lad out, we'll gladly enrol
For a fighting campaign, to press on to our goal.

If this isn't plain enough, let me repeat —
We're aiming at victory, not defeat,
So why do you ask us to make *a retreat?*

Rumer Godden to F.C.   *22 January 1962*

It was a sad blow not to be able to see you. This letter isn't from
me. Siegfried Sassoon asked me to bring you this photograph of
him unveiling the plaque to Walter de la Mare in St Paul's, and
to give you his anxious sympathy. He was really upset when
we told him you had 'flu, and walked about as if on strings
saying, 'She shouldn't have it! She should *not* have it.' It was
all that I hoped. *Why* I wanted to go so badly I didn't know
then (have always preferred to keep away from writers), but
it was unforgettable — the great house with its fallen-away
shrubberies and terraces overgrown with grass and moss — the
neglected park — the gate that wouldn't open — the bell that
wouldn't ring — and then, he living there, like a very clear
flame that would presently be burnt out, and everywhere we
looked, beauty — not a single incongruous note — as if a line
had been drawn from the little boy to the old man, and however
wound and mazed, never broken.
    He showed me, or rather gave me, *Lenten Illuminations,*

which I do think extraordinarily fine. It made me wonder why you didn't put it in whole into *The Path to Peace*. In fact, there is so much to wonder over and remember. He has asked us to come again.

Rumer Godden to F.C.
22 Aurangzeb Road
New Delhi, India
Ash Wednesday, 12 February 1964

As this letter is written on the first day of Lent I don't know if you will be able to have it, but, selfishly, it has cleansed as it were this Lent from various ungracious and unbecoming habits — not easy as I am alone in this large house, like a solitary pea in a large pod, though there are about twelve servants in attendance. Anyway, it will be waiting for you at Easter if you can't read it now, and it *was* meant to be written in Copenhagen, because I have two to thank you for.

To answer the first — this coming to India is a *rest*, a *holiday*, which is perhaps why I feel a bit lost . . . am not suffered to work but have begun collecting notes. I am not pushed out here by my publishers but by James to have some fun and sun, so please don't be anxious. India, remember, is my natural habitat and Delhi is at the moment so lovely. The 12th of February is the beginning of the Indian spring and the garden, made by my sister, is a sight, all the English flowers muddled with cascades of orange creepers, bougainvillaeas, jessamine, plumbago, morning glory, and fountains playing for refreshment. Such birds too, and it is cool, at night cold enough for blazing log fires — my sister and brother-in-law are away in Calcutta — he is now a real tycoon and the houses are like young hotels — but I go there on Tuesday. Its odd to think it takes longer to go from Rye to London than from Delhi to Calcutta, though that, of course, is by air. A childhood friend of ours is now commander in chief and he is taking us up to Jodphur and out into the desert of the Princes — something I have never seen. And then I am going down to Cochin to see one of the game reserves. I must say the new Indian India is, to me, far more interesting than the old and it is good to see the friendliness

everywhere — both Nancy and Dick (my sister and her husband) love these Indians dearly and are loved. I always hated
the manners of most English here —

This home is New Delhi and one begins to see the magnificence of Lutyens' plan — though they spoiled his approach —
it is truly impressive, and the wide tree-shaded roads are beautiful — soon all the trees will be in blossom, but, of course, it is
Old Delhi that fascinates with its huddle-muddle of teeming
streets, though the refugee squatters on the outskirts of the
town are piteous — as are the animals. What is wonderful is
Mass to which I go at the Apostolic Internuncio's. The chapel
was meant to be his private one but the people came and as he
would not turn them away, it has become public. The Embassies
use it so that one has people of every nation and of every kind,
a humble little Indian woman with her baby on her hip next to
the Italian ambassador. Another glimpse of what it means to
belong to a universal Church! The masses are beautifully said,
chiefly by Indian priests.

Do you remember once talking to me about the Immaculate
Conception and showing me where the authority for the doctrine came in the Bible? I wish you would do the same about
the Assumption. I am the only Catholic in a pool of Protestants
and Indifferents, while my sister thinks all religion nonsense.
I'm still such a novice at answering questions.

To go back in time — Copenhagen was intensely hard work,
which was why I didn't write, but was finished and we had a
wonderful session with the Wilhelm Hansen sisters. They run
a large music publishing firm and are impresarios who will, I
think, back it and, thank God, they were quite carried away
with it. I took my secretary and we worked, hammer and tongs,
but it got done!

I am heartened by all you say of the Villa Fiorita, and you
are quite right, it nettled many of the critics. So many wanted
it to end the other way! I'm sorry Pia seemed a prig — she is
a very typical little Italian girl, and I thought more pathetic
than priggish. They *are* like that, honestly. And I'm sorry the
sanctuary lamp jarred you, but you see it was Fanny thinking,
not you or me, and very, very many Church of England people
have not the faintest idea what the lamp means — yet the high

churches do have them. My sister, my own sister, would think
I was out of my mind if I told her! There isn't the first faint
ray of comprehension. I look at her, so good, so wonderfully
unselfish, the way she supports her husband, and looks after
this procession and multitudes of guests and think of Martha,
that 'one thing needful', and one's whole heart cries out, 'Why?
Why is someone so good and sweet without it?'

You made me laugh about the parlouring — wish I could
have seen you listening to the budgerigar record! And the Tail
Waggers' Tales. Here I'm in the midst of 'horse' (though mustn't
complain as I do love watching polo) but would give much for
a really good *parloir*, half of me so happy here, half so dismayed.
Do hope Doctor Latto has remitted the diet, but Lady Abbess
said you were better, so I hope the endurance has been
rewarded.

For St Martha's Day (but only doggerel I fear)

The House in Bethany

I think often about that house in Bethany:
it would have a flat roof, thick walls, a trellis of morning glory
perhaps, in a courtyard open to sun and the Jerusalem stars.
Dark cool rooms inside; in the kitchen a clay oven and water-jars
(I think of the wedding in Cana when water was changed into wine)
There was an arbour perhaps, where, on His visit, He sat in the
        shade of a vine
looking out over Lazarus's almonds and lemons, the sun-eaten olive
        groves,
while from the road came whip-cracks, footsteps in dust, the pricking
        of donkey hooves
and, from the house, a coin-toss bustle and quiet, Martha and Mary.
Yes, I think often about the house in Bethany:

because it is no legend or old history:
Bethany is my village, your town or street, everywhere.
Martha's brisk plaits, the veil of Mary's hair,
both throw my shadow on the wall of the lighted sitting-room,
antagonists in every woman as every day she makes her home:
and Martha forever has no time to waste—
her tribute is the supper — Mary knows a richer feast.

Yet there is a sigh.
Wistful, eternal:
'If I could be that worth of rubies.'
'Could find that single pearl.'

'If I could talk to Him as Mary can.'
'If I could welcome Him as Martha can
with a fragrance of baking, and spiced and sizzling meat.'
'But Mary brought the ointment to pour out on His feet.'

'I shrill into talk or gossip.
Mary listens; her voice is low
but her words are a blossom that bears.'
'If I had Martha's hand with dough.'

'Jesus! To see this picture
my eyes need Your touch of spittle and clay.'
'Martha's busy spindle
shames my dreaming day.'

'The great names belong to Mary,
Sappho, Beatrice, Teresa, they echo on and on.'
'Martha is more than names,
she is everyone.'

'Mary takes an adventurous road;
a squirrel's wheel taunts my dailiness.'
'How scarred and stained I am
beside Martha's cleanliness.'

'If I had loved as she loved
greatly.' 'If I knew her content.'
'How wisely Martha saved.'
'How magnificently Mary spent.'

But He said He would be
in bread
as well as wine;
and there was something
else He said:
'Let your light
shine' —
homely, votive, midnight
and when the everyday of every
day, January to December,
acquaints
us with our dim flickerings,

remember:
Martha and Mary,
both were saints.

H. F. Rubinstein (lawyer and playwright)
to F.C.   *29 July 1956*

Please forgive an unknown reader of 'The Nun and the Dramatist' for writing to you, but I want to thank you very sincerely
for the joy you have given me. First, in making known the life
and beautiful character of Dame Laurentia, with those two
wonderful speaking portraits. And, again, for telling the literary
world just what it needed to be told about Bernard Shaw. To
explain what that has meant to me (for my own satisfaction!),
I have to send you the enclosed little play,* in which I was
attempting to describe the Shaw who asked for the prayers of
your Abbess, and which, had I known of the correspondence
when I wrote it, might have been better. There is nothing else
in it worthy of your notice.

H.F.R. to F.C.   *12 August 1956*

The reason I haven't written before to thank you for your letter
is that I wanted to say so much more than 'thank you', and
have found it very difficult to know where to begin.
    Well, to begin with Shaw. I've been reading his first novel
Immaturity, written in 1879 when he was 23 — and first published 42 years later. Four years after that (in 1925) he writes
to Dame Laurentia: 'I exhausted rationalism when I got to the
end of my second novel at the age of 24.' The second novel
was *The Irrational Knot*. The main interest of both these early
works is that they contain portraits taken of himself, while he
was a complete nonentity in the world, before his conversion
to any political 'idea', but after the birth in him of what he
later called 'moral passion'. He was already a man in whom

---

* *Bernard Shaw in Heaven*

conscience was working. The central character of *Immaturity*, a youth named Smith, is, in the eyes of the world, an efficient and completely trustworthy prig, detached from all the excitements and ordinary ambitions of life. Most of the other characters are caricatures, but there is an outstanding exception, a Scots girl Harriet, to whom Smith is attracted from the first. They enter into a strange friendship, with admiration and a subtly implied adoration on his side and, on her side, respect and a subtly implied maternal interest. This relationship survives her marriage with another man, and the story concludes with a scene between the two (Harriet and Smith), after she has put her infant son to bed, Smith leaving the house 'to meditate on his immaturity, and to look upon the beauty of the still expanse of white moonlight and black shadow which lay before him'. Haven't I here detected the first 'Hail, Mary' from Shaw's pen? (Was *Candida* the second?) The Shavian joke is that this Scots Madonna, with all her beauty and her virtues, displays a rationalistic contempt for all churches — which, needless to say, is fully shared by Smith. It all seems to make sense only in the light of the explanation furnished on pages 438–440 of *The Cornhill*,* for which I can never cease to thank you.

Well, at least I've begun this letter, but I don't seem to know how to go on. Perhaps I'll write again one day. I think you won't mind.

F.C. to H.F.R.   *26 August 1956*

Your stimulating letter arrived when I was swallowed up in Martha-like activity. On Tuesday we plunge into our yearly ten-day 'Retreat', so I am trying today to take a deep breath and cope with arrears of correspondence.

I feel as if we are both attempting to fit together a jig-saw puzzle and your last move fits most satisfactorily into the pattern. Thank you for a much-enjoyed synopsis of *Immaturity*

---

* 'The Nun and the Dramatist', a chapter from *In a Great Tradition* (John Murray 1956) was published in *The Cornhill* (summer 1956).

and that beautifully-evocative quotation. Your intuition may very well prove right. I wonder whether you have read Paul Claudel's *Le Soulier de Satin*? (English translation *The Satin Slipper* by John O'Connor has been published by Sheed & Ward, I think; but I know it only in French). Both in the play itself and in *Bernard Shaw in Heaven*, Candida reminds me forcibly of a scene in Claudel's play in which the heroine's guardian-angel dangles the soul like an expert angler: '*C'était mon hameçon au fond de tes entrailles*', he tells her. '*Et moi je réglais le fil comme un pêcheur longanime. Le pêcheur amène sa prise du fleuve vers la terre. Mais moi, c'est vers ces eaux que j'habite que metier m'est de ramener ce poisson qui leur appartient*' ['It was my fish-hook that pierced your innermost self', he tells her. 'I played the line as a tireless angler. The fisherman hauls in his catch from the river towards the bank, but my work is to return to the waters in which I myself live the fish who belongs there'].

I do not consider that I have any right to give an opinion as I do not know G.B.S.'s work sufficiently, but in all I have read, I sense the deep compassion underlying the outward mockery, an intense religious spirit in its real most vital meaning, even when he is superficially irreligious. I cannot believe that a man such as he was did not lead a profoundly spiritual life, although its characteristics could be expressed in none of the usual terms of religious jargon. I am afraid I may be talking *ut minus sapiens* — like a little fool. But Shaw's complete lack of realization of the sanctity of the human body, with all its consequent sacramental implications, seems to provide the key to his failure. Does he ever show any love for children? He denied the Incarnation: all the rest follows naturally. It is useless to wish it otherwise, but I think it explains much in his life and thought. Chesterton had much to teach him when they met at that second crossing.

It may amuse, or possibly even please you to know that Lady Abbess and I both wished we might have been present at the midnight matinée of your play. The duty of chanting Matins nightly however rules out all possibility of such jaunts.

H.F.R. to F.C.   *5 October 1956*

Your letter is so graciously friendly that 'I's in me, disposed to
start an argument about this or that were, from the first reading,
defeated by overwhelming majorities; isolated cries of 'I am *not*
introspective!' and 'I *won't* be called a nasty Manichee!' being
drowned in cheers from all parts of the House. ('Isn't he touchy!
Fancy taking the "nasty Manichean" personally. Dear, oh dear,
I suppose I shall have to go into all that now . . .')
    No, dear Sister, it isn't necessary. If any apologies are due, I
owe you a large-sized one for lecturing a Benedictine of Stanbrook on how to control the kingdom of the mind — much as
if a junior art-student were to tell an R.A. how to paint. But
I'm not going to bore you with an apology, and I *am* going to
try and make myself clearer. The point is that I know I have
these touchy 'I's in me ('I's whose self-love is easily offended),
and I find it helpful, when I can, to notice — *constater* — their
manifestations by means of an Observing 'I' that owes allegiance
to Christ. By watching these low-class 'I's as they assert themselves (in my name, as if they were the whole and real me,
confound their cheek!) I am enabled to discover something of
the shape and dimensions of the 'beam in my own eye', which
makes it possible to avoid condemning and disliking my brother
when I notice a mote in his. So long as I can keep this practical
object in view, *and* keep in charity with myself, I think I am
steering clear of introspection, which I take to be an unhealthy
indulgence in self-analysis.
    But — and here is the rub: to try and practise this technique
is one thing; to do it whilst at the same time trying not to get
immersed in the distractions and stress of a busy life in this
world is more difficult. One gets caught up, hypnotized, and
forgets one's aim, forgets the high origin of what is real in
oneself (as the Prince from the East found in the *Hymn of the
Soul*) — which is another way of saying that one loses real
consciousness and simply falls asleep in life. And this happens,
not once or twice, but over and over again every day of one's
life. Of course I agree with everything you write about handing
over the keys to Christ. 'Who shall deliver me from the body
of this death? I thank God through Jesus Christ our Lord.' Who

shall deliver me? — but I alsc find myself agreeing with every word in Romans 7 that precedes the outcry. 'For the good that I would, I do not: but the evil that I would not, that I do.' St Paul knew all about this multitude of 'I's — irritable, impatient, resentful, self-justifying, self-deceiving, boasting, lying — all need to be tamed or changed as surely as the heathen to be converted. All of which I meant to convey in my apology for Brother Bernard.

I'm not going to attempt to tell you yet how much I'm treasuring *In a Great Tradition*: I read such books very slowly. I seem to have new Catholic books all about me at present, written by a cross-section of friendly acquaintances: the Jebbs, G. B. Stern (old friend), Barbara Lucas, Louis de Wohl. Are you pro or anti Graham Greene and Evelyn Waugh? And now you have the 'I's that swank about 'my Catholic friends'. God bless you all.

F.C. to H.F.R.   *18 November 1956*

'If it be not now, it will be to come; if it be not to come, it will be now; if it be not now yet it will come' — that is what my correspondents gradually learn about my letters. Life has been and is so busy. However, having polished off an archbishop, an abbot, and a countess in the last forty-eight hours, I turn with positive relief to a mere man-of-law.

Thank you for your last letter. I have to admit that I laughed at the 'I' who bridled at the terms 'introspective' and 'Manichee'. You know perfectly well that I did not mean it personally. I am in complete agreement with you when you observe that self-love and self-interest benumb the divine element within us. We are all sleep-walkers to a greater or lesser degree — certainly I am. But there are two ways of transformation, purification, enlightening, whatever you like to call it. I like Henry Suso's simile of the washerwoman taking stains out of linen. One may either scrub and scour with caustics, or simply put the thing to bleach in the sun. I prefer the latter. If one lives with our Lord (*O sacrum convivium* we say after Holy Communion. It is badly translated as 'O sacred banquet': it should be rendered literally as 'most holy living-together'), one becomes not less but more conscious of one's failure and betrayal. But somehow it ceases to matter. We are earth, and what more can you expect? Earth yields its fruits: nettles, briars, weeds and suchlike. Julian of Norwich says 'He is the only Doer', and he is quite capable of saving and sanctifying you and me. Why worry? He will do the cleansing and the changing and the taming in ten thousand hidden but sure ways. We often spoil the work by trying to do it ourselves. We ought to become humble, simple and joyful — even about our sins! I don't think you *really* do, but you sound as if you look upon the duties of your professional and social life as though they had no connection with the life of faith and the service of God. The psalmist would reply: *Illic iter, quo ostendam illi salutare meum* — It is by that very road that I shall show him my salvation. So many people waste time and opportunity hankering after a spiritual life that can never be theirs: they take it for granted that God has made a mistake in putting them where he has.

May I disabuse you? I am not in the smallest degree literary or cultured or familiar with any of the people you mention. I know them by name of course, all except Barbara Lucas. If she is Christian Lucas's sister, then she is Alice Meynell's grand-daughter, but beyond that I cannot go. Graham Greene? Evelyn Waugh? I have been immured since 1933, and a monastery is not a literary club. Waugh was a rising star of the late twenties, but I was busy studying music, and had neither time nor money to devote to books. I have read a good deal *about* Graham Greene, but someone who wished to give me one of his novels last Christmas was prevented from so doing by — Sir Sydney Cockerell who thought it 'against the rules'. Evidently Dame Laurentia's training was not in vain. Evelyn Waugh's son, Auberon, is at Downside, and has evidently inherited his father's gift of words. In the summer number of the School magazine, he has published two extremely interesting prose experiments. I should imagine the world will hear more of him one day.

Advent is near, and with Advent, silence; we do not write letters during that time. I wonder whether it is necessary to wish *you* what Dame Laurentia wished Sydney Cockerell — 'the full and perfect faith in him without whom we should never have known the graces and joys of Christmas:

Gift better than himself God doth not know,
Gift better than his God no man can see.'

You can guess the question I have not fully formulated.

H.F.R. to F.C.   *3 May 1959*

It was a great joy to receive your letter and to know that you
approved the play, *The Prison and the Vineyard*. Also I enjoyed
the delightful libretto of *Ophelia, or The Beefeater's Daughter*,
only wishing I could have been present at the performance. . . .
Yesterday I was taken to Brighton to attend a reading of *The
Prison* by a group of fellow whatever-we-are, including a marvellous King James, whose broad Scots was irresistible. I read
Shakespeare very badly. The reading was followed by a discussion, which produced some interesting thoughts as to the
psychological meaning of 'digging and dunging', in relation to
the fig tree of the parable. I wished I had been able to follow
up the interesting reference in your letter to a discourse of St
Gregory, on the nature of dung. Ivor Brown, the dramatic critic,
with whom I was at school, wrote: 'I really can't excite myself
about that fig-tree . . . four verses of agricultural advice with
the implication that investors should not cut their losses without
giving the investment another chance — all right, but nothing
very impressive or original.'

F.C. to H.F.R.   *13 June 1959*

If you can come over from Stratford in July, it will be a joy to
see you. Shall we regard it as a date? (When in hospital in
London in 1947, I was amused to overhear the very Irish voice
of a night-nurse protesting to the nurse going off duty: 'Dame?
Dame? I can't possibly call her Dame. That's what the American
boys say: "I've got a date with a dame!" ')
. . . I have been on the hunt of the muck-and-mystery in St
Luke (Londoner that you are, I wonder whether you have ever
read anything by Lady Eve Balfour about her compost research?

In the years I spent growing vegetables, I was an ardent disciple of the muck-and-mystery school, and a fierce opponent of all chemical fertilizers.) I knew I had read the passage from St Gregory in my Noviceship days — but where? At last I traced it — it forms the 31st of his Forty Homilies on the Gospels. I know of no English translation.

Monday. Have given you on second thoughts *such* a rough translation of a few lines of the homily. It is probably not at all to your liking, but is a typical bit of patristic exegesis. The Fathers like to call a spade a spade, and dung, dung. Do not trouble to answer. Hope the bairns are bonny.

Sancti Gregorii Magni Romani Pontificis XL Homiliarum in Evangelio

Now let us listen to what the dresser of the vineyard has to say: Lord, let it alone this year also until I dig it about. What does digging the fig-tree signify but reproaching barren souls? For a trench is dug deep in earth. And the sharp rebuke which reveals self to the soul humiliates it. As often therefore as we correct a man for his sin, we dig a trench. And when the trench is dug? 'I will give it', he says, 'a load of dung.' What does the load of dung denote if not the recollection of past sins, for sins are the body's dung. 'The beasts have rotted in their dung', says the prophet Joel. These represent carnal-minded men spending their days amid the stench of dissolute living. But if the grace of compunction follows upon the remembrance of past sins, fresh life so to speak springs out of the dung. Then, after the soul has roused itself through penance to contrition, and reformed by the grace of good works, the root of a man's heart at contact with dung returns to the fruitfulness of an upright life. He bewails his past misdeeds, finds no pleasure in the kind of man he once was, and directs his accusation against himself, so awaking his soul to strive after higher things — the dung has restored the tree to life and fruitfulness.

et cetera!

F.C. to H.F.R.   *31 October 1961*

I have never subjected you to the indignity of a typed letter from my monastic cell — where such gadgets should be debarred — until this moment. But we are just out of Retreat, and

All Saints is a long and heavy Office leaving little time for such frivolities as letter writing, so I ask you to accept and if necessary forgive the use of a machine to speed things up and save energy. (And anyway I am recovering from a super-bilious attack. In the middle of the Retreat, I beat a hasty one not allowed for on the time-table. As Mr C. J. Yellowplush would have put it, 'A feelin', in the first place singlar, in the next place painful, and at last compleatly overpowering had come upon me, until I found myself in a sityouation which Dellixy for Bids me to describe . . .')

What I'm really trying to do is to thank you for *This House had Windows*. Reading it has been in itself an experience. The book was *really* my Retreat. I derived far more profit from it than from the spiritual conferences given by the Ampleforth monk who conducted the Retreat. Let me tell you a story. On October 25th I rose from bed rather troubled about something. 'Really!' I said to myself, 'there are times when life seems most intractable and perverse. I feel I simply can't cope. However, it's no use crying about it. Tears won't mend matters.' But to tell the bare truth there *were* tears. Outside the wind was terrific, and as I sat in the refectory during breakfast, I watched the trees, black against the lowering clouds that heralded a storm. The thousands of leaves on a great elm were every one a-quiver, with each gust, elms, beeches and firs swayed and dipped with such wonderful grace. 'If only one could bend like that to God's will and the wind of the Holy Spirit', I thought. 'It's resisting that causes all the stress and strain.' As we went to Mass Dame Scholastica could not resist whispering to me: 'Agincourt Day. Henry V attributed his victory to St John of Beverley whose feast it is.' But I was feeling anything but valiant. When I finally reached my cell, I felt too tired for specifically 'spiritual' reading, so I took up the book you had sent me. I had reached Chapter six. And there I found myself as it were gathered up and wrapped into a nice neat parcel: 'Which would you rather do, cry or not cry? Bend to the wind and innerly be whole, or fierce be broken?' Do you realize, it WAS the Holy Spirit speaking? I cannot tell you what I felt as I read that whole chapter in the mood of mine. I came away with an overpowering impression of what we mean by the Communion of Saints. I took David Blackhall and put him into the chalice at Mass to unite his sacrifice and life and merits with our Lord's and with my own (if I've got any!) and with all Christian folk, and I blessed and thanked him for having lifted me out of the Slough of Despond at his own expense. But isn't that precisely why he was made to suffer? When one meets men such as he (and its extraordinary how one feels one HAS met him), the age-old riddle, 'Why does God allow suffering?' is at once solved. Why, to make sons of God out of mere sons of men.

There were times when the reading became too poignant and I simply had to put the book down. And yet it is so gloriously humorous as well. How right you were to liken it to George Thomas's life. Both bear the mark of authenticity. One simply says, 'The finger of God is here'. Do you know that they sometimes use the same terms? Time and time again, I could have supplied absolutely parallel passages. They both regard *understanding* as the touchstone of true knowledge. His contemplative experience in the churchyard when he was thirteen was so like G.T.'s when he was in St Mary's Hospital, Paddington. (By the way, I assume that D.S.B.'s hospital unnamed was St Mary's Moorfields? A brother-in-law of mine was blinded in one eye and for a time it seemed as if he would lose the sight of the other during the war, when he threw himself across my sister to protect her from a falling beam. Their house received a direct hit. He spent many weary months in that hospital.)

But we can discuss all this when I see you. I felt I had to send this little word of thanks meanwhile. Shall I confess that there was one tiny sentence that perhaps jarred? Why on earth should Mr B. have felt 'uncomfortable' at being sent a nun's love? Has the greatest thing in heaven and earth become so debased in meaning in these our days? Of old, the pagans cried out in wonderment: 'See how these Christians love one another!' And the early church could think of no nobler term to describe the Holy Eucharist than *agape*, the love-feast — a term which is happily returning to use in present-day theology. Our late Abbess, Dame Laurentia, was once asked whether a nun could 'love' another safely. She sent from her sick bed the following reply: '*Dominus autem dirigat corda nostra in caritate Dei et patientia Christi* ['May the Lord guide our hearts in the way of God's love and Christ's patient endurance']. We have only one love to give, and with it we love God and men. I mean we don't give bits of our heart but we love all with the love we give to God. That keeps it safe and enables us to include all that he loves. What we have to avoid is loving our love of God and man, for that is loving our own pleasure. Our Holy Father, St Benedict, wants us to run to God with dilated hearts — wide enough to embrace the world. As if we love we don't criticize harshly.'

F.C. to H.F.R. *12 September 1962*

A typed letter calls for explanation and apology. For the past three weeks I have had a poisoned finger. Wasn't there a king of Israel whose wickedness oozed out of his body? — I feel he'd have been companionable of late. Lady Abbess's feast will mean a long recreation, and a visit afterwards to view the display of gifts: every one is hard at it to complete vestments, bookbinding, printing, illumination, and so forth, and I shall be necessary to the music. I can free myself on any other day that week, and shall expect you to lunch *always*, so shall not repeat the invitation.

Siegfried Sassoon was here for six days, and has sent a 'poem' by way of thanks. Entitled 'Hallow End' he asks:

> Why call a village Callow End
> That's able to mature and mend
> The soul of one impulsive ass
> Befriended by Felicitas? (etc)

He lent me a book, 'For Mamsy from Siegfried' containing original poetry and prose written by himself in green and silver between the age of ten and eleven for his Mother's birthday, copiously illustrated by the author. One page, badly smudged, bears witness for ever to the nudge his brother Michael gave the leg of the table, for which he was repaid by a badly bleeding nose. But it is the prose that is so remarkable, with a fine irony and subtle humour that is characteristic of S.S. to this day.

F.C. to H.F.R.   *15 November 1966*

'Gratitude is a fruit of great cultivation; you do not find it among gross people.' Thus spake the Great Cham. You exemplify it, for what have we done to evoke gratitude? Your flowers before our Lady of Consolation look as lovely as ever, they are lasting wonderfully well. But your news of Victor Gollancz's illness was sad. I hung up a notice at once to ask the community to support both him and Lady Gollancz with their prayers. If you have the chance, please tell him that we are holding him in our capacious cowl-sleeves before the Lord. To all the wonderful prayers in his Anthology, he can now add the touching one of St Peter Canisius, that doughty warrior of the Counter-Reformation:

> I am not eager, bold,
> Or strong — all that is past.
> I am ready *not* to do,
> At last, at last!

A Tibetan Buddhist recently talked informally with small groups in the parlour. This climate of communication, knowing one another better, learning from one another and so deepening one's own insights is a good thing. He spoke of the Buddhist *ascesis*: the mental concentration on one point, the harmonizing of all physical and mental activity (walk, stance and so on), the drawing in and drawing together of the whole personality. And then the reverse process, the emptying, the losing of oneself in the greater Whole: 'not an empty void, not a static peace, but a living infinity, a living peace', he said. I went to choir and sang: *Fons vivus, ignis, caritas* — living water, living fire, living love, living bread, peace that surpasses understanding. Obviously both sides were thinking in terms of God's Holy Spirit, whatever the label.

I wonder whether you know Benjamin Britten's *Curlew River*, a marriage of Japanese Nō and Gregorian chant, *most* beautiful? I should like to write to Benjamin Britten for several reasons: first, to tell him how magically wonderful it is. Then I'd like to offer him a gift of our English Benedictine *Hymnale*, so that he should not be misled into selecting the text of the Roman Breviary when he should have used the monastic and older version, nor a French melody when a superior English variant was at hand! The setting of *Curlew River* as you probably know, is East Anglia; the *dramatis personae* are, among others, an abbot and his monks. But oh! the photograph! Such a travesty of history, to say the least. How many can distinguish between monk, friar, and clerk regular? The 'monks' of *Curlew River* wear a Franciscan friar's frock with a Dominican cappa. Franciscans would be ruled by a Guardian, Dominicans by a Prior, yet these singular brown and cream wildbeestes have an abbot clad in white. I give it up. Even Osbert Lancaster draws an abbot wearing a cord round his middle, and actually portrays a Dominican — nice premature baby he must have been — as present at the Siege of Acre.

I send a photograph of our statue of St Joseph carved in cedar wood. He is holding the Child Jesus by the hand and carrying a Jewish loaf of bread. The Child has a bunch of grapes. Shall I eat that Paschal meal with you in Paradise?

F.C. to H.F.R.   *4 November 1974*

It is typescript or nothing. Your plays are safely in my keeping and I hope to recreate myself with them during the Retreat, which opens half an hour hence. Fancy you, a lawyer, retaining such a belief in human honesty as to expect to recover your brief case from a Lost Property Office. The amazing thing is that your belief was justified! But if mine was the most valuable content, no wonder the case was returned to the LPO. I've spent a simply horrific fortnight. *In this House of Brede* is being filmed, and poor Rumer was reduced to tatters by the film-script writer from California, who was here for two days. After attending the recording from 9.30 a.m. to 5.40 p.m. (having coped with the Director, the Chief Producer, the Mistress of the Wardrobe, and four technicians), I had to climb on to the organ stool anew at 6 p.m. and play grand First Vespers of All Saints. What I really wanted to do was to summon Charon and order him to ferry me across the Styx, and lay me down in the nethermost hell of the City of Dis. However, everything in this world comes to an end. I suppose you'll one day sit back with an apple and some cheese biscuits and soup, and transport yourself to Stanbrook while you view the film. By the way, I'd love to see G. K. Chesterton's article in *The Illustrated London*: if you can send it along — perhaps when I come out of Retreat?

F.C. to H.F.R.   *24 November 1974*

This letter should have been written yesterday, when we were observing the martyrdom of St Clement of Rome, Pope. I have spent the last two hours in your company amid the assembly of all the creatures of your splendid imagination — Clemens, Domitilla, Linus, Elissa, Josephus, Berenice, Seneca and the rest. Such a fascinating tapestry. Am I correct in deciding that at this point in your own personal history, all this writing is largely autobiographical? It is in a very real sense a history of H.F.R.'s mind, or perhaps I should go further and say 'of H.F.R.'s soul'? I have read and re-read your plays during the last fortnight, and they have driven me to *Rome on Fire* and *Hated Servants*. Yes, I've had a good time, thank you. I have even made Seneca's acquaintance. The trouble about you is that you are so confoundedly erudite; you presuppose learning that this reader at least just hasn't got.

I think the plays need reading together exactly as I have done — they form a logical and admirable sequence. I found the situations dramatic, and the dialogue full of verve and significance. Perhaps as a square 'R.C.' I boggled at an 'obscure Linus holding a key position in the Church throughout the most critical and bloodiest ordeal in its whole history' portrayed against a background of domestic bliss, but you *do* suggest that the bliss is to be shattered, or rather sacrificed. And the situation is historically at least not impossible.

But of greater interest to me is the Jewish predicament of strong attraction to Christ versus loyalty to Jewish tradition. Or you would possibly argue that Saul of Tarsus invented Christianity; whereas I should reply that the Jews knew Christ only according to the flesh (hence the prominence of circumcision in their thinking), while Paul knew only the risen Christ (hence the prominence of the Holy Spirit and baptism in his thinking). But Christ remains yesterday, today, the same for ever.

I am returning the G.K.C. page having read it and deeply pondered it, puzzled as to why it has offended you. To accuse it of anti-Semitism is to read into it what isn't there. But oddly enough, all G.K.C.'s charges are supported by the Sassoon dynasty. They married into the Rothschilds, didn't they, and controlled the banks of almost the whole world; yet in a single generation they had got into Parliament in England, married into houses of the ancient nobility, and owned *The Observer* and *The Sunday Times*. Q.E.D. Chesterton isn't tilting at all at refugees or immigrants, but at power finance, graft, and politics. Surely he is right to do so? His exaggerations are obviously meant in jest.

H.F.R. to F.C.   *14–16 February 1975*

Your letter happened to arrive just after commencing on the 5th draft of my new little play. I found I had dried up. This has happened before and there is nothing one can do about it, except wait patiently. But your letter has helped. . . . My brother Stanley, after much suffering and affliction bravely borne, was mercifully released on Friday night. Old age ('the out-patients' department of Purgatory' — Lord Hugh Cecil) has one great advantage. It brings one nearer to God. If Teilhard had discovered Shakespeare, he'd have found the basis of his optimism paralleled in King Lear: therein is the basis of my optimism anyway.

F.C. to H.F.R.   *17 February 1975*

Five minutes after reading your letter, I heard this read in choir, from the *Dogmatic Constitution on the Church*, of Vatican II:

The Church was prepared for in a remarkable way throughout the history of the people of Israel, and by means of the Old Covenant. At the end of time, all just men from 'Abel the just one, to the last of the elect', will be gathered together with the Father in the universal Church. In the first place, the people to whom the covenants and the promises were given, and from whom Christ was born according to the flesh. On account of their fathers, this people remains most dear to God, for God does not repent of the gifts he makes, nor of the calls he issues.

On the strength of that, I am putting your brother's name on the community's list for the public *Commemoratio Defunctorum* at Mass, to pray that he may be admitted to the place of 'refreshment, light and peace' promised to the children of Abraham whom *we* call *Pater fidei nostrae* — our father in the faith. So tomorrow morning our two chaplains will pray aloud for Dom Joseph Woods, Dame Hildegard Mortimer, and Stanley Rubinstein, all three members of holy Church. After all, I have as good a chance of being proved right as you. *Requiescat.* You know Helen Waddell's translation of Alcuin's

> Come, make an end of singing and of grieving,
> But not an end of love,
> I wrote this song, beloved, bitter weeping,
> And yet I know 'twill prove
>   That by God's grace,
> We two shall see each other face to face,
> And stand together with a heart at rest.

F.C. to H.F.R.
(Helen Waddell's literary executor)   *3 December 1973*

That is honour indeed, and I thank you for your trust with all my heart. But you will be the first to appreciate that I cannot commit myself to anything, until I have been able to examine Helen's papers. She 'rarely assembled her papers . . . never numbered them, most of the originals are handwritten, books, poems, lectures and miscellaneous writings'. These phrases, culled from Monica Blackett's *The Mark of the Maker* are a bit daunting.

Here are some of the pros and cons:
PRO:
1. An immense veneration amounting to love of H.W. She has

always been deeply appreciated in our house, and for years we have regarded her almost as one would a member of the community.

2. We possess what few libraries in the country possess: the complete Latin works of John of Salisbury. Whew! One whole tome, double-columned, microscopic type of something like 1,400 pages, and that doesn't include his life of Thomas Becket.

3. The nun most closely acquainted with Helen's poetry threw out her arms when I approached the subject with a despairing gesture: 'I can't tell you what Helen's work does to me. Her medieval lyrics have become part of the patrimony of English literature.' That's exactly how I feel about Helen's output as a whole, but if you and Miss Martin will entrust her papers to us, we should love to see whether we could consider the task. . .

F.C. to Dr and Mrs J. White   20 *September* 1974

Among your many gifts, you once sent me Canon Philip Martin's *Mastery and Mercy*, that splendid study of G. M. Hopkins's *The Wreck of the Deutschland* and T. S. Eliot's *Ash Wednesday*. I think it had just been issued by the Oxford University Press, you were captivated by it, and had to share your enthusiasm. You were right. Over the years it has provided me with never-failing inspiration and spiritual strength. Under the title *Earnest-Pennies*, the Stanbrook Printing Press later issued Canon Martin's anthology of Eucharistic Prayers drawn largely from 17th century Anglican sources, in an ordinary and special edition. In that way, the author came into personal contact with us. When he consented to devote a whole afternoon to giving us a kind of spiritual retreat — he called it 'a day of recollection through poetry' — based on the poems of Hopkins and Eliot, I leave you to imagine my excitement and eager anticipation. Lady Abbess decided to enlarge the audience and make the occasion a fully-Christian meeting-point so, in addition to our own sixty-five-strong community, some fifty guests filled the sanctuary and Extern chapel, among them an abbot and several monks, clergy of all kinds, notably Catholic, Anglican and Methodist, a group of our Anglican sisters from Malvern — altogether a mixed and most responsive audience. Let me try to give you some account of a really memorable day. Housman opined that religious poetry is likely to be most justly appreciated by the undevout, and that even when poetry has a meaning (he generously concedes that it usually has), it may be inadvisable to draw it out since perfect understanding will sometimes almost extinguish pleasure. To judge by Tuesday afternoon's experience, Housman's observation is out of key and wrong from the start.

Canon Martin had deliberately made choice of the date — 17th September, feast of the Stigmata of St Francis of Assisi, for he had selected stanzas 21–24 of *The Wreck*, with its cry of 'Joy fall to thee, father Francis, Drawn to the Life that died; With the gnarls of the nails in thee, niche of the lance, his Lovescape crucified . . .' This fact heightened the emotional appeal, and over against it, acting in some ways as a foil, he dealt with Eliot's *A Song for Simeon*. Canon Martin argues, and surely truly, that both poems were written from within the Church, and therefore the great Christian truths which they necessarily contain deserve as serious a consideration as their literary form. Moreover he feels — and again, surely rightly — that Christian truths have been communicated far too long and too often in rational terms and purely intellectual concepts, so that men are too rarely MOVED by their beliefs. Poetry may lead to a much deeper apprehension of truth because the imagination (in the Coleridgean sense of that word) and affections are brought into play as well as the mind, and so God's truth is grasped at a more profound level. At the end of the afternoon, he had triumphantly vindicated this thesis of his. We began at 3 p.m., broke off at 4.15 for tea, resumed at 4.45 for an hour, saw the guests for a few minutes in the parlour at 5.45 and concluded the memorable service with Vespers.

Possibly from the outset, one was inevitably reminded of J. H. Newman, for Canon Martin went from Newcastle to be Vicar of St Mary the Virgin at Oxford, before accepting the chancellorship of Wells. As he stood in the sanctuary, his whole stance, appearance, personality recalled the fact that he had stood in the pulpit which had held the preacher who once spellbound Oxford. Of medium height and slender build, in his simple cassock bound by a plain buckled girdle, his slightly self-depreciatory air, his intellectual and highly sensitive features (and later in the parlour his delicious sense of humour), Canon Martin seemed a not-unworthy successor — and higher praise than that, it is impossible to give. He read the difficult poetry with an ease and naturalness that bespoke consummate artistry — not for nothing has he studied Hopkins and Eliot for a lifetime. Not a syllable was missed throughout the whole afternoon, as he dealt with the occasion of each poem, its subject-matter, its imagery, its theological truths; he punctuated his talk with spells of complete silence for personal meditation, each time concluded by a prayer, beautifully wrought and yet completely from the heart. Common to both poems was the theme of death as potential sacrifice, and the Christian challenge as 'crisis' or judgement — our Lord's demand that his followers should see that it is only from 'the dense and driven Passion' that redeeming love can be released, and reproduce it in their own lives.

It was obvious that Canon Martin had several leading ideas, and these were powerfully illustrated time and time again. In every trial, every desolation, the Christian finds the material of the road that leads to God, because God is in every happening, every contingency, and man is never out of his hand. So to the five Franciscan nuns facing death on the night of December 7th, 1875, the 'Storm flakes were scroll-leaved flowers, lily showers — sweet heaven was astrew in them.' Christianity, he kept repeating, is meant to turn the world's values upside down. To a non-Christian there is something ludicrous perhaps in the Christian's constant meditation on the juxtaposition of life and death, life out of death, — 'drawn to the Life that died'. Isn't death the very negation of life? No; the Christian is drawn, not to a memory, but to 'him that liveth and was dead' and 'is alive for evermore'. Every sacrifice is a kind of death that releases a redemptive power that sanctifies the world. So it was that the tall nun on board the *Deutschland*, helpless amid the swirl of wild waters, recognized the presence of God and cried out with joy: 'O Christ, Christ, come quickly'. At this point, before quoting the last line of the 24th stanza, the speaker admitted that he had made it the meditation of many years and never plumbed its depths:

The Cross to her she calls Christ to her, christens her wild-worst Best.

As Canon Martin has written: 'The crucifix, rather than the cross, is the Christian symbol; what gives strength and fosters devotion is not an empty nameless cross, an emblem of stark torture, but the fact that the Son of God died upon a cross. The christening of suffering and desolation brings joy to God and also to those who are enabled to do it.' It is when we accept positively the world's worst that we find Christ nearest to us and discern the invincible mastery of God.

Happily there was a break of half an hour between Parts I and II when we passed to a consideration of Eliot's *A Song for Simeon*: perhaps inevitably I found myself thinking in terms of a transition from one of Bach's great Preludes and Fugues *organo pleno* to the Choral Prelude of the *Nunc Dimittis* — from thundering diapasons and trumpets to viols and flutes, from difficult language and construction to a concentrated simplicity laden with reference and allusion. But again we found ourselves contemplating death: 'My life is light, waiting for the death wind, Like a feather on the back of my hand.' It was Canon Martin's task to give us the clues that unlocked the rich contents of the poem, and to do this he went backwards and forwards, now to the Old Testament, to Isaiah and the prophets, now to the New,

> Before the stations of the mountain of desolation,
> Before the certain hour of maternal sorrow! . . .

now to the context of the Agnus Dei of the Mass: 'Grant us peace.' But here I voice a personal reaction. Bach's *Nunc dimittis* is one of the most intimate and personal things he ever wrote, and there are certain passages which always cause a constriction in my throat as I play them — the controlled joy of the tenor line that wells up and spills over, so that I always feel convinced that when holy Simeon finally gave back the Child into his mother's arms, his heart simply broke with joy and he went forth 'to join his fathers' as the Scriptures put it so often. But in Eliot's

Grant Israel's consolation
To one who has eighty years and no tomorrow . . .
. . . I am tired with my own life and the lives of those after me,
I am dying in my own death and the deaths of those after me.
Let thy servant depart,
Having seen thy salvation.

I found Simeon's experience incomplete — possibly because at the time of the poem's composition, Eliot had not yet found that joy expressed so powerfully by Bach. It only came later. However I must come to an end, and can only place on record here and now our immense gratitude to Canon Martin for opening wide windows on to the horizon of God's life and love and beauty; fresh air from the Sea Pacific, as Catherine of Siena calls the Trinity, blew lots of cobwebs away and left us toned up realizing the blessedness of being a Christian.

F.C. to Dr and Mrs J. White   *6 September 1979*

Today as you, May, will remember (even though Jack may forget), marks the anniversary of my entrance into Stanbrook on a journey that was more of a fare forward than a farewell. Footfalls echo in the memory, don't they, as we approach the terminus? I have just come in from the garden where I have been sitting happily in a little sacred space, completely concealed, in the heart of a weeping willow tree down near the pond, 'annihilating all that's made/To a green thought in a green shade': Curtains of shimmering silver-green leaves drifting in soft billowing waves under brilliant sunlight, and opening to reveal clumps of bamboo along the edge of the pond, and moorhen chicks, tiny balls of smoke-blue, disporting themselves on its surface. Yet such is the contrariness of the human mind that the leafy screen lured my thoughts away from English sights and sounds to a screen of brightly-coloured paper ribbons forming a doorway and barrier against the tropical heat and glare and noise of the Nigerian village of Abakpa, where the Little Sisters of the Poor cared for destitute old people. In mindsight I passed along the crowded market-place with its streams of enormous lorries lurching dangerously under their human cargo of traders from the North and labelled 'Gents Only', past the uninviting shack bidding 'Welcome to Liberty Hotel. Home of Comfort and Happiness', threaded a path through children, vendors and cocks, deafened by the blare of horns and pop music pouring from juke boxes, and turned off into a quiet white road leading to the paper streamers of a doorway. Part them, and you find yourself in a silent oasis of prayer — the Convent chapel, always peopled by a few old men and women, their lips moving in silent supplication, and ready to greet the visitor with exquisite courtesy. Probably all this was simply a 'distraction' during my own prayer today — wasn't it an Indian sage who likened the human mind at prayer to a tree filled with chattering apes? So I shall invoke a blessing on the heads of my dear 'Little Sisters' to whom I owe much and pass on to whatever else there is to tell.

We spent such a memorable afternoon of pure pleasure on 30 August when Joy Finzi, wife of Gerald the famous song-writer and musician (she was a schoolfellow of Rumer Godden incidentally), brought over Myfanwy Ann Thomas, younger daughter of Edward and Helen Thomas, to acquaint us all with recollections of her famous father and mother. She told their story and read passages of poetry and prose simply exquis-itely — oh, such a rare delight. One could see in her still the small child to whom her father so tenderly bequeathed 'Steep and her own world/And her spectacled self with hair uncurled.' That self is so lovely now and so like her noble mother (I fear I have punned). She was driven here by Joy Finzi (I find it impossible to call such vibrant personalities Miss or Mrs) who added to the feast of good things by her recollections of her husband Gerald's schooldays and youth. She made us a gift of two recordings of his music — his settings of Wordsworth's *Ode on the Intimations of Immortality*, and Thomas Traherne's *Dies Natalis*. Like Edward Thomas, Gerald Finzi is being accorded posthumous recognition, and I find a strange affinity between the two: their feeling for Nature and sensitive spiritual response to beauty, but above all the way they both point to a world of mystery and desire that lies just beyond the borders of sight. A young nun stopped me to thank me for the immense enjoyment of the afternoon. She confessed the reading had moved her to tears, and added: 'Helen and Edward had such a sense of the holiness of everything that is — they found it in such unexpected places — Edward in the dust on nettles, Helen in a kitchen range of steel polished until it SHONE!' Even fire tongs were apparelled in celestial light — a lesson that Women's Lib could well take to heart? At one point, Joy was discussing the eurhythmics learnt at school. The details of one complex exercise evoked merry laughter: 'Could you still do it?' someone asked, whereat she jumped to her feet, thought a moment, and then beat two with her head, three with her right arm, four with her left, and tapped five with her foot simultaneously. I leave you to imagine our reaction. It was a memorable visit, and I hope our guests realized that the silence with which we greet things that deeply move us is more full of sound than the loudest clapping or acclamation.

Rule of St Benedict Chapter 4

Live in fear of judgement day and have a great horror of hell.
Yearn for everlasting life with holy desire.
Day by day remind yourself that you are going to die.

God hath given me peace in my soul, and what can one desire more, coming to die? Methinks I have nothing at all to do but to leave myself wholly to his disposition and let him do what he pleases.

DAME GERTRUDE MORE 1633

Circle of priests surrounding William Bernard Ullathorne, monk of Downside and Bishop of Birmingham, as he lay dying in 1889: 'From the snares of the devil deliver him, O Lord.' Response from the figure on his deathbed: 'The devil's a jackass!'

I lift up my eyes to the hills

All day has raged the rough November wind;
   Now, glancing towards the sunset, half-aware,
   I see, through lacing tree-tops newly bare —

With sudden joy — the rugged hills aligned
Purple on gold, too long unseen behind
   These beechen boughs, while leafy summer's fair
   Soft loveliness enmeshed the languid air,
Veiling the sterner peaks from sight and mind.
So, Lord, when Time relentless strips away
Like autumn leaves, friends, joys, yea all I prize
   On earth, and comfortless my spirit chills,
Let me not shrink dismayed, but lift mine eyes
Calmly, a vaster landscape to survey,
   And rest them on thine everlasting hills.

'I am going to God. That is what I came for — what we all came
for — to go to God.'

ABBESS LAURENTIA MCLACHLAN 1953

10

Dame Scholastica Hebgin

11 OCTOBER 1973

Praise God for the mill by the harnessed stream,
For the hard stone quarried and hewn aright,
For the pitiless grinding, smoothly slow,
For the flour perfected, pure and white.

This stanza from her own 'Song of Praise', with its echoes of *Tunsionibus, pressuris/Expoliti lapides* ('With hammer-blows and grinding weights/are the stones polished') from the hymn of the Dedication of a Church, and the *Frumentum Christi sum* ('I am God's wheat') of St Ignatius of Antioch, provides a fitting epitaph perhaps for Dame Scholastica's fifty-six years of monastic life. Five hours before her death, she had sat with me in the parlour, her last act being to scrutinize a difficult letter I had passed over to her to read. 'That's all right,' she said, 'you have been determinedly non-committal.' How many times have I not been greeted with her invariable smile of welcome and, 'Yes, my dear, what can I do for you?' She stood in the parlour doorway as I teased her about her slowness in getting to bed for supper. An hour later she had a serious stroke, received the anointing of the sick at 8 p.m. and died at 9.40 on Thursday, 11 October, the former feast of our Lady's motherhood. She had left me, a tiny figure bent double over two sticks, her poor body encased in a thick leather and steel harness to protect her spine and give her the necessary support to stand at all. When I saw her in death, an amazing transformation had taken place. I don't think it an exaggeration to say that I have never seen anyone so beautiful. She lay tall, slender, agelessly immortal, with face uplifted in sheer ecstasy. And yet it was herself and none other. Everyone gazed long at her and came away with a tender and delighted smile. 'Did you see that square stubborn chin of hers?' her fellow-novice Dame Werburg asked me. 'She has taken it to heaven all right. I used to tell her that I foresaw her arrival in heaven, and her coming down next morning, looking round expectantly and announcing, "I want my breakfast." "Sh!"'I'll say, "you don't have breakfast in heaven." "But I've ALWAYS had breakfast. I want my breakfast!", and then with shame and embarrassment, I'll go and pluck a fruit from the Tree of Life and hand it to you, just to keep you quiet!' Yes, she could be endearingly stubborn. I recalled a story she told me of her very early childhood — she was only about two. Her mother had taken the protesting mite to church, a 'very Low' evangelical one with hymns and a long sermon. Small Sybil found her way to the floor, sat down, gazed up at the wooden angels supporting the roof, and began to murmur across the preacher's voice: 'Pitty angels'. 'Sh!' came her mother's warning admonition. Louder rose the cry, 'Pitty angels . . . Pitty angels!' The battle was on, and at the mother's final 'SH — sh!' the rebel shouted defiantly, 'Shawnt!' Kicking and repeating 'Pitty angels!' she was carried home in disgrace, sat in a high chair, and her misdeeds were reported to her father. He looked at her for a long time in silence and she looked tremblingly at him. Then very quietly, he said, 'YOU said SHAWNT' . . . 'And you said SHAWNT to your MOTHER!' . . . 'And you said SHAWNT to your MOTHER in CHURCH!' At this she burst into tears: 'Daddy, Daddy' . . . To the end of her life, one only had to hear her refer to 'my Daddy' to realize how she worshipped him. She was the eldest of his three children and all the happiness of her childhood stemmed from him. Her two brothers were too young to be companionable, and her mother never understood the daughter who refused to like being dressed in pink ('I had the prettiness of a barmaid', she used to say) and demanded to have her curls shorn. Throughout life she could be counted on to provide from her voluminous pocket a needed piece of string, a jack-knife, some paper clips, a rubber, a magnifying glass, and she was never happier than when up a tree sawing and pruning, or tearing her arms to pieces picking gooseberries. She was an East Anglian farmer's daughter, proud of a yeoman ancestry traceable for four centuries at least. I can see her in mindsight surveying a newly-laid crazy paving with cool disdain, and then observing truculently: 'It's these tidy suburban minds — how I dislike them, so there. Heaven for me will not be a town park, it will be grass and speedwell and willow-herb and heartsease and forget-me-not.' And then she'd take me, the townee, for a ramble and point out the lovely pattern of the mugwort by the bog garden; pick a cluster of rayless mayweed, crush it and fill the air with the smell of apples, while she dilated on its history — brought over on the keel of a ship from its native America, and now to be found all over Britain; she would nod at the masses of ground elder and chuckle over the Scottish retort which named it Bishop's weed. A walk with her was always an adventure — and an education. I remember once we were by the pond when she suddenly ran and dived, and I saw her pressed to the ground, her magnifying glass out, examining a tiny flower. 'Come and look', she cried. 'I haven't seen this in the enclosure for thirty years. Only the Almighty can make such beauty!'

I am rambling too, without plan or any aim except to talk about her. For we were the closest of friends. Was it she or Lady Abbess Laurentia who called us 'the Seidlitz Powder' — two opposites complementing one another. She had the intellectual weight, I the mere effervescence; she the analysis, I the synthesis. We fought like mad but never quarrelled. When we were translating Augustine, she'd run an eye over my translation and wrinkle her nose: 'You want to put him in a beret and a Fair-isle sweater', she'd say. 'And you', would be the hot rejoinder, 'want to put him in a shovel hat and gaiters.' We did our last piece of work together in the early months of this year when I recorded a talk on Julian of Norwich for the monks of Mount St Bernard. I very much doubt whether there is anyone who had a more intimate knowledge of *The Revelations* than she, and my paper made it pretty obvious that in my own mind there was a certain identity between the two. For it is my very considered opinion that Dame Scholastica was possessed of rare holiness, and had been specially favoured by God.

I have already mentioned her father. He was ostensibly at least an agnostic, and died when Sybil was only fifteen years old. As she stood by his grave and listened to the rattle of the earth thrown on his coffin, she decided there could be no God, for no one who was good could have dealt her such a cruel blow. For years she nursed her resentment and rebellion, while her mother tried to make ends meet and educate the three children — she, at Norwich, a city she knew inside out; her two brothers at Thetford Grammar School. From Norwich, she went up to Bedford College coming out top of the Cambridge Senior examination. 'Did you know she took a First in Logic at London University?' her brother John once asked me with awe in his voice — it was on his last visit from Canada, shortly before his rather sudden death. She read English at Bedford, and retained an enviable knowledge of Anglo-Saxon and High German. Her first-class analysis of the twelfth-century Aelfric's *Grammar*, one of Worcester Cathedral Library's treasures, should certainly have been published in the English Association Papers, but when I said so, she greeted the remark with nothing more than polite interest. She had simply done the piece of research because Lady Abbess Laurentia asked her, and she thought no more about it. She might easily have retorted: 'Working for God, no work is lost. Work on.' Never did she look for reward — I almost added, never did she get it.

At this point, I am going to make a strange leap and take you to the day of her burial. 13 October, festival of St Edward the Confessor — nothing could have been more fitting, for it was when she was standing in the cloisters of Westminster Abbey in her final year at Bedford College that she was suddenly overwhelmed with the realization that the cloisters had once been peopled, not by tourists and sight-seers, but by English Benedictine monks. The sense of the past was always strong in her, and she had an expert knowledge of English Cathedral architecture. At that moment, all her agnosticism was swept away, and along with her new vision came the call to monastic life, pretty well simultaneously with the gift of faith. Her mother was already dead and her two brothers' education almost completed. She was received into the Church by Fr St John SJ at Farm Street on 7 December 1915, and entered Stanbrook as a postulant on St Michael's Eve, less than two years later.

A friend has just sent me a Mass offering, and I have asked for Mass to be offered for Dame Scholastica on 7 November, for the joy it will give me to hear proclaimed at the Memento of the Dead on that day, Lady Abbess Caecilia Heywood whose anniversary of death it is, and her daughter Scholastica. In her abbess, she found all the love, the understanding and the guidance denied her in youth, and the fourteen years she spent under her rule were the halcyon days of her life. She who so rarely betrayed deep emotion admitted that after Abbess Caecilia's death, she cried daily for a year — she, who in forty years, only broke down once in my presence. Her own summing-up of her abbess is to be found in *In a Great Tradition*, for I asked her to write the pen-sketch. God gave mystical graces out of the ordinary run to Abbess Caecilia, and he gave them likewise to Dame Scholastica. This was the classical prelude, in Dame Scholastica's experience, to the trials of faith which St John of the Cross calls the Dark Night of the senses, followed by the far more searing Dark Night of faith. She was to endure aridity for the next forty years, and would be increasingly and relentlessly stripped of all she held humanly dear and divinely sacred. I can speak from first-hand knowledge of just one event. Her greatest love was the Blessed Eucharist, and naturally this was the trial of faith. (How far does grace build on nature? She was by everything in her a rationalist of the first water. 'I loved her,' Dame Werburg said to me last week, 'she was tough, unsentimental, cerebral, and deeply affectionate.') One day when her anguish was at its height and reason mocked faith, the celebrant at Mass dropped a host at the grille while distributing Holy Communion. The host rolled down the steps of the choir and came to rest at Dame Scholastica's feet. She had to pick it up and restore it to Dom Philip Langdon. In that moment she was 'out of herself' as St Augustine would say, and it was characteristic of her that later she burst into one of Elizabeth Barrett Browning's Sonnets from the Portuguese to voice her rapture:

> The first time he kissed me
> He but only touched the fingers of this hand . . .

To the end of her life, she re-consecrated to God the two fingers which had held Infinity that morning.

If I'm giving an impression of pie-jaw, I'm putting her over all wrong. 'Piety' was abhorrent to her, so was a long face. After a bad night, she'd show the same welcoming face and say in amused tones: 'It's one of those days when you have to pin on a large smile.' Her prayer was one and the same thing as her breathing, I think. It went on day and night, no matter what she might be doing outwardly. One winter she was my aid in the vegetable gardens, and she used to spend a long time in the cellars among the apples and stored carrots and so forth. I don't know how Dame Katharine came to tease her about the time she spent down there, but that evening a truculent D.S. put on D.K.'s door this verse:

Retort Courteous

According to K.
S. doesn't pray
In the cellar all day.
S. won't tell her
She prays in the cellar
As well (or weller)
As curled in a ball
Asleep in her stall –
So there! That's all.

Oh, how can I convey the delicacy of her perception and mind? One day I asked her in exasperation what the *Ante torum hujus virginis* of our Lady's office could possibly mean. Within hours I received on a bit of paper, this:

Ante torum

Maidens, weave your wreathed chorus
Twining arms and twinkling feet;
Her, whose beauty smiles before us,
Raise your rhythmic chants to greet.

And one remembers with a smile how she disliked the annual retreat, and most of all its name:

Misnamed

To attack or defend I will do my endeavour,
To advance or explore I'm as ready as ever,
But you ask me to make a Retreat — well I never!

It would be impossible for me to tell how much I shall miss
her. I found her, only some ten days or so before her death,
standing in her cell separating lavender cuttings from flower-
bearing stalks. Reflectively she observed that Dame Maura (our
nonagenarian niece of Abbess Caecilia Heywood) was slowly
climbing up her stalk and would soon reach the top — a reference to the caddis-fly's gradual journey from the mud of the
pond, up a reed, into the sun and thence, dried in the warm rays
and hard sheath burst and cast aside, into the near-miraculous
transformation of a dragon-fly. This had been much in D.S.'s
mind as a symbol of the resurrection, and as Dame Maura had
suffered a series of heart attacks, she concluded that she was
next in the queue for Paradise. Unwittingly, however, she was
speaking of herself, for it was she who was journeying to the
sun. 'But that shimmering and natural beauty was always there
in her and I felt it a privilege to know her', Rumer has written.
To return, she held out to me the few discarded stalks of lavender, reserving the cuttings for the noviciate to plant. After her
death, I placed between her fingers along with her well-used
rosary the stalks of lavender. My dragon-fly had reached the
top and flown into the rays of the sun beyond the reach of
human eye. As sacristan I had the adornment of her cell. Two
large white Paschal candles stood on wooden bases, a sheaf of
corn at her head, and tendrils of vine leaves round the body.

Board and provision for that marriage-feast
To which he calls alike the greatest and the least.

She would undoubtedly have reckoned herself among the very
least, and yet we buried her with greater splendour than we
have witnessed since the death of Abbess Laurentia. And our
new sanctuary made such a lovely setting. It all came about
seemingly accidentally. Mother Prioress gave me leave to ring
up Prinknash on the morning after her death, to inform her old
friend, Dom Michael Hanbury. To put things in a nutshell,

Father Prior answered the telephone and suggested bringing Dom Michael over with a dozen or so of his brethren to represent Prinknash. Mass was sung at 2.45 p.m. to allow of easy assembly, and Lady Abbess ordained that it should be the Latin Mass *de Requie*. Father Prior and two of his monks concelebrated with Dom Dominic Allen, our chaplain, and a choir of white-robed monks made a corona in the sanctuary, and added a note of joy and peace — quite impossible to describe. No room really for grief. The monks sang much of the Mass, alternating with our community, and at the end, with monk cross- and torch-bearers we bore her body to her resting-place in our little God's acre with songs of victory and resurrection. Her nephew, Peter, husband of Alice, her so-loved niece, bore her coffin as she had asked, and ten-year-old Penny came into the enclosure with her mother, dangling a little beaded gourd just given her from Dame Scholastica's prie-dieu where it had often held wild flowers. Alice lifted her head at the graveside to listen with joy to the birds who added their song — not dirge — to ours. Later she wrote: 'She stayed with you as long as she could until she could stay no longer.' Yes; the crushing and grinding of the corn was done, and the pure bread ready.

11

Seeing is Believing

I should like to publish a number of articles on prayer that could be given to interested people who feel themselves to be beginners, not highly technical pieces for experts. Would you contribute?

The Editor of *The Clergy Review*

If anyone is asked to do the impossible and his representations are set aside, let him obey out of love, trusting in God's help.

Rule of St Benedict, Chapter 68

Will the veiled sister pray
For children at the gate
Who will not go away and cannot pray.

T. S. ELIOT, *Ash Wednesday*

Prayer is the great adventure of faith. If we would see, then we must believe. It involves a journey into the unknown, different for every one of us. God has made hearts *singillatim*, one by one (Psalm 32:15) — there is no mass production with the Almighty. Throughout all the aeons of time, there never has been, never will be an exact replica of any one individual. Each has a vocation, a name, a place which is unique. While that makes any general 'map of prayer' a near-impossibility, it is a fact of the deepest significance and encouragement. For each can say with perfect truth: 'God loves me as nobody else loves me, and as he loves nobody else, I love God as nobody else loves him, and as I love nobody else.' It also carries a responsibility. If I withhold my worship then, humanly speaking, earth's praise of its Maker is defective. To want to see him is a need written into the law of our being. 'You have said, "Seek my face." My heart says to you, "It is your face, O Lord, that I seek." Hide not your face from me' (Psalm 26:8, 9). And we have our Lord's specific invitation, 'Come and *see*!' (John 1:39).

It was precisely to reveal the Father that the Son came into the world. St Paul tells us that in the hearts of all believers, the Spirit ceaselessly murmurs, *Abba*, Father! The same cry, re-echoed by Ignatius of Antioch, disciple of John the Evangelist, on his way to the lions in the Roman amphitheatre, 'There is in me a living water which speaks and tells me: Come to the Father!', leaves us asking with St Thomas, 'How do we go?' To that, our Lord returns the answer: 'I am the way. No one comes to the Father but by me' (John 14:6). Paradise, where Adam walked and talked with God face to face among the trees at eventide, was forfeited by disobedience. In the incarnation the Son of God once more walked with man, and by the grace of the Holy Spirit has enabled us to renew our intimate relationship with the Father. 'That they know thee the only true God, and Jesus Christ whom thou hast sent' is both eternal life, and the foundation of prayer (John 17:3).

I Am (Exodus 3:14)

Prayer is the meeting of two persons: God Eternal Being, and myself, out of his infinite love called into being from nothingness. Having once created me, even God himself cannot get rid of me for all eternity. And this, the first question of the despised Penny Catechism, makes a good starting-point.

Who made you? God made me.
I am who am. You are, who are not (to Catherine of Siena).
Behold, I AM. And now *thou* art and prayest me (to Julian of Norwich).

Read and pray the 138th psalm:

> It was you who created my being,
> knit me together in my mother's womb.
> I thank you for the wonder of my being,
> for the wonders of all your creation . . .

We stand, stripped and defenceless, like that naked babe, symbol of the soul, lifted high on two arms, that the medieval illuminator so often enclosed in the large gilded A of the Introit, *Ad te levavi animam meam* of the 1st Sunday of Advent. But there must be no illuminated addresses, no pious pose before

God. He who walks simply, walks confidently (Proverbs 10:9). Whenever God speaks in the Bible, his words are short and incisive, and the more we use the word of God in our prayer, the better. No other words are big enough, bold enough, tender enough, pithy enough, strange enough.

Our Lord has himself taught us all the technique we need. 'When you pray, go into your room and shut the door and pray to your Father who is in secret . . . and in praying, do not heap up empty phrases' (Matthew 6:6). 'Go into your room.' At first you may feel at ease only in the comforting clean space of a church where you can kneel before the Blessed Sacrament. Don't despise the scaffolding of a tag — tags can prove very useful. To remember the word 'A-C-T-S' — adoration, contrition, thanksgiving, supplication — can be a stimulus and prevent mooning. Be on the alert against 'empty phrases'. Keep questioning your assumptions. Are you addressing God as he is, beyond all intellectual concept and human imagining, or an image constructed in your own mind? You 'love' violets. You 'love' your friends. What exactly do you mean by 'love' of God? Does the mere saying 'I adore' really do it? Don't be like Samuel Johnson's Poll Carmichael who, when he talked to her tightly and closely, was all wiggle-waggle and never categorical.

'Shut the door.' Accustom yourself to pray anywhere, under a tree, in your own home, and especially in that 'cell of your heart' dear to Catherine of Siena. If possible, take our Lord's injunction literally, set aside at least a quarter, preferably half an hour every evening, when you can slip away from television and gossip, and 'go into your room' apart. It is easier to see the unseen in darkness. Shut the door of your heart and mind. See that your body is comfortable so that you can forget it, gently blot out all the internal noise, drop things, keep dropping them, if necessary look over the shoulder of your distractions, as the *Cloud of Unknowing* puts it, and then listen at least as much as you speak:

Be still, and see that I am God (Psalm 45:11).
I shall see your face, and be filled with the sight of your glory (Psalm 16:15).
Fear not, for I have redeemed you; I have called you by name, you are mine (Isaiah 43:1).

Here I am, Lord, I have come to do your will (Psalm 39:9).
You are precious in my eyes and honoured, and I love you (Isaiah
    43:4).
I love you, Lord, my strength, my rock, my fortress, my saviour
    (Psalm 17:2).
Son, give me your heart (Proverbs 23:26).
What have I in heaven, and apart from you, what do I desire upon
    earth? You are the God of my heart, the God that is my
    portion for ever (Psalm 72:25).
My house shall be called a house of prayer (Luke 19:46).
Lord God, in simplicity of heart, I have joyfully offered you
    everything (Offertory of Mass of Dedication of Church).

You may find it helpful to utilize for prayer psalms characteristic of the liturgical season: during Advent, the 24th; throughout Lent, the battlecry of the 90th; at Easter psalms 112–117,
the *Hallel* of praise sung by our Lord and his apostles after
the Last Supper (Matthew 26:30); at Whitsuntide, the 'Golden
Sequence' the *Veni Sancte Spiritus* of the Mass. The Mass texts
are treasuries of doctrine and prayer. Each Sunday they can be
used as the key to that week's prayer, for they ring the changes
over the whole range of emotions, love, gratitude, sorrow, trust,
petition. Begin a collect or psalm reflectively and then stop —
possibly at the first invocation of God. Repeat the phrase slowly
until it springs to life: when it is fully alive, stop saying words
at all. Do the same with the next phrase and so on. Carry away
a word or idea, and use it as your daily aspiration. These
'seeings' or intuitions renew the morning Mass, and gradually
simplify and silence the soul.

Acquire a deep love of the psalter for it was our Lord's own
breviary. He learned it at his mother's knee, sang it in temple
and synagogue, prayed it on the cross. The psalms abound in
primal symbols — earth, sea, sky, cloud, bird, rock, trees and
so on — strong enough to carry the whole weight of human
existence, and can open out infinite horizons if, when saying
them, we lend our voices to the Word and become the mouth-
piece of the mystical Christ as he prays, works, suffers, rejoices,
now as Head, now as Body — for nothing that we can experience lies outside the cognizance of this Man. The psalter lifts
us above all pettiness, gives us a vision which aims at self-
effacement rather than self-expression, and subjects us to the

Holy Spirit. Nor need we feel squeamish about cursing psalms if we recall the cold-blooded murderers, the torturers, the drug-pedlars, the child-corrupters — for all of whom it would be better if a millstone were hung about their necks and they were cast into the sea (Luke 17:2).

I in Them (John 17:23)

So far, you may have been thinking of God as outside yourself, 'over there' in the tabernacle under the sacramental form, 'up there' in starlit infinity, or as an unseen presence facing you. But there are two kinds of presence, the presence outside, and the presence within us. 'If a man loves me, he will keep my word, and my Father will love him and we will come to him and make our home in him' (John 14:23). The words 'outside' and 'within' neither describe nor define, and are used not spatially but purely symbolically. Nothing is conscious, and the growing inwardness depends on faith, on the awakening to God, listening to the Word, living in the light.

This brings us up against the necessity for purification, for clean worship. Read Ezekiel 16; the whole of Hosea, especially 2:14–23; Isaiah chapters 49–52. When Henry Suso, the four-teenth-century Dominican mystic, wanted to go straight to the Godhead, our Lord assured him: 'You will never arrive at my naked divinity unless you first break through my suffering humanity.' For the Christian there is no road other than the Cross. 'His member he is not, who hath no ache under such a painfully aching head', says the thirteenth-century Ancrene Riwle. And St Paul makes our divine sonship dependent on our sharing in the passion of Christ: 'When we cry, "Abba! Father!" it is the Spirit himself bearing witness with our spirit that we are children of God, and if children, then heirs, heirs of God and fellow-heirs with Christ, provided we suffer with him . . .' (Romans 8:16). So faith itself must be purified if the darkness surrounding the mystery of God is to glow with light. Sooner or later, consolations and delight in prayer vanish, supports crumble, attempts to reach God meet with baffling silence, thought is famished, heart empty. But God is now known in a different way, for he reveals himself just as truly in absence as in presence. He is the watchman in our night (Isaiah 21:11) calling to us to search to the depths of our need of him — *abyssus abyssum invocat* (Psalm 41:8). He, God of gods, Lord of lords, with sovereign freedom has given us being. And sinners as we are, we respond by a total gift of self that looks for no rewards, knowing that only through death can we find true life. Isn't this the Offertory of our Mass? No longer does the Holy Eucharist arouse feelings of tenderness and devotion, but God's gift of himself becomes a hungry necessity:

> *Mange ton Dieu et tais-toi! Marche, travaille, obéis! . . .*
> *Pourquoi regretter le Chaos?*
> PAUL CLAUDEL *Hymne de Saint Benoit*

Now the *sacrum convivium* — not a sacred banquet but quite literally a holy living-together — takes on a nuptial dimension that belongs to the inexpressible. Its fruit is the consent to peace.

One in Us (John 17:21)

'Lord, show us the Father, and we shall be satisfied.' In reply, in the very act of manifestation, God hides himself more deeply: 'Have I been with you so long, and yet you do not know me, Philip? He who has seen me has seen the Father; how can you say, "Show us the Father?" ' (John 14:8). In dealing with the divine, we must be prepared for mystery, paradox and apparent contradiction. We are craving to see the God who dwells in inaccessible light, whom no one can see and live. If we are never to be shown him, what becomes of our Lord's mission? In his twelfth Sermon on the Passion, with our Lord's *transitus* to the Father clearly at the back of his mind, St Leo the Great uses an unforgettable phrase, so compressed as to defy translation. 'To share the body and blood of Christ', he says,

effects nothing less than this: by a Passover, we pass into what we consume, and as in him we are dead, buried, and risen again, so everything we do whether in body or soul is done in him, as the Apostle teaches, 'You have died, and your life is hid with Christ in God.' *Non enim aliud agit participatio corporis et sanguinis Christi, quam ut in id quod sumimus transeamus.*

For a Christian our Lord remains the sole Way, but that way

passes through a terrain of varying contours during life's pilgrimage. For many perhaps the graph goes something like this.
To begin with, we receive Holy Communion as a somewhat
isolated event, confined to Mass; we make our thanksgiving, go
about the business of the day, recall at intervals some incident
in the life of the Christ of the gospels to rekindle our prayer,
and look forward to our next Communion. Then suddenly we
find that the risen Christ here and now is permeating our lives,
and Holy Communion has become a partnership, an *admirabile
commercium*, that dominates all our thinking, so that prayer
revolves around his presence within our souls. There is a further
shift of emphasis when, instead of God entering into us (to use
the stammering tongue of human speech), we enter into God.
We become what we eat, as St Leo so boldly says; the Holy
Spirit takes over, our life becomes centred on the Blessed Trinity,
and our prayer *Deus solus*. The early Fathers never tire of
dwelling on the wound in Christ's side, the door into the ark,
the cleft of the rock. Hidden in that cleft, we look up at the
Father through the eyes of his Son, and we rest in his infinite
knowledge of the Infinite: God seeing God, God adoring God,
God praising God, God loving God. Our incorporation in Christ
by baptism and the Eucharist has made us bone of his bones,
flesh of his flesh, and has bestowed on us through the Holy Spirit
this capacity for receiving God through Christ, with Christ, in
Christ, so that we can confidently pray: 'O God our Protector,
look upon me, and look into the face of your Christ' (Psalm
83:10). St Clement of Rome tells the Corinthians:

Through Jesus Christ we look straight into the heights of heaven and
see mirrored there the faultless and transcendent face of God. Through
him, the eyes of our heart are opened, and our dull-witted clouded
mind shoots up into the light.

Senses, emotions, even thoughts however spiritual, are largely
left behind during actual prayer, although at other times meditation will be constant. Language becomes stripped and reduced
to its essential form: Fiat. Amen. Alleluia. We join our Fiat to
the three great Fiats of holy Scripture — the Fiat of Creation:
Let there be light; the Fiat of the Annunciation: Let it be done
to me; and the Fiat of Gethsemane: Not my will but thine. In

so doing, we at last give full and free consent to God's ordering of our life.

> Because I have believed, I bid my mind be still.
> Therein is now conceived Thy hid yet sovereign Will.
> Because I set aside all thought in seeking Thee,
> Thy proven purpose wrought abideth blest in me.
> Because I can no more exist but in Thy being,
> Blindly these eyes adore; sightless are taught new seeing.
>
> SIEGFRIED SASSOON 'Proven Purpose'

A cluster of biblical images seems to say all that can be said:

> You who seek the Lord, look to the rock from which you were hewn (Isaiah 51:1).
> And the Rock was Christ (1 Corinthians 10:4).
> One of the soldiers pierced his side with a spear (John 19:34).
> Moses said, I pray thee, show me thy glory. And he said, I will make all my goodness pass before you, and will proclaim before you my name. But you cannot see my face; for man shall not see me and live. And the Lord said, Behold there is a place by me where you shall stand upon the rock; and while my glory passes by I will put you in a cleft of the rock, and I will cover you with my hand (Exodus 34:6). In the clefts of the rock, in the covert of the cliff, let me see your face, let me hear your voice (Song of Solomon 2:14).

Prayer and life may become inseparable and powerfully apostolic but, because we are still *in hac lacrymarum valle* ['in this valley of tears'], buffetings and trials both without and within may increase. The Irish Dominican, the late Archbishop Finbar Ryan, a man of dynamic holiness whose life mirrored his doctrine, spoke with the voice of a lifetime's experience as friar, priest, spiritual guide and bishop when he gave this warning:

> Your soul will be pierced to the inmost recesses of your being. The disciple is not above his Master and, like his Master, must be prepared to go to the very end in growing loneliness of heart, darkness of mind, and bitter abandonment. You will meet with your Annas and Caiaphas and Pilate. Yet God is there all the time. You need not be surprised or afraid. Keep tight hold of that verse of the *Veni, Creator: Per te sciamus da Patrem* ['Through thee may we know the Father'] — the realization that God is our Father and holds everything in his hand. *Noscamus atque Filium* ['May we discern the Son'] — to live in the love of his Son, our Lord. He who has called you will sustain you. As Julian of Norwich would say: 'Thou shalt be tossed, thou shalt be

tempested, but thou shalt not be overcome.' And you must learn to
say not only Amen, but Alleluia.

Especially in our spiritual life, we need to preserve a sense of
proportion and a sense of humour, to turn disappointments and
falls into fun, to remember sometimes that our Lord is completely human, Divine Wisdom still playing in the world, *homo
vere ludens*, and that in a sublime sense Plato was right when
he declared men to be playthings in the hand of God. Under a
hail of afflictions, Teresa of Avila irreverently retorted with wry
amusement: 'If this is the way you treat your friends, Lord, no
wonder you have so few!' Did heaven ring with the delighted
laughter of the Son of Man at finding himself so perfectly
understood? We must never forget that God is a Person, not a
machine to be taken to pieces and reassembled. He has made
all things with incredible wisdom, love, sympathy and humour.
He has made me. How then should I not know him?

This wholly inadequate treatment of prayer with its three
neat divisions is reminiscent of a slice of rainbow cake: a layer
of chocolate sponge, the second of raspberry, the third of van-
illa, bound by ligatures of jam and butter-cream. In fact, prayer
resembles far more closely childhood's game of snakes and
ladders, archetype of ascent and strife between the Great Above
and the Great Below. Just as you were inching with bated breath
towards the goal, a throw of the dice cast you headlong into
the jaws of the dragon, that old serpent, which is the Devil, and
down you went with despairing moan to the nether hell of
Square One. Prayer can be just like that. Job's anguished cry,
Ut videam bona — oh, let me see good things — will reverberate
in the human heart until the end of time. In the tenth-century
Codex 339 of St Gall, *Ut videam bona* forms the Offertory
verse of the 21st Sunday after Pentecost. Emphasized by the
expressive traceries of neumatic musical notation, the text runs:
*Quoniam quoniam quoniam non revertetur oculus meus ut
videam bona, ut videam bona, ut videam bona, ut videam bona,
ut videam bona, ut videam bona, ut videam bona, ut videam
bona, ut videam bona.* No fewer than nine times the imploring
voice rises in crescendos of billowing melody until, at the final
repetition, the scribe's quill takes wing and flies right off the

folio. Apt symbol of the prayer of beseeching. The psalmist takes the phrase and answers it with the confident assertion of faith: 'I believe that I shall see the good things of the Lord in the land of the living' (Psalm 26:13). The Evangelists take the phrase and bring it into sharp focus. 'If you then, who are evil, know how to give good gifts to your children,' our Lord tells the crowd surrounding him on the Mount of Beatitudes, 'how much more will your Father who is in heaven give good things to those who ask him?' (Matthew 7:11). But Luke makes this significant change in the reporting: 'How much more will the heavenly Father give the Holy Spirit to those who ask him!' (Luke 11:13). *Per te sciamus da Patrem*. In my beginning is my end. In my end is my beginning. 'Oh, these good things of the Lord', St Augustine exclaims,

sweet, immortal, unchangeable. Let us listen to the voice of courage and consolation 'O wait for the Lord' (Psalm 26:14). By patient waiting for the Lord you will possess him, you will possess him for whom you wait. If you can find anything grander, better, or sweeter, set your heart on that. Yes, wait for the Lord. (On Psalm 26)

Don't despise tags — they can be so useful that the advice is worth giving twice. Like the seventeenth-century Dom Augustine Baker, Archbishop Finbar Ryan was very fond of them. He made this one his farewell:

> Working for God
> No work is lost:
> Work on.
> Praying to God
> No prayer is lost:
> Pray on.
> Waiting for God
> No time is lost:
> Wait on.

12

The Spiritual Teaching of St Benedict*

ABBESS LAURENTIA MCLACHLAN

One

It is often said, and truly, that we Benedictines have no hard and fast system of spirituality, any more than of theology or art or architecture. We do not claim any exclusive theory on the Divine Office or prayer or asceticism. We use the riches of the Church which are the patrimony of all Christians. But this does not imply that St Benedict has given us no spiritual guidance, that he has pointed out no preferences, that he has taught us no way of going to God. It is for us to discover his special ways, and to find them in his code of monastic laws, as someone has said, 'a thousand-years-old instrument of sanctification'; and we children of St Benedict should know how to find there his ideal of Christian perfection in the ascetic life and prayer. Founded as it is on the gospel it never grows old or out of fashion, it is as practical today as in the sixth century and is so far from exclusiveness that it can run alongside more modern schools of spirituality and mingle with them according to the tastes and needs of souls. During Lent this year we shall see what the chief principles are that our Holy Father lays down in his teaching as fundamental to the spiritual life or asceticism. They are quite clearly set forth though we shall not find them tabulated or numbered as perhaps we might in a modern rule or spiritual way. In St Benedict's mind the ruling principle of all action, of all attempt at serving God, is God himself. God is ever considered as our first beginning and last end. In order

* Four Conferences given by Abbess Laurentia McLachlan to the Stanbrook Community Lent 1937

to carry out his acknowledged dependence, a man subjects himself to God's guidance and strives to shake off all bonds of self, to grow in virtue and open his soul to the freedom of grace. With St Benedict there is no question of seeking moral perfection as an end in itself; everything tends to God first, and is made an act of homage to God's will, and so every effort in the spiritual life becomes purely *religious*, directly related to God. The value of this attitude of soul is very great; it puts God in the first place as our Ruler, and it removes all self-complacency, all fancying of ourselves or of our progress. The soul seeks God and his will more than its own perfection, and so all efforts after the best are made solely to please and glorify him. When life is ruled by this great yet simple principle there is nothing too great or too small to be fitted into God's service; or rather, everything in life becomes great; because the smallest actions are connected with the thought of direct service, and instead of being delayed by a lower view of things we pass on to their higher and eternal value. By this means we look on God not as an abstraction outside our life, but as involved, so to say, in every effort of our daily life, in our moral progress; and this consciousness of our immediate dependence on God and of his action at every turn purifies and elevates our whole life. In many places in the Holy Rule we find justification for what I have just said. In the Prologue after asking with the Psalmist: 'Lord, who shall dwell in thy tabernacle or who shall rest upon thy holy hill?' he hears God's answer: 'They who fearing God take no pride in their good observance, but know that any good in them comes not from themselves but from him, glorify his work in them saying: "Not unto us, O Lord, not unto us, but unto thy name give the glory"; or with St Paul: "By the grace of God I am what I am", and: "He that glorieth let him glory in the Lord." '

And what means should we take for acquiring this habit of simple childlike dependence on God? 'To know for certain that God beholdeth us in every place' (Ch. 4.49 'Instruments of Good Works'). I think I am justified in saying this because St Benedict in Ch. 7 which deals not merely with humility but with the whole of the interior life, puts in the first place this remembrance of God's presence. 'The first degree of humility is that a man always keeps the fear of God before his eyes. . . . Let him consider that he is always beheld from heaven by God, and that his actions are everywhere seen by the eye of the Divine Majesty, and are every hour reported to him by his angels.' And in the chapter on the manner in which we should perform our direct service to God in choir (Ch. 19) he says: 'We believe that the Divine Presence is everywhere . . . especially do we believe this without any doubt when we are assisting at the work of God. . . . Therefore let us consider how we ought to behave ourselves in the presence of God and of his angels. . . .' Even when not actually expressed in words the thought of our being continually in the divine presence runs through the Rule and is at the root of St Benedict's frequent injunctions to see God in everyone; in our brethren, in strangers, in the sick and weak, in the Abbot. During these holy days when we are striving to repair the negligence of other times, let us take heed of this ruling idea in our Father's teaching, a teaching backed by his own practice as described so beautifully by St Gregory: *Solus in superni inspectoris oculis habitavit secum* — 'Under God's all-seeing gaze, he dwelt alone with himself.'

Two

We have considered the first means for carrying out our Holy Father's programme of the spiritual life, the continual reference of all to God in whose presence we live. And taking the Prologue and Ch. 7 as our guides, we shall go on trying to follow St Benedict's thought and to recognize his principles. In the first degree of humility after laying the foundation of the presence of God, we find:

We are forbidden to do our own will by Scripture which says to us: 'Turn away from thine own will.' And so too we beg God in prayer that his will may be done in us. Rightly therefore we are taught not to do our own will, if we take heed to the warning of Scripture: 'There are ways which to men seem right but the ends thereof lead to the depths of hell.'

— And in the next paragraph linking up the idea to his previous thought by the words:

If therefore the eyes of the Lord behold the good and evil and the Lord is ever looking down from heaven upon the children of men to see who has understanding or is seeking God ... we must always be on the watch, brethren, lest as the Prophet says in the Psalm, God should see us at any time declining to evil and becoming unprofitable, and though he spare us now because he is merciful and expects our conversion, he should say to us hereafter: 'These things thou didst and I was silent.'

We know the prominent place that obedience holds in St Benedict's ideal and here we have the key to the stress laid on this virtue. In the first words of the Prologue we are told that we are to go back to God by obedience, using it as our best weapon — 'the bright and shining armour'. In Ch. 4 we are admonished to hate our own will and to obey in all things the Abbot's command. There is a whole chapter on obedience, containing the strongest and clearest teaching as to its theory and practice; another chapter tells us to obey one another and to be convinced that obedience is our road to God. In the chapter on Good Zeal, which is a bird's-eye view of our Holy Father's teaching, we are told to be eager to obey one another. There must be some very important principle behind this insistence on obedience and the words of Ch. 7 are, I think, the key to St Benedict's meaning: 'Rightly are we taught to avoid doing our own will.' We saw in the last Conference on this subject that our approach to God should be as direct as possible and that our life should hang on to the fact of his presence and even our efforts after perfection and our good works should be directed to him and to our desire for union with him and not to our moral improvement. Looked at in this light what is the meaning of obedience? It cannot be just a material performance of commands or even merely the supernatural spirit in which we obey. The virtue of obedience is concerned with teaching us the right use of the will, than which nothing is more important in the spiritual life. It is not a question of breaking the will; if you break a will, you risk breaking a personality. The object of obedience is to make the will supple in response to God's orders, to turn it into a perfect instrument. There is no particular virtue in having our will thwarted except as part of our exercise (*ascesis*) for keeping spiritually fit. At the present moment there is a campaign for fitness being launched in England and people are being taught, with Government support, to do certain physical exercises, not for the sake of the exercises but because these practices will strengthen the muscles and give them suppleness and resilience. So in our monastic life we have a regulated day, for each one has her time-table, tasks are not chosen haphazard, things are done in a certain way and by appointed people. For the most part this obedience works automatically without definite orders. At times, though, such orders are given, notices are put up and they must be obeyed exactly. Obedience does not *interpret* orders. They are given for a purpose and the spirit of obedience should welcome them as opportunities of checking our own will and doing things in someone else's way. Our own way might have been better in itself, but obedience gives value to the other. These are commonplaces and I need not dwell on them further, for the Conference is not on obedience, but on the use and purpose of obedience, which is the training of the will. Our will is our most precious faculty and therefore the vow of obedience by which we subject it to another is the highest of the vows and indeed includes the others. It stands to reason that this high value is not derived from the mere performance of someone else's will, but in the fact that supernatural obedience of the will is the highest homage we can pay to God. From the ascetical point of view the value of obedience consists in the *result* of such submission, and the result is to make the will a very bright and strong weapon, the strongest and brightest weapon of our spiritual warfare. If we are to serve God consistently and perseveringly we must rely on something more stable than our feelings, even good and pious feelings. We must have our will rooted in God, and the whole object of our life being to reach conformity with God's will, i.e., union with him, the proper use of our will is of the utmost importance.

Three

In two previous Conferences we have been studying the characteristic teaching of St Benedict underlying the Holy Rule, in order that by following it we may the better be what we are, i.e., true Benedictines — true children of St Benedict. We saw that his first idea on which he builds all that follows is the continual thought of the presence of God, living always in his sight, going to him by a straight way; and directly following from this comes the command 'Do not your own will'. This leads to obedience which we find running all through the Holy Rule and in its most searching forms — we saw last time how this obedience is not merely an outward practice of doing what we are told by a Superior but much more a voluntary surrender of ourselves to God — the surrender of that most precious faculty, our will; and we exercise our will making it pliable and readily submissive by our outward practice of obedience. In our kind of life the proper use of the will is of even greater importance than in the case of religious of active orders. We live in seclusion, left much to ourselves, occupied for the most part in duties which have no wider scope than our enclosure walls. Our noblest and chief duty, the Divine Office, is performed with God and the angels for the listeners mostly, our private prayer and the spirit of prayer that runs through the day is not heard even by our Sisters. The days follow one another with little external relief. What is to keep us from becoming mechanical, or depressed, or slack in our duties, or too much absorbed in their active side, or inclined to seek relaxation by excess in talking or by interesting ourselves in things (even good things such as systems of spirituality) that do not fit into the true spirit of our life? What is to keep us ever steady, ever true, to save us from vagueness which is one of the worst evils? The grace of God alone can save us from all these things, the grace of God acting on a will that is trained by obedience to disregard feelings and imagination, to respond easily to the call of duty, to know that what God asks from us is not achievement or enjoyment in our prayer and service, but a sincere desire to serve him in spite of our feelings and moods, in spite of the tiresomeness of those with whom we live (who may sometimes include our Superior), in spite of the weather and our health etc. (we can each make out the list for ourselves). This steady purpose keeps us faithful, first in prayer, makes us eager to be in choir and to do our best there in spite of our own deficiencies or those of our neighbour, it prevents our fervour being dependent on the mere outward circumstances; it holds us up in our private prayer when things are dark and we are dry; it maintains us in a supernatural spirit towards our Abbess, our Sisters and our work; it forbids us even the gratification of grumbling while carrying out our duties. St Benedict's closing words in the chapter on Obedience when he says that even though we obey but murmur, we shall get no reward but rather the punishment of a murmurer, coupled with his other strong denouncement of grumbling in any way for any cause, show what a good psychologist our Holy Father is, and follow self-will into its last retrenchments. Murmuring is really a shabby way of getting our own way. This is to thwart the whole purpose of obedience, and instead of becoming supple and supernatural in our life, we become hard and materialistic. How foolish to misuse our opportunities of self-surrender for the sake of a slight assertion of our own will! If we miss the road of obedience we miss the road of freedom, we take the responsibility on ourselves instead of throwing it on God and on authority. The obedient free soul has a song ever on its lips, it is ready to serve joyfully because it has cast off its burden, it keeps its thoughts on those things that are above all day long and when it comes to prayer it is exempt from thousands of wearying and distracting thoughts which assault us when we have plans and ideas of our own. The Church in her collects is always praying for this freedom of mind, especially at this time — in the prayer for Easter Monday we find her asking that we may deserve to obtain 'perfect liberty'. This aspect of obedience seems to me to be of the greatest importance in our life as children of St Benedict. He was the blessed man whose 'will was in the law of the Lord' and by that stability and steadiness, St Gregory tells us he kept his mind in heaven while he was still on earth, *in terris positus in coelis habitavit*; he lived an angelic life, *vitam angelicam gerens in terris*, and the chief feature of the angelic life is an absolute readiness of will to do God's bidding without delay and without afterthoughts. Guided, therefore, by St Benedict's words and example we should make it our business to aim at this suppleness of will and independence of circumstances which will establish us in freedom of spirit.

Four

The third of St Benedict's principles is the most important and
the most potent as a formative influence. For him the ruling
thought, the only motive we might say in life, is the love of
Christ. Our Lord is the centre towards which everything else
must gravitate. We are to 'prefer nothing to the love of Christ',
elsewhere we are 'to set nothing whatsoever before Christ'. If
we obey and subject our wills in the way we discussed in a
previous Conference, we do it for the love of God as we find
laid down in the third degree of humility; and in the chapter
on Obedience the motive is given — obedience 'becomes those
who hold nothing dearer to them than Christ', though the fear
of hell is given as an alternative for those who cannot rise at
once to love. The love of Christ is so dominant that every
person, from the Abbot to the guest, and even the beggar at the
door *is* Christ, and offers an opportunity of showing our love
for God hidden behind the poor mortal. The sick are especially
commended to the care of the Abbot and officials, in fact
nothing is to be considered more important than their service,
because they are Christ in his weakness and suffering and our
love for him is poured out on them. It is not surprising that the
value of this love as a principle of the spiritual life is recognized
by our Holy Father, who was full of the spirit of the gospel and
of the early Fathers and Saints of the Church. Our Lord's
reiteration of the first and greatest commandment as his own
special legacy makes it the sum of all his teaching. St John
carries on the lesson in his Epistles. St Paul is constantly urging
it: 'The love of Christ urges me' — 'Who then shall separate us
from the love of Christ?' and he goes on to show us that nothing
exterior to us can separate us from 'the love of God which is
in Christ Jesus our Lord'. St Augustine makes it the one thing
necessary: *Ama et fac quod vis* he says, meaning, of course,
that if you really love you will only be able to do what that
love dictates. There followed centuries of a more complicated
spirituality but the Holy Ghost always brings back the teaching.
St Bernard makes it his chief theme in all his teachings. St
Francis of Sales in an age of ultra-sophistication takes as his
summary of the spiritual life the love of God and writes his

wonderful book. Again in our own days St Thérèse of Lisieux gives the same lesson and I believe that she gets very near to our Holy Father's meaning of preferring nothing to Christ. It is a long jump from the twentieth century to the sixth but truth never dies. St Benedict's thought seems to be that instead of labouring at attaining virtues in turn or simultaneously, or working at *our* perfection as we call it, we should aim at having as our motive and our goal the love of Christ. Instead of setting ourselves the task of accepting every opportunity of humiliation or patience or whatever virtue we might choose, we simply on *all* occasions ask ourselves what is demanded by love of our Lord, what will please him who has all our love.

This method has many advantages. It makes God and not self the prominent figure, the centre of our actions, and checks any temptation to tabulate results, for we have nothing to show except an increase of love and that is not measurable. It gathers all the virtues together under one head which is St Paul's theology, *plenitudo legis est dilectio* — love is the fulfilling of the law — love of the neighbour flowing from love of God, love being the meeting place of all the virtues. Furthermore, by this way of love all service becomes personal and direct. We are trying to serve not an abstract idea, not a virtue, not a system, but a Person, the second Person of the Blessed Trinity, God himself. Every little act of self-denial, of patience, of humility, of obedience, of silence, of mortification, becomes not mere worshipping at a shrine, but actual service of a Person. And the more we love, the more we serve by love, the keener becomes our insight into the ways of God. Love opens our hearts to God and God's heart to us. No wonder that our Holy Father gives as our watchword the love of Christ and makes it his last exhortation to his children: 'Let us prefer nothing whatever to Christ, and may he bring us all together to life everlasting.'

CHRISTO OMNINO
NIHIL PRAEPONAT. QUI NOS
PARITER AD VITAM PERDUCAT
AETERNAM
Amen

PAX